Economic and Human Development in Contemporary India

This book deals with issues in economic development in India. It highlights those factors that are indicative of India's emergence in the global economy yet indicates negative "trickle down" effects, such as malnutrition, poverty, bonded labourers, high adult unemployment and the widespread use of child labour.

Focusing on structural deficiencies for a steady growth rate, and how to make growth inclusive, the book examines duality in development and the factors standing between national economic prosperity and human development. The author analyses issues concerning international trade, technology, access to food, inequality and poverty, and the "catching up" of developing countries. A novel approach to the analysis of the Indian economy and other developing countries in the twenty-first century, this book advocates development as a form of governance.

With India as a case study, this book provides a solid framework for looking at developing economies which will be useful to policy-makers and to graduate and post-doctoral students and researchers in the areas of development studies and economics, industrialization and structural change.

Debdas Banerjee is Professor of Economics at the Institute of Development Studies Kolkata, India, and former Fulbright Senior Fellow at MIT, Cambridge, USA. He has authored numerous books and articles on industrialization, international economy, regional disparity, knowledge economy and aspects of labour economics.

Routledge contemporary South Asia series

1. **Pakistan**
   Social and cultural transformations in a Muslim nation
   Mohammad A. Qadeer

2. **Labor, Democratization and Development in India and Pakistan**
   Christopher Candland

3. **China–India Relations**
   Contemporary dynamics
   Amardeep Athwal

4. **Madrasas in South Asia**
   Teaching terror?
   Jamal Malik

5. **Labor, Globalization and the State**
   Workers, women and migrants confront Neoliberalism
   Edited by Debdas Banerjee and Michael Goldfield

6. **Indian Literature and Popular Cinema**
   Recasting classics
   Edited by Heidi R.M. Pauwels

7. **Islamist Militancy in Bangladesh**
   A complex web
   Ali Riaz

8. **Regionalism in South Asia**
   Negotiating cooperation, institutional structures
   Kishore C. Dash

9. **Federalism, Nationalism and Development**
   India and the Punjab economy
   Pritam Singh

10. **Human Development and Social Power**
    Perspectives from South Asia
    Ananya Mukherjee Reed

11. **The South Asian Diaspora**
    Transnational networks and changing identities
    Edited by Rajesh Rai and Peter Reeves

12. **Pakistan–Japan Relations**
    Continuity and change in economic relations and security interests
    Ahmad Rashid Malik

13. **Himalayan Frontiers of India**
    Historical, geo-political and strategic perspectives
    K. Warikoo

14. **India's Open-Economy Policy**
    Globalism, rivalry, continuity
    Jalal Alamgir

15. **The Separatist Conflict in Sri Lanka**
    Terrorism, ethnicity, political economy
    Asoka Bandarage

16. **India's Energy Security**
    Edited by Ligia Noronha and Anant Sudarshan

17. **Globalization and the Middle Classes in India**
    The social and cultural impact of neoliberal reforms
    Ruchira Ganguly-Scrase and Timothy J. Scrase

18. **Water Policy Processes in India**
    Discourses of power and resistance
    Vandana Asthana

19. **Minority Governments in India**
    The puzzle of elusive majorities
    Csaba Nikolenyi

20. **The Maoist Insurgency in Nepal**
    Revolution in the twenty-first century
    Edited by Mahendra Lawoti and Anup K. Pahari

21. **Global Capital and Peripheral Labour**
    The history and political economy of plantation workers in India
    K. Ravi Raman

22. **Maoism in India**
    Reincarnation of ultra-left wing extremism in the 21st Century
    Bidyut Chakrabarty and Rajat Kujur

23. **Economic and Human Development in Contemporary India**
    Cronyism and fragility
    Debdas Banerjee

Economic and Human Development in Contemporary India

Cronyism and fragility

Debdas Banerjee

Routledge
Taylor & Francis Group
LONDON AND NEW YORK

First published 2010
by Routledge
2 Park Square, Milton Park, Abingdon, Oxon OX14 4RN

Simultaneously published in the USA and Canada
by Routledge
711 Third Avenue, New York, NY 10017

Routledge is an imprint of the Taylor & Francis Group, an informa business

First issued in paperback 2011

Typeset in Times New Roman by Glyph International

British Library Cataloguing in Publication Data
A catalogue record for this book is available from the British Library.

Library of Congress Cataloging in Publication Data
Banerjee, Debdas.
Economic and human development in contemporary India : cronyism and fragility / Debdas Banerjee.
p. cm. – (Routledge contemporary South Asia series ; 23)
Includes bibliographical references and index.
ISBN 978-0-415-55974-4 (hbk. : alk. paper) – ISBN 978-0-203-86643-6 (ebook) 1. India–Economic policy. 2. India–Social policy. 3. India–Economic conditions. 4. India–Social conditions. I. Title.
HC435.3.B347 2010
330.954–dc22 2009018313

ISBN 13: 978-0-415-50213-9 (pbk)
ISBN 13: 978-0-415-55974-4 (hbk)
ISBN 13: 978-0-203-86643-6 (ebk)

Sudeshna, Arka
and to all those who motivated me

Contents

Figures

Tables

Boxes

Preface

The completion of the draft of this monograph coincided with the beginning of global meltdown. Which order of sequence the national economic prosperity (narrowly defined as growth in per capita income) and human development should follow is still a live intellectual issue in India. I began with the objective of inquiring into the sources of India's income and wealth, and the ways of translating those into well-being of the population as a whole, at a time when Indian planners and *India Inc.* started thinking of the economy as finally launched on the steady-state growth path. The Eleventh Five-Year Plan (2007–12) document notes:

> India has entered the Eleventh Plan period with an impressive record of economic growth. After a lacklustre performance in the Ninth Plan period (1997–98 to 2001–02), when gross domestic product (GDP) grew at only 5.5 per cent per annum, the economy accelerated in the Tenth Plan period (2002–03 to 2006–07) to record an average growth of 7.7 per cent, the highest in any Plan period so far. Besides, there was acceleration even within the Tenth Plan period and the growth rate in the last four years of the Plan has averaged 8.7 per cent, making India one of the fastest growing economies in the world.
>
> (Planning Commission 2008, vol.1: 1)

Generally, the government and international funding agencies became content with a high GDP growth rate and bullish stock market, and regarded these as the "black box" of the economy. Since many other indicators of development were found to be inconsistent, an examination of the constituent components of the GDP growth rate was felt necessary. True, the current rate of growth has been persisting for the last four consecutive years, but in the past India did achieve in quite a number of years an annual growth rate of greater than 8 per cent. These figures used to be followed immediately by opinionated rhetoric (as found in GoI, *Economic Survey*, various issues) such as: 'we have the capability of being in line with the best in the world and aiming beyond that'; 'India is well-poised to reach the stage of developed countries and is set to make rapid strides'; or 'the country is in the periphery of developed countries and would soon enter the stage of developed countries'. But why didn't it materialize? Were there institutional and/or organizational hurdles? If yes, what are those?

The current reality is rather rough and points to a graph of development that has two vertices with a flat but fattened middle, plotted against percentage of Indian population. It sounds surreal to a neoliberal economist obsessed with the tricky idea of the "trickle down" effect and who does not consider entitlements of the general population to factor endowments as necessary determinants for a diffused aggregate economic prosperity. Nonetheless, a number of non-fiction titles have a fictionalized "emerging giant", or "the Indian tiger", which sounds quite predatory in this region of Asia. Some books have collated the chronology of macroeconomic policies in India and suggested further reforms. Policy choices are certainly important, but under what conditions those produce positive results are rather more important. The failure to appreciate the *real* fundamentals produces inferences that have little prognostic virtues: as it happened, India is now caught into the gloomy cycle despite a series of so-called reforms.

Indian billionaires are leading the list of world's richest individuals, and many Indian tycoons are building up colonies overseas. On the other hand, India is worse in human development indicators and is leading the world in absolute poverty, malnutrition, infant mortality rate, use of child labour (despite widespread adult unemployment). There is mass demand from about four-fifths of the Indian population for cheaper cotton cloth, yet the century-old cotton mills in Ahmedabad (Gujarat) Mumbai (Maharashtra), Delhi, Kanpur (Uttar Pradesh) and in other "older" cities have been closed for a decade or so, and many of these have made rooms for high-end shopping plazas, entertainment centres and gated communities on the same land.

India had appeared in the global industrial atlas in the third quarter of the nineteenth century with cotton textiles and engineering industries, when German industrialization was making headway. Later, the two countries diverged. The colonial rule did not set hurdles for Indian cotton mills producing and exporting coarse cloth up to 20–25 counts. Besides, the coercive rule ended in 1947, leaving wide scope of speculation as to what impeded Indian industrialization afterwards. Briefly, while the principles of growth in income and wealth were overrepresented in the institutions in India, the principles of human development were not considered as critical. These varieties of dualism warrant explanation for a better understanding of the functioning of the economy and entrepreneurship, and also for redesigning development policies in the twenty-first century. The focus in this book is thus on the structural deficiency of a positive relation between national economic prosperity and human development.

'I don't want India to be an economic super power. I want India to be a happy country.' This was said by J.R.D. Tata (1904–93), the previous head of the TATA business house, which is one of the few pioneering Indian entrepreneurs who directed large-scale investments in basic and heavy industries and wanted to see a self-reliant India. The message was communicated to the nation through a dedication from the Tata house in many of the Indian daily newspapers on the occasion of JRD's 104th birth anniversary, on 29 July 2008. The late JRD made the point long before "superpower" caught the imagination of the Indian *nouveaux riches*. So: is there a conflict between becoming a superpower and happiness? Perhaps, JRD thought in that way, we guess.

We ought to strive for "happiness" as the principal agenda in the twenty-first century, after a pretty long voyage through industrial civilization. In the contemporary world, the earliest assurance of "happiness" came from the economic (mostly, trade-centric) arguments of globalization. It was later confirmed by the Millennium Declaration and the Millennium Development Goals (MDGs) as declared by the United Nations for a shared future for all. 'The MDGs are still achievable if we act now. This will require inclusive sound governance, increased public investment in economic growth, enhanced productive capacity, and the creation of decent work' (Ban Ki-moon, the Secretary-General, United Nations, Foreword to *The Millennium Development Goals Report 2007*, New York: United Nations, 2007). This exercise is a modest attempt to make out the right conditions for a "shared future". My friend and distinguished social scientist Jan Breman, who has worked extensively on destitute and disadvantaged communities in India and China, quite often feels uncomfortable with economists and the discipline of economics as currently practised. He thinks the great divide between the economic sector and the social sector is a creation of the contemporary economists. Perhaps he is partially right; there is a need to revive the liberal tradition. This book makes an effort to highlight the inseparability of economic development and the development of the social sector; one may find out the *alternatives* implicit here.

The book avoids an exhausting mountain of facts, the linear narrative and a narrow Paretianism. It highlights factor endowments of individuals/communities as related to income and wealth distribution. The understanding is that the nature of income distribution is intrinsically connected to the kinds of assets – share-scripts and bonds, real estate, agriculturally productive land, human capital and skills, social capital, and so on – generated in the development process. A few issues are chosen – viz. international trade, technology, access to food, inequality and poverty, and the "catching up" of the developing countries – around which the global civil society would like to have a consensus. I have refined data to the extent that they do not make the primary information incomprehensible. I am one of those who believe in statistics only as a "tool" of economics, and am not very friendly with the branch of knowledge which prefers to "plot the scatter, draw conclusion(s)" that ignore *history*. Finally, the aim is to provide a template by which to think about the Indian economy and similar other economies in the South.

I am very thankful to the MPhil students (in Development Studies of the Calcutta University) at IDSK as well as those of the graduate programme of Sciences Po (Paris) whose probing classroom questions helped me plug many loose ends. Parts of this study were presented at the Institute of Advanced Studies, University of Western Australia (Perth); in the China–India joint seminar organized by the Indian Council of Social Science Research, Institute for Human Development and China Academy of Social Sciences; and in the 49th annual conference of the Indian Society of Labour Economics. I am very thankful to all whose comments have enriched the text. I am thankful to Alice Amsden who read the first draft. I am grateful for the thoughtful comments and suggestions that I received from the anonymous referees. I am also very thankful to Dorothea Schaefter, who discovered the manuscript. I am especially appreciative of the assiduous, careful, and creative copy-editing of lan Guy. I am also grateful to the staff at Routledge and at Glyph International who took care of various aspects of the production of the book. I am very thankful indeed to various government ministries and departments in India including Reserve Bank of India, Central Statistical Organization and National Sample Survey Organization for making available all the official data on respective websites, and the online service. I also deeply acknowledge the online data services of different departments of the United States, various UN organizations and the World Bank. I have used information available at numerous other websites; all of them deserve my sincere gratitude for posting information for wider and easier access, especially when free of costs.

Debdas Banerjee
Institute of Development Studies, Kolkata

1 Emerging India

Issues in development

Obscurity to prosperity

'[T]he economy has moved decisively to a higher growth phase ... with growth in GDP at market prices exceeding 8 per cent in every year since 2003–04' asserts the government of India (GoI) (*Economic Survey 2007–08*: 1). The document also says there was an acceleration in domestic investment and saving rates to drive growth and provide the resources for meeting the 9 per cent (average) growth target of the Eleventh Five-Year Plan (i.e. during 2007–12). GDP at current market prices is expected to cross US$1 trillion (at market exchange rate) (ibid.). In a slightly longer time-period, India did attain the level of a 7 per cent *plus* growth rate in couples of years in the so-called conservative regime,[1] and even had a growth rate of nearly 10 per cent in 1988–89. However, the distinction of the current phase is that it gives the impression of equilibrium at a higher level.

India's wealth *vis-à-vis* the world has grown simultaneously (Merrill Lynch and Capgemini 2005). No matter whether India lags far behind in terms of per capita income, the number of her high-net-worth individuals (HNWI, each holding at least US$1million in financial assets) exceeds that of such global business hubs as Singapore and Hong Kong, the oil-rich United Arab Emirates, middle-income South Africa, and is narrowing the gap with the "Miracle on the Han River", i.e. the high-tech economy of South Korea. The HNWI population growth in India was even higher than that of the early developed countries (EDCs) such as Spain, the UK, or even the US.[2]

A different estimate of private wealth, i.e. the American business magazine *Forbes* lists for the last couples of years, shows that the spatial distribution of the world's richest individuals is undergoing changes. In 2000, almost all of the world's richest people lived in North America, Europe, and rich Asia-Pacific countries. Each of these groups of countries contributed about one-third of the members of the world's wealthiest 10 per cent. China occupied much of the middle third of the global wealth distribution, while India, Africa and low-income Asian countries dominated the bottom third. Matters have been changing quite dramatically since then. First of all, the number of billionaires in the world is increasing at an unprecedented rate.[3] Total net worth of the billionaires has increased from $3.5 trillion in 2006 to $4.4 trillion in 2007. By nationality, most surprisingly, the third place is occupied by India.[4] Much richer countries, namely

Japan, France and Italy, are trailing behind India.[5] Even China, despite its sharply increasing inequality, fails to match India.[6] The combined wealth of Indian billionaires – which increased from US$106 billion to $170 billion in a single year, i.e. 2006–07 – is about 19 per cent of India's GDP. Their combined wealth is now larger than the gross national income of such rich countries as New Zealand, newly industrializing countries in Asia, namely Malaysia, Philippines and Singapore, Latin-American countries like Venezuela, Chile and Colombia, and evidently larger than in its immediate neighbours, excepting China. Forty-eight Indian firms, led by Ambani's Reliance Industries, have made it to the *Forbes 2008* list of 2,000 biggest global companies. For sure, public enterprises such as State Bank of India and Indian Oil Corporation are in the list, but otherwise most of the 48 Indian firms are private enterprises. Moreover, out of the 75 richest families in the world, seven are Indian nationals; of these, four held ranks within the top 10.

Gross income and wealth

The gross national income (GNP) of India (in US dollars) in 2006 exceeded that of Australia, Brazil, South Korea, Mexico, and many EU countries such as the Netherlands (World Bank, WDR 2008). More revealing is the fact that, in purchasing power parity (PPP) dollars, India's GNP is double the amount of Europe's largest economy, i.e. Germany, and is at par with Japan. The upper 15 per cent of the population in the income distribution – the middle and high income groups – provide a domestic Indian market for industrial goods, which is larger than that of many of the developed countries.

The per capita consumer expenditure of the high income[7] and middle income[8] groups in India is found to have grown at the rate of 6.2 and 4.3 per cent, respectively, between 1993 and 2005 (NCEUS 2007). On average, the annual expenditure of the 253 million high- and middle-income people grew at the rate of 5 per cent per annum, which is greater than the GDP growth rate of an average EDC. One would witness the rapid horizontal spread of expensive multistorey air-conditioned shopping malls beyond the class-I metropolitan cities to the class-II and class-III cities across the length and breadth of the country in the last couple of years. The expensive restaurants, the number of which is increasing so rapidly, are overbooked for dinner. Brand shops of all sorts of luxurious consumer articles were doing business beyond their expectations until the global meltdown put a brake on their growth. Never before has the big domestic capital as well as the foreign transnational corporations (TNCs) showed so much interest in opening retail chains in India as they are doing now, and that too in a very big way. Further, the number of domestic passengers using air traffic was nearly 51 million in 2005–06. Despite there being one of the best railway networks in the world available in the country, considerable improvements in passenger comfort in the trains, and substantial differences in the prices of rail and air travel, there was a stupendous 39 per cent increase of domestic air passengers, to 71 million in 2006–07 (GoI, Ministry of Civil Aviation 2007–08) – a strong indicator of economic growth, of course. A large part of these was for the bullish stock market.

Beyond the realm of financial wealth, the stock of "knowledge capital" in the country has also enlarged notably if the numbers of science and engineering graduates are counted. Indian emigrants nowadays corner most of the US H1B (Indian nationals accounted for 38 per cent of the 409,619 admissions in the US in 2008) and high-skilled H2B visas. As for L-1 visas, which are primarily used for intra-company transferees, leading source countries in this category were India (17 per cent), Britain (14 per cent) and Japan (9.8 per cent) in 2008 (US Office of Immigration Statistics 2009: Table 4). If the trend continues, by about 2020 most of the skilled jobs occupied by the international migrants in the ten largest developed host countries would be of Indian origin. Not least important is the fact that today India is the sixth nation – after the EU, the US, Japan, Russia and China – to buy nuclear merchandise and retain a nuclear arsenal, without being a member of the G-8 and other such groups, the gatekeepers of high technology. India has moved from nuclear pariah to a member of the club in just 10 years after the Pokhran-II (in the deserts of Rajasthan) nuclear test in 1998 which had led her to the nuclear doghouse. Thus many, including the corporate media, started dreaming of an India that is certain to emerge as *superpower* in the coming 10–12 years; only the Indian people ought to ensure the current rate of GDP growth to sustain, as we are told.

The rate of growth of total output in the economy can be expressed as the sum of two factors: the rate of increase in the number of hours worked, and the rate of increase in the output per hour worked (the productivity of the labour force).[9] The growth in total hours worked occurs because the labour force has a "natural" growth rate. It could also be the case that while the employment remains constant the regular working hours of the existing workforce have lengthened. One would then expect an increase in the wage level and thereby rising living standards of the existing workforce. The second factor, i.e. the growth in productivity, is the key to rising living standards. The size of the Indian population itself, besides being instrumental to enlarging the consumer market, is one of the factors fuelling the dreams of gaining the status of economic superpower. The world population projection for the year 2010 by the US Census Bureau shows that the Indian population (1,155 million) would be greater than the aggregate population of Europe and the New Independent States (NIS) (which would be roughly 810 million), as well as that of North America (344 million).[10] Therefore, the productivity growth of the Indian people would be "rampaging" in the near future!

Reverse colonization

Until a couple of decades ago, the TNCs were, exceptions notwithstanding, the icon of the "West", establishing leadership by superior technology, brands, and selling power. The image of *India Inc.* was that of "low cost – low price – low margins", especially in pharmaceuticals, textiles, software and engineering industries such as automobiles. The latest sensational global news was Indian giant Tata Motors' takeover of the British luxury car brands (Jaguar–Land Rover) (see Box 1.1). Developing a car from scratch would have taken the Tatas three to five years.

Box 1.1 TATA Group's empire building

- Apr 2008 — Tata Motors acquires Jaguar and Land Rover from US carmaker Ford
- Mar 2008 — Telco Construction Equipment Company (Telcon: a 60:40 joint venture between Tata Motors and Hitachi Construction Machinery, Japan) acquires 79 per cent in Spain-based Serviplem, one of the world's leading manufacturers of transit mixers, dry bulk tankers and pumps. The company has a strong presence in China and the acquisition gave Tata an entry into the Chinese construction space
- Feb 2008 — Tata Chemicals buys US-based General Chemicals
- Jun 2007 — TRF acquires control of Singapore's York Transport Equipment
- Jun 2007 — Tata Power picks 30 per cent stake in Indonesia's PT Kaltim Prima Coal and PT Arutmin
- Apr 2007 — VSNL (Videsh Sanchar Nigam Limited, in which Tata has substantial shares) acquires Transtel Telecoms of South Africa
- Apr 2007 — Tata Tea buys Poland's Vitax and Flosana
- Apr 2007 — Indian Hotels acquires Campton Place Hotel in the US
- Mar 2007 — Tata Power picks stake in Indonesia's PT Bumi Resources
- Jan 2007 — Tata Steel acquires Anglo-Dutch steel maker Corus
- Aug 2006 — Tata Tea acquires 30 per cent stake in USA Glaceau (Energy Brands). Later sells it to Coca-Cola
- Jun 2006 — Tata Tea acquires US-based Eight o'Clock coffee company
- Dec 2005 — Tata Chem picks up 63.5 per cent stake in UK's Bruner Mond Group
- Dec 2005 — Tata Steel acquires Millennium Steel of Thailand
- Nov 2005 — TCS buys Chilean BPO firm Comicorn
- Oct 2005 — Tata Technologies purchases INCAT International, UK
- Oct 2005 — Tata Tea acquires Good Earth Corp
- July 2005 — VSNL acquires Teleglobe International
- Aug 2004 — Tata Steel buys Singapore's NatSteel
- Mar 2004 — Tata Motors acquires South Korean Daewoo's Commercial Vehicle Company
- Feb 2000 — Tata Tea buys Tetley

The firm now gets access to readymade engine and design technology that will allow it to compete with high-end carmakers like General Motors. Also, the company gets access to engineering technology that has been designed and manufactured since the 1950s. This was originally developed by British Leyland, British Aerospace and BMW, and is now part of Ford. It also helps Tata Motors to cut down its time period (perhaps not less than five to six years) for R&D in the luxury car segment. This type of colonization, based on the capital market, is distinct from the colonialism of the EDCs in the past with their superior technological and military prowess.

Then there is the thrilling rise of the London-based Indian Lakshmi Mittal – who began his career working in the family's steelmaking business in India – the richest man in Europe and fourth richest person in the world. The Mittal family owns 44 per cent of Arcelor Mittal, the world's largest steel company, with assets in France, Belgium, Romania, Bosnia-Herzegovnia, South Africa, Poland, Czech Republic, Indonesia, Kazakhstan, Canada, Bulgaria, United States, Trinidad, Brazil and Mexico. Further, the Anil Ambani group firm Reliance Big Entertainment acquired the digital images business of US-based DTS Inc. in April 2008. DTS Digital Images is a leading firm in the field of digital restoration and enhancement of moving pictures and uses proprietary tools and algorithms. It used to work with Walt Disney, Paramount Pictures, MGM and 20th Century Fox, among others. This was the first acquisition by Reliance Entertainment overseas in the digital services space. On the whole, in a telling demonstration of reverse outsourcing, 12 Indian companies have invested billions of dollars in the United States, creating and retaining more than 30,000 American jobs.[11]

In a nutshell, the accumulation of capital is unhindered, perhaps because of not experiencing diminishing returns. One possibility is that technological progress in the economy helps capital to steer clear of diminishing returns. A second possibility could be that developed human capital – education, skills and health – gave the physical capital a piggyback ride to avert diminishing returns. And a third possibility could be that neither continuing improvements in technology nor developed human capital was responsible, but constant, if not rising, profit-share (and diminishing wage-share despite productivity growth) in gross income of firm or country, which was the likely outcome of the state's direct and indirect subsidies to capital. We will inquire into the alternative possibilities.

The best of times, the worst of times

The ever-growing capital accumulation by the Indian corporate sector, notwithstanding a deeper scrutiny of economic and demographic statistics of India, lands us in great paradoxes all around. Let us begin with the frequently used summary indicators of development, namely per capita income and human development index (HDI). By the former indicator (in PPP dollars), India is marginally above the average low-income country but much below the average lower middle-income country. India is even worse in the HDI – the rank was 128 in 2007 – which tells us the PPP GDP per capita rating *overstated* the country's overall level of development. The aggregates look stronger, yet at the average individual level one gets stuck: can the population be blamed, then?

Of course not, because there was a 50 per cent increase in population as compared to 234 per cent growth in real GNP between 1985 and 2005. So, apparently we are clueless as to why the bulk of the population is languishing or has remained "excluded" in the processes of visible economic growth. More precisely, nearly 836 million or 77 per cent of the Indian population were living with a per capita daily consumer expenditure of less than half a US dollar (i.e. less than Rs 20) at the end of 2004–05. Since 2000 (when world leaders endorsed the Millennium Declaration) and up till 2004, extreme poverty and hunger have engulfed yet another 25 million people in India alone.[12] India is home to roughly one-third of all the poor people in the world, which is pegged at 1.4 billion people. It also has a higher proportion of its population living on less than $2 a day than even sub-Saharan Africa (Chen and Ravallion 2008). India, according to the new estimates, had 456 million or about 42 per cent of the population living below $1.25 per day in 2005.[13]

Considering the lower bound of the poverty line of $1.00 a day at 2005 PPP – which is very close to the national poverty line used by the government of India – 24.3 per cent or 267 million people were living below the poverty line (BPL).[14] And, if we consider the upper bound of $2.50 a day, then 86 per cent of Indian population was BPL in 2005 (Chen and Ravallion 2008: Table 6). What is more disturbing is the slowdown of the rate of decline in the poverty ratio – either with the $1.00 or the $1.25 line – following neoliberal reforms between 1990 and 2005, as compared to that in the 1980s (based on Chen and Ravallion 2008: Table 7).

As one looks further into the social categories, 88 per cent of the Scheduled Castes (SCs) and Scheduled Tribes (STs), 80 per cent of the "Other Backward Class" (OBC) population and 84 per cent of the Muslims in India are condemned to absolute poverty. In many Indian states such as Gujarat, Maharashtra, Orissa and Rajasthan, the share of tribals out of the poor population is about 40 per cent.

> They have remained poor at a bare subsistence level without any job or social security, working in the most miserable, unhygienic and unliveable conditions, throughout this period of high economic growth since the early 1990s (NCEUS 2007: 8).

The illiterates have a high probability of being poor or vulnerable if one follows the logic of "human capital". However, it is found that 83 per cent in the poor and vulnerable group are receiving education up to the primary level (NCEUS 2007). Therefore, these people might be suffering, one does not know for sure, because of their low productivity (mostly in agriculture and allied economic activities) and perhaps need relocation in the higher productive economy. But what does the occupational status of the "working poor" tell us?

Working poor

The share of the working poor (at US$1 a day) in total employment in India was 39 per cent in 2005. If we consider $2 a day earnings, then 81 per cent of the Indian working population was living BPL (ILO, KILM, 5th edn: Table 20). One of the probable reasons, as argued by many, for the very high incidence of poverty among the working population is the low rate of industrial growth; otherwise the low-wage syndrome would have been history.

Certainly, the agriculture to manufacturing wage ratio was 1:1.9 – i.e. the manufacturing wage was nearly double the agricultural wage rate in India, in 2004–05. However, first, the *gap* between wages in agriculture and manufacturing itself tended to decline since at least the mid-1980s when the manufacturing wage was about two and a half times the agricultural wage (Abraham 2007).[15]

Second, the workforce participation ratio of men and women in general, and women in particular, is considerably higher in agriculture than in manufacturing. The share of women in wage employment in the non-agricultural sector is miserably lower in India (only 17.5 per cent) than in any other country in Asia and the developing member countries of the Asian Development Bank in the Pacific – the only exception is Pakistan where the share is 8.7 per cent (ADB 2005: 126). Globalization has feminized the industrial workforce elsewhere, but not much in India and Pakistan.

To summarize, the relative wage is low in agriculture, but the sector is conducive to higher (than urban) annual family income of an average household with work participation by both the male and female adult members, especially as the number of days of wage employment available to rural agricultural labourers, annually, happened to be at least 227 for male and 184 for female in 2004–05 (NSSO 2006d, Report no. 515).

The wage labourers get engaged in other activities as well such as animal husbandry, the products of which have ready markets. On the other hand, once these people are "pushed out" to the urban industrial economy most of them become self-employed in the periphery of the capitalist economy – the products produced by them face uncertain and discriminatory markets – and others turn into casual workers, given their levels of skills. The distribution of workforce by gender, activity-status and rural–urban location shows that nearly 45 per cent of urban males and 48 per cent of urban females were self-employed, while 15 and 17 per cent respectively were casual labourers and the rest regular waged/salaried, in 2004–05 (NSSO 2006d, Report no. 515). In a nutshell, the prospect of greater opportunities for better livelihood in the urban industrial economy confronts the rude reality: the poverty ratio (by the Indian official yardstick) among urban unorganized sector workers has increased.[16] Ironically, during the period of speedy global integration of the economy, the self-employed (male *plus* female) working poor (i.e. BPL) in rural India declined,[17] while increasing in urban India. While there is a decline in the number of working poor among the rural casual labourers, the same has increased in the urban areas.[18]

The second line of argument is that as the *market* hegemonizes, life and livelihood income distribution becomes more asymmetric. This may be true, but only partially, because the century-old market institution in the EDCs was not found to have generated income inequality to the extent it is evident in India. Both the labour laws and the civil laws in the EDCs facilitated defences of the weaker competing agents against the asymmetric consequences of labour market flexibility and capital market restructuring which, at a first glance, appear to be complementary and symmetric policies. Yet another line of argument is that the market is there to rule, but the government must not shy away from its role in ensuring distributive justice. However, keeping aside taxes and subsidies, it is difficult to establish serious lapses on the part of the government of India in allocating budgetary resources for such distributive schemes as poverty eradication, rural employment generation, improvement of the socio-economic conditions of the STs, the most disadvantaged, and other means of social sector improvement.

Of course, one can challenge the schemes on the ground that these are not given to the beneficiaries as a matter of entitlement. Anyway, the allocated financial resources in these projects might be inadequate, but one needs to inquire: why has the money spent not produced the "expected" outcomes?

The central government expenditure (planned and non-planned) on social sector and rural development has gradually increased and constituted more than 16 per cent of the total in 2007–08 (GoI, Ministry of Finance, *Economic Survey* 2007–08: Table 10.2). The total combined social sector expenditure by the central and state governments constituted about 28 per cent of GDP in the year. A large part of this is spent through the so-called decentralized power institution, i.e. the three-tier *Panchayati Raj* Institution (PRI, elected local self-governments) in rural India. Ironically, the huge social expenditure of the government has been instrumental in only strengthening the *intermediate regime* of the politician-bureaucrat-local elites (see Chapter 7). Hardly a fraction of the actual allocation reaches the targeted population,[19] which deepens both the absolute as well as the relative deprivation, thereby weakening substantive democracy in India. The enlarged middle class could have been a boon for democracy provided the foundation at large was not corruptive and parasitical, unlike in the West (see Chapter 6). It is important to recognize that mass deprivation is a hindrance to intelligent participation (against demagoguery) by the mass of population in politics.

Development of underdevelopment

During the last two decades, more than 2.4 million hectares of arable land and additionally 1.06 million hectares of pastures in India (FAO 2007: Table A2) have changed to non-agricultural uses, mostly to develop into cities and towns. It has not only been the loss of livelihood of the farmers and their family members; several other people such as sharecroppers and landless wage labourers, local grocery shop owners and people engaged in transporting the agricultural products to the market places, have also lost their livelihood in the process. On average, about 10 jobs, direct and indirect, are dependent on one hectare of cultivable land; therefore, at least 24 million people were forcibly displaced from the farm sector and have been desperately searching alternative jobs. As the elasticity of employment in the organized factories is on the downtrend, the outcome is the swelling informal or unorganized labour market – the twilight zone. Even the unorganized sector cannot provide so many regular jobs. Most of the jobseekers, as stated earlier, ultimately become self-employed "market entrepreneurs".

On the whole, the income-share of the unorganized sector[20] – in net domestic product (NDP at factor cost) – has been nearly three-fifths. Despite the rising employment share, the income-share of the unorganized sector in manufacturing as such has been declining. The declining share of the unorganized sector in the country's value-added is not unlikely, because of the greater weight of the low value-added (i.e. low priced) products in the sector's total output than it is in the organized or corporate manufacturing sector. The growing contribution of the unorganized sector in the economy is further visible in "financing, insurance, real estate and business services", "construction", "transport, storage and communication" and as in many developed countries, in "trade, hotels and restaurants" (Table 1.1).

As regards the crucial "wage–export" relations, the gems and jewellery industry, for instance, is now India's single largest export earner and constitutes 24 per cent of exports of manufactured goods. India is the world's biggest diamond and gemstone cutting centre, and polishes more than 80 per cent (in weight) of the global diamonds yield, engaging more than a million workers. The trade consists of importing, polishing and cutting (or otherwise treating) and then exporting diamonds, gold jewellery, coloured gemstones, pearls, non-gold jewellery, synthetic stones and fashion jewellery. The United States is the single largest importer of gems and jewellery from India, followed by Hong Kong, Belgium and Japan. The diamond and gemstone industry generates hundreds of millions of dollars as profits around the world. Yet the workers who cut and polish the precious stones often receive poverty wages and work in conditions which leave them with lung disease or half-blinded.

Overall the labour costs in the diamond industry amount to just 1 per cent of total costs, and most workers do not receive any social benefits. Despite this, workplace conditions are generally bad, with workplaces being congested and poorly lit and ventilated. Over half of the industry's workforce suffers from work-related ailments such as kidney dysfunction, tuberculosis, lung disease, stomach problems, wheezing, pains in their joints and eye sores, because of exposure to crystalline and amorphous silica (ILO 1997). There is no comprehensive official survey on how many workers have died of quartz dust or other serious occupational illness. However, it will not be surprising if the total mortality caused by work-related diseases is found to be highest in this export industry among all domestic industrial activities. The information in this regard generally remains partial because roughly 95 per cent of the workforce are not unionized, and also because the government shows apathy to collect information from the unorganized sector. Workers' incomes are not settled through collective bargains, and depend on whatever the employer or the labour recruiting agent decides to pay them (ibid.). In many cases, workers trying to organize or join unions have been dismissed and even threatened with guns. Further, according to the most conservative estimate, over 30,000 children are working in diamond processing in India (ibid.).

There were about 10 million working Indian children in 2000 (Lieten 2004a), despite the Child Labour (Prohibition & Regulation) Act (1986). If all children not going to school are counted as child labourers (UNDP India Homepage) – i.e. all children who were deprived of the right to education and childhood and are out of school – India has around 100 million child labourers (Lieten 2004b). A large number of those tens of millions of children work 8–14 hours a day in shops and establishments, in manufacturing units, in auto workshops, substituting that many adults, who are therefore out of employment, and depressing the wage market further.

Table 1.1 Share (%) of the unorganized sector in the net domestic product (NDP at current prices) of various economic activities, in 2005

Industry	*1999–00*	*2000–01*	*2001–02*	*2002–03*	*2003–04*	*2004–05*	*2005–06*
Agriculture, forestry and fishing	91.7	91.7	91.2	90.8	92.0	90.8	90.8
Mining and quarrying	8.4	9.0	9.4	9.1	9.9	8.4	10.4
Manufacturing	37.5	36.5	34.9	34.3	33.8	32.6	32.1
Electricity, gas and water supply	2.7	2.8	3.2	3.3	3.4	4.9	5.4
Construction	59.0	58.7	57.5	59.8	59.8	64.5	57.7
Trade, hotels and restaurants	84.8	84.1	81.8	81.4	80.6	80.1	80.7
Transport, storage and communication	52.6	53.8	53.9	57.9	58.3	61.4	64.1
Financing, insurance, real estate and business services	48.4	49.3	47.3	44.9	44.3	44.0	43.1
Community, social and personal services	23.1	23.7	24.7	25.9	26.8	27.4	28.0
Unorganized sector (total) in NDP at factor cost	59.5	59.0	58.5	57.2	57.9	57.5	57.4

Source: CSO, NAS (2005–06).

As such, the unorganized sector accounts for most of the extremely poor, poor, marginally poor and vulnerable people. By international standards, especially those of East and South East Asia, India's labour force participation rate, which is 40–42 per cent, would not be considered as high. However, the number of workers is a staggering 457 million by the latest count in 2004–05. Of this, more than 92 per cent are unorganized – the number includes informal workers in both the unorganized and the organized sectors – having no entitlement to job, decent wage and social security. Of these, the number of non-agricultural unorganized workers is quite large, i.e. 167 million. The wage rate ranges from half-a-dollar a day — for 10–12 hours — to $3 at the most. And, of course, the wage structure is gendered. Considering an average of three dependents per worker, the wage income clearly does not allow these unorganized workers to break away from the shackles of poverty.

The National Commission for Enterprises in the Unorganized Sector (NCEUS) prepared reports along with draft laws for covering social security for more than 300 million unorganized workers that would have required an expenditure of barely 1 per cent of GDP at the most. The proposal had the potential of a pronounced social reform – through empowerment – but ultimately was ignored and turned into a titbit by the pro-reform government. The Unorganized Sector Workers' Social Security bill (2008) – a systematically revised version of what was prepared by the NCEUS – was passed by both the upper and lower houses of parliament; still pending is the enactment (i.e. notification by the central government) of the Act. In a nutshell, "social welfare" (a new term among many others) thus prevailed over "social security". Any law that does not deal with the issue of employment, its regulation, wages, conditions of work and so on, will be not merely incomplete but also dysfunctional if it proceeds to deal with social security on a stand-alone basis (for details, see Sankaran 2009).

The sector is equally neglected by the national trade unions. It is thus apt to describe the sector as "underworld" in the parlour of the privileged citizens of India.

What has worsened the matter is the drying up of sources of alternative employment abroad for the "residuals" from the poor developing countries, since the total labour force in the developed countries is likely to decline progressively (Table 1.2). The General Agreement on Trade in Services (GATS) is an ambitious effort to expand international labour migration to help developing countries. Labour typically accounts for 70–80 per cent of the cost of producing services as against 10 per cent (at the most) of the cost of producing manufactured goods. Therefore, labour migration from the low-wage developing countries to the postindustrial economies in the North would help the latter to lower prices of many labour-intensive services. However, most industrial countries have been reluctant to liberalize their immigration rules, thereby encouraging undocumented migration of low-skilled desperate workers. Hence, the urgent development agenda is to have domestic growth of the "modern" sector *à la* Arthur Lewis (Lewis 1954; 1979), the classical Marxian historical materialism, and the post-World War II neoclassical development economics.

Table 1.2 Size of labour force in high income and developing countries, in 2001 and 2025 (estimated)

	2001					*2025*			
	Migrants (million)	*Share of migrants in total labour force (%)*	*Total labour force (million)*	*Share (%)*	*Migration (million)*	*Migrants (million)*	*Share (%)*	*Total labour force (million)*	*Share (%)*
			High-income countries						
Migrants from LDCs	28	6	479		14	28.5	6	475	
Unskilled	25	7	332	69	10	25.3	8	324	68
Skilled	3	2	148	31	5	3.2	2	145	31
			Developing countries						
Total labour force			2,596					3,561	
Unskilled			2,396	92				3,294	93
Skilled			200	8				267	7

Source and notes: Martin (2006: Table A2.1). The table summarizes a World Bank effort to project the gains from adding three per cent developing-country migrants to the labour force of high-income countries between 2001 and 2025 via increased migration, i.e. adding 14 million migrants to the current 28 million. These 2001 migrants, who included 25 million unskilled and 3 million skilled workers from developing countries, would be augmented by 10 million more unskilled and 5 million more skilled workers, so that in 2025 there would be a total of 35 million unskilled and 8 million skilled LDC migrants. However, with the labour force of high-income countries projected to shrink slightly to 475 million, LDC migrants would constitute a larger share of high-income-country labour forces. Meanwhile, developing-country labour forces increase by one billion, to 3.6 billion.

Comparing relative "social productivity"

The increase in social productivity – which takes an economy to a higher production frontier – reduces the expenditure of social labour necessary for the production of a given product or service, and consequently its cost, but not necessarily its value. In this light, let us examine the consequences of displacement. Evidence suggests that the displaced people later swell the slum population in the cities and towns. The slum population constituted 43 million or 23 per cent of the total population of cities and towns in India in 2001. Most of the municipal corporations – with population above one million and experiencing considerable growth of the so-called modern sector – are having a slum population of more than a quarter of the total population.[21]

Workers living in slums constitute at the most one-third of the slum population in the million-plus cities (Office of the Registrar General and Census Commissioner 2001).[22] More than 95 per cent of these workers are engaged in the non-household unorganized units. It is anyone's guess how the rest eke out a living without access to common property – some types of land, forest products, fish and vegetation in the water sources, etc. supplying nutrition at low cost or free of costs – which they previously had before eviction.

The rate of growth of real wages of urban casual workers had always been lower than that of rural casual workers in the decades of 1980s and 1990s, but not negative.

So, if wage is considered as proxy for productivity, the data are not encouraging for an alternative social productivity of labour. The relative wages changed between 1999 and 2004: there was an absolute decline in the real wage of urban casual workers, while it increased for casual workers in the rural areas.[23] Surprisingly, many of these urban casual workers are actually engaged in the deregulated and growing export sector. The trade-theoretic argument thus takes us nowhere, except to a "wasteland" where the number of working poor, in other words the BPL households, is enlarging. It is perhaps not a game of chance that the states (and union territories) which are still to witness across-the-board industrialization – namely Himachal Pradesh, Sikkim, Arunachal Pradesh, Nagaland, Manipur, Mizoram, Daman and Diu, Dadra and Nagar Haveli, and Lakshadweep – happen to be states with no slums at all (Office of the Registrar General and Census Commissioner 2001).

Hopes and fears of the slum dwellers in the metropolis are that they will lose *numbers* – yes, this is their acquired new identity – in the near future, following another round of evictions as the legal system increasingly becomes hostile to them and as the land-price in the metropolis is skyrocketing, thanks to the prosperity of the big real-estate developers, many of whom find places in the *Forbes* list. In the landmark Olga Tellis case in 1985, the Supreme Court affirmed that the right to livelihood was inherent in the right to life, and that if the state decides to evict pavement and slum dwellers, it must do so only in conformity with procedures established by law, including sufficient notice and rehabilitation. Those days are gone with the wind. The Delhi High Court held in the Okhla (Delhi) Factory Owners Association case in 2003 that displaced families are *not* entitled to any resettlement, as this would put extra burden on the state exchequer. The Supreme Court went further in the Almitra Patel case in blaming – even stigmatizing – the victim by declaring that rewarding an encroacher on public land with an alternative free site is like giving a reward to a pickpocket (Mander 2008).

In fact, in the class-I cities (with a population of 1 million and above), in general, and in Chennai (Tamil Nadu), Delhi, Kolkata (West Bengal), Lucknow (Uttar Pradesh), Ludhiana (Punjab), Patna (Bihar), Pune and Thane (both in Maharashtra) and Vadodara (Gujarat), in particular, the number of usually employed persons aged 15 years and above (according to principal and subsidiary status taken together) has declined between 1993 and 2005 (NSSO 2007, Report no. 520: Statement 3.2). So now it is the turn of the medium-sized towns and cities to witness a rising slum population. However, the problem of these places is that there are not enough jobs for the migrants from the metropolis. The class-II towns (with a population of 50,000 to less than one million) and class-III towns (with population less than 50,000) also experience a declining capacity to generate employment.

As such, decent jobs for relatively longer duration are fast drying up in the Indian cities and towns, if the trend between 1993 and 2005 was any indication and the economy's choice of technology does not undergo radical changes. Partial exceptions are the jobs that are specifically performed by women, like the domestic work of utensils cleaning, housekeeping, or as washers, all of course at

BPL wages (NSSO 2007, Report no. 520: Statement 3.2). What is more, the latter jobs are not "new products", rather a change of location of already existing jobs, thus raising doubts about aggregate productivity growth in the economy as a result of the displacement.

To summarize, it may be a coincidence, but the fact is that the major victims of displacement are the tribals and other backward classes. The distressed areas turn out to be the "labour catchment areas" of activities that use primitive technology and pay poverty wages such as, in the brickfields, stone quarrying and crushing, road construction, and domestic help, and in the numerous "sex colonies". In course of time, the issue of entrepreneurship acquires an added dimension in India.

Rise of "political entrepreneurs" and social tension

The assumption of perfect competition is incompatible with the case of increasing returns to scale (IRS). Yet IRS is considered as the source of economic development in the Smithian theory of division of labour. The proactive state might consider acting over the market – for speedy expansion of the social division of labour, leading to a rise in social productivity in a shorter time-span – thus planning to allocate entrepreneurship to those selective few who assure IRS (included in the list are mega dams, power projects and so on). This act could breed conflict in certain situations.

The scale economies determine the shape of the scale curve, while the position of this curve depends on: (a) change in technology (improvement in techniques); and (b) changes of factor prices in the industry. One needs to distinguish between *real economies* and strictly *pecuniary economies* of scale. While the former are realized in production – from, say, specialization and skills, inventory economies, managerial, selling or marketing, transport and storage, etc. – the latter are economies realized from paying lower prices for the factors used in the production and distribution of the product.

So far as (a) is concerned, the productivity cycle of a machine or technology – often inverted-U shaped – generates two types of tension. At the beginning of adoption of a revolutionary technology, the social reaction might become *Luddite* in appearance. On the downtrend of the U-curve, the reaction type is *passive* resistance to work-intensity by the knowledge workers (Banerjee 2006). Information technology – especially when it is embodied – is the best example.

So far as factor (b) is concerned – more relevant in the present context – the public institution or organization plays a decisive role. The institution creates positive externalities for private entrepreneurs in broadly two different ways: first, in general, by the development of knowledge/skills in the society or community through education, and in making provisions for better health of the workers; and second, in particular, by providing cheaper inputs – land (by the exercise of eminent domain), power, water, finance, etc. – to a selective few. So long as the beneficiaries are the selective few – for example, the industrial entrepreneur gets, among other things, finance at, say, one or two per cent interest rate while the farmer is at the verge of committing suicide, being unable to obtain this largesse from the state – the perception (among "the rest") of relative deprivation leads to a conflicting and, quite often, violent situation.

Ultimately, what the entrepreneur initially thought to be "positive externalities" later turns out to be an anticlimax. Why had she then opted for it? Maybe, she is the third generation or later in the "life cycle" of the firm. Alfred Marshall refers to the sequence of three generations in control of a typical firm: the founder, endowed with above-normal organizational and innovative ability; her immediate heirs, grown up in the hard school of the founder and used to at least a rigorous management of the family business; the third generation, grown up in prosperous conditions and less ready to make the sacrifices that are often necessary in a competitive environment characterized by continuous technological change and hence by the need to save and invest in order not to lose ground to their competitors. The rent-seeking behaviour of this firm ultimately takes it to the state in order to obtain pecuniary economies of scale.

Compare this with the situation of perfect competition, where the government is indifferent and the rival entrepreneurs offer equal compensation for the resulting dispossession, if any. Therefore, if the enterprise needs to acquire property rights on land, the land-loser has a fair chance to get a bargain price. By contrast, if the state prefers the route of IRS of a selective few for development, it fuels hostility of the deprived – they too can be disfavoured entrepreneurs. Given a choice between "market" and the "state", the deprived would then prefer the former since the state appears to them as a predator. But then they are in the midst of another problem.

If the market is to allocate entrepreneurship, the selection of the project by reasoning with costs and benefits and applying market-based exhaustive valuation still tends to ignore crucial informational inputs regarding consequences for the victims, which only a representative government or the civil society could supply. It leads to social tension when dispossession from the earlier forms of property ownership means sequential disadvantage for the dispossessed. Maybe (since return to individual labour is most likely to vary, especially in the informal economy) social productivity in the available alternative for the victims is lower (e.g. a farmer finding a job of domestic cook). Further, in the course of evaluation of the property rights, what are usually lost sight of are the economic rights (or the usufructuary rights) on the same asset by many others – e.g. the wage labourers or the tenant cultivators on a piece of agricultural land – who are left to lose their livelihood. Thus, inclusiveness of growth prompts us not to ignore the "consequential evaluation" that allows relevant consequences to be included in the calculations of costs and benefits (see Sen 2002). This necessitates an intelligent coordination between government and the market since both are prone to failure. These understandings of economics are in retreat when "free market" is merely demagoguery and crony capitalism is in full swing.

Special Economic Zones

A Special Economic Zone (SEZ) is a geographical region that has more liberal economic laws than the country's typical economic laws. SEZ covers a broad range of more specific zone types, including Free Trade Zones (FTZ), Export Processing Zones (EPZ), Free Zones (FZ), Industrial Estates (IE), Free Ports, Urban Enterprise Zones and others. One of the earliest and the most famous SEZs were promoted by the Chinese government in the early 1980s. Following the Chinese model, SEZs have been established in several countries, including Brazil, India, Iran, Jordan, Kazakhstan, Pakistan, the Philippines, Poland, Russia and Ukraine. A single SEZ can contain multiple specific zones within its boundaries. SEZs have been implemented using a variety of institutional structures across the world ranging from fully public (with exclusively government operator, developer and regulator) to exclusively private (private operator, developer and regulator). In many cases, public sector operators and developers act as quasi-government agencies in that they have a pseudo-corporate institutional structure and budgetary autonomy. SEZs are often developed under a public–private partnership arrangement, in which the public sector provides some level of support (provision of off-site infrastructure, equity investment, soft loans, bond issues, etc.) to ensure higher profitability for the private sector developer.

The SEZ policy in India was announced in April 2000, and was intended to make the SEZs an engine for economic growth through multifold increase in exports. It was supported by quality infrastructure complemented by an attractive fiscal package, both at the centre and the state level, with the minimum possible regulations. The SEZs functioned under the provisions of the Foreign Trade Policy (FTP) from 1 November 2000 to 9 February 2006, and fiscal incentives were made effective through the provisions of the relevant statutes. Briefly, according to the estimate of the union minister of Finance, the central government would lose about 37.8 billion US dollars as tax concessions on an estimated investment of $78.2 billion by these SEZs. (More on this is discussed in Chapter 2.)

The software technology parks of India (STPI)

STPI was established and registered as an autonomous society under the Societies Registration Act (1860), under the union ministry of Communications and Information Technology, Department of Information Technology, in 1991 with an objective to implement the STP scheme and to set up and manage infrastructure facilities, among others. Specially designed for the development and export of computer software, the STP scheme is essentially export-oriented with a focus on quality initiatives and, in addition, it facilitates exports of professional services. This scheme is unique in its nature in that it focuses on one product/sector, i.e. computer software. The scheme integrates the schemes of 100 per cent export-oriented units (EOUs) and the export processing zones (EPZs) of GoI. Briefly, under the STP scheme: (a) 100 per cent foreign equity is permitted; (b) goods imported or procured locally by the STP units are completely duty free; (c) second-hand or used capital goods may also be imported; (d) sales in the domestic market are permissible up to 50 per cent of the export; (e) income tax (on profits and gains from exports of software) benefits under sections 10A/10B of the Income Tax Act; and (f) there is minimal export obligation with positive net foreign exchange.

The STPI clause, which was originally slated to lapse on 31 March 2009, would have hit the earnings of companies the following year by raising the tax outgo to 18–22 per cent depending on the operational structure of individual firms. So there was a hue and cry from the entrepreneurs. In a relief to the IT and BPO industry, the Union Minister of Finance has declared that the two sections (10A and 10B) will be amended and the tax exemption available to companies under the STPI will continue until 31 March 2010. This kind of protection is not quite unusual since it is being practised in many EDCs. The infant industry argument is an economic reason for protectionism. The crux of the argument is that nascent industries often do not have the economies of scale that their older competitors from other countries may have, and thus need to be protected until they can attain similar economies of scale. However, since this is basically an export industry, the protection – by various forms of subsidies is most likely to distort trade relations in globalization. So, on the one hand, the neoliberalism of the Indian state is selective. On the other hand, despite state protection – especially as the entire profits and gains do not form part of total income under certain provisions of the Income Tax Act which the privileged entrepreneurs are entitled to – for a pretty long period there is no strong indication of a breakthrough by Indian industry from the "tail-end product" syndrome (see more on this in Chapters 2 and 3). Instead, these state subsidies are making the earnings distribution in the economy more skewed (see Chapter 6).

The Singur lessons

Tata Motors Ltd (TML), in order to set up a small car factory (*Nano* car), made a deal with the government of West Bengal (India) on required land, power, water and loans and subsidies, which is still undisclosed. The complete information as to the terms and conditions of the land-use by TML is, at the time of writing, preserved as a "trade secret" by both the parties. Even the supreme audit institution of India – the Comptroller and Auditor General of India (CAG) – failed to examine in audit, due to non-production, many parts of the agreements and related records (see CAG 2008b). Ironically, in the information age of market and free contract, the global entrepreneur – i.e. TML – had appealed to the High Court in West Bengal against disclosure of any part of the agreement with the state government. However, by that time the government, responding to the public reaction, had disclosed some parts of the contract.[24] According to that part of the Agreement, TML was supposed to pay a lease of Re 0.015 per month per square foot of land. Note that a lower middle class family pays for a modest residential accommodation a lease-rate which is 660 times more than that. Second, at a time when many of the developmental projects are stalled in the state because of the resources crunch of the government, the group – which has acquired, among many others, the British steel major Corus – was given a Rs 2,000 million (nearly US$ 44 million) loan at 1 per cent interest rate. Not only this, the state government would make good the loss that the TML suffer if and when there was an upward revision of excise duty and corporate income tax during the current decade.

And alternatively, if and when the excise duty and corporate tax go down, the benefit would go entirely to TML with the state government having no share in it. Moreover, the Nano project was assured power at 28 per cent less than the existing industrial rate of electricity per kilowatt-hour (kWh) in the state. If the rate went up by more than Re 0.25 per kWh in every block of five years, the government would provide relief through additional compensation to neutralize such additional increase. For every Nano sold in the state, the government *de facto* was to refund the value-added tax (VAT) and sales tax collected on each sale of Nano. There is far, far more that we do not even know. In sum, although the car is advertised as the cheapest one in the world, what transpires is that for a single car costing Rs 100,000 (declared ex-factory price) the subsidy that the government would be giving is roughly Rs 38,000. Ultimately, the TML project had to beat a retreat in the face of strong mass agitation in the state as well as the country as a whole, and the vast stretch of farmers' land still remains unutilized. Subsequently, the CAG unearthed the financial irregularities in land acquisition and subsidy payments, as well as the misuse of the state industrial development corporation, which is not a subordinate office of the state government (see CAG 2008b: 105–8). In short, it was *state capitalism* minus the state entrepreneurship.

It is important to recognize that the central issue in violent reaction to private entrepreneurship was fertile agricultural land in Singur and not land as such. Moreover, the negative reaction in general is not with industry as such but with the type of industry (in this instance car production, with not even a critical number of buyers in the markets around) that has either very poor or no *backward* linkages – contrasting the case that would be with an agro-based industry to the high-productive and multi-crop region that Singur is.

For the project, the government had acquired 1,006.45 acres of land in Singur (about 40 kilometres away from Kolkata) from about 12,000 landholders in 2006.[25] The doctrine of eminent domain permits the state to acquire private land for a public purpose. However, the Land Acquisition Act (1894) of the British colonial government, which encapsulates the doctrine, was invoked in the immediate post-Independent India to dispossess *zamindars* and feudal landlords, unlike in the present when it has become the draconian and coercive instrument of mass displacement. Since TML is neither a joint-venture project nor a project for "public purpose", the government of West Bengal took a zigzag in bypassing the century-old and archaic central Land Acquisition Act of 1894 to acquire land for private industry.[26] The whole land is part of an area which is one of India's richest alluvial soils, endowed with a developed irrigation system and yielding six crops a year.

To make the matter worse, the state has already been in the grip of food shortage since 2006 (Banerjee 2007b). After all, out of the more than 12,000 land-losers in Singur, 65 per cent are small and marginal farmers who used to make provisions for their own food security. The misery of Singur's land-losers is pathetic since over 60 per cent of them are the weaker sections of the society, i.e. the SCs and STs. None of their grievances and apprehensions about future livelihood and sustainable income were addressed following the National Rehabilitation and Resettlement Policy (of 2003 and 2007). Under this policy, if the government and the Tatas were to fulfil all the "safety requirements" and directives about the types of land to be acquired, the "illegal" acquisition of highly fertile land could not have taken place.

The "1,000 acres" is not just an end in itself in this fertile agricultural region, rather the beginning of a process through which the multi-cropped farm land in the vicinity would soon turn into non-farm land by the infallible laws of the market as land prices increase. Why blame the market alone? The air- and water-polluting industries will ensure that a given area no longer remains conducive for farming around a radius of 5 to 7 kilometres, and will also affect the food chains, forcing human habitation to move elsewhere. These are well known facts, yet the auto-lobby in the country acquired immunity from various central environmental rules and regulations by a GoI Order of 14 September 2006.

Is it obsolete technical knowhow of the entrepreneur, or state-sponsored *rentier capitalism*? One cannot be sure about it, but TML was given a plot of fertile agricultural land which is more than double the size required by the Maruti–Suzuki auto plant in Gurgaon (Haryana), to produce double the number of small cars to be produced by Tata Motors in Singur, or what the latter needed earlier to set up the auto plant in Pune. This is relatively too large when compared to what the Boeing plant occupies, which the *Guinness Book of World Records* acknowledges as the largest building in the world by volume.[27]

Singur is not a lone exception. Both South Korean steel majors Posco and Arcelor-Mittal have signed Memoranda of Understanding (MoUs) with the government of Orissa for constructing 12 million tons per annum steel projects in one of the poorest states in India. Although the capacities for both the Posco and Arcellor-Mittal projects are same, Posco has asked for 4,004 acres of land, while the latter has asked for 8,000 acres (Pattnaik 2007). Incidentally, the 16 million tonne capacity steel plant that Posco has in the South Korean city of Pohan is built on nearly 900 acres. So what explains Posco's demand for 4,000 acres for a 12 million tonne plant in Orissa? Further, in Naraj in the district of Cuttack (Orissa), the Tata house put forward a demand for 1,500 acres of land – agricultural, as it happened, – to build a 1,000 megawatt capacity thermal power plant, which far exceeds the techno-economic necessities when compared to similar projects elsewhere. Is it because the land currently is cheaper here for building up colonies in future?

Actually, the not-well-defined land rights in many places, coupled with the method – best to call it the bookkeeping method – followed by the state agencies to determine land prices, grossly underestimate the "value of land" in a land-scarce and overwhelmingly land-dependent economy. And so land has become an instrument in the hand of the state to show largesse to the big corporate houses in the changed circumstances.

"Exclusionary" growth

The crux of the matter is that the labour force is growing at a rate that is higher than the growth of the workforce. Despite billions of dollars of investments (see RBI, *Handbook*, various issues) in the modern sector, net manufacturing employment in the private corporate as well as the public sector (see GoI, Ministry of Finance, *Economic Survey*, various issues) has turned out to be negative in the last 10 years or so. Perhaps, because of the effective demand problem, corporate downsizing – as the labour productivity increases – has worsened the situation.[28] This is of course a worldwide phenomenon and puts a big question mark on the "future of work". However, in none of the industrialized countries has the legitimate share of the workforce in the productivity gains been denied to the extent it is evident in India. Here, the wage share has been declining with stagnant real wage, which – together with direct and indirect government subsidies – has fostered rapid capital accumulation by the Indian large business houses and helped them to acquire foreign assets.

To elaborate further, the icons of commercial and manufacturing hubs of the country, i.e. Maharashtra and Gujarat, have been attracting most of the foreign direct investment (FDI) and domestic investments during the last two decades. Yet they are the laggards as regards creation of non-farm and manufacturing jobs. While manufacturing establishments grew by more than 56 per cent, employment growth was a mere 1.1 per cent in Maharashtra between 1998 and 2005. Gujarat closely followed Maharashtra in this respect (CSO, *Economic Census*, 4th and 5th). By contrast, a mere increase in land productivity (by dint of improved irrigation or other such measures), with labour productivity remaining constant or even experiencing a decline in some years — led to an increase in gainful employment in agriculture, thereby reducing the burden of rural poverty.

On the whole, it is more or less a situation of "jobless growth" reinforcing backwardness – i.e. a stunted social division of labour – in the larger part of the economy. Employment elasticity in India, for both men and women, is not only very low in comparison with many other Asian countries, namely Bangladesh, Malaysia, Pakistan, Philippines, South Korea and Vietnam (excluding China), but has been reducing, while the GDP growth rate has surged ahead (Table 1.3). Employment elasticity gradually falls as a country becomes more developed and labour more scarce. Labour-abundant economies, especially those with relatively

Table 1.3 India: employment elasticity (male and female), 1993 to 2005

	1993 to 1997			*1997 to 2001*			*2001 to 2005*		
	Male	*Female*	*MF*	*Male*	*Female*	*MF*	*Male*	*Female*	*MF*
Elasticity of employment to total GDP	0.30	0.24	0.29	0.36	0.33	0.35	0.25	0.25	0.25
Average annual GDP growth rate (%)			6.8			5.5			7.4

Source: ILO (KILM). Note: MF = male *plus* female.

high incidences of poverty, need to achieve a relatively higher employment intensity than do less labour-abundant economies. A study by the ILO suggests that employment elasticity in developing economies, until these economies attain upper-middle-income status, should ideally be around 0.7, whereas in India it was 0.25 (Kahn 2001).

The unemployment rate has been growing since the early 1990s despite the transition from a moderate to a high economic growth rate. The latest estimate shows the number of unemployed as 34.7 million (Table 1.4). The figures, however, do not capture the fact that the number of days worked per person per annum has considerably declined, especially in areas where a huge agricultural labour force has been displaced by the government or the SEZs. A survey shows that – before nearly 1,000 acres were acquired by the government of West Bengal for the TML – about 94 per cent of the economically active women in the affected area used to get jobs for 200–250 days a year. Now, the percentage of women finding jobs has drastically declined to 31. Moreover, they don't find work for more than 120 days. The access to food per head in the affected families has generally reduced to 330 grams a day from the previous 670 grams.[29] If we take into account similar instances elsewhere, the rising economic disparities in aggregate become unambiguous.

Dilemma of the classical development model

Many believe the current model of economic development is not at all riding on the bumpy road of ideology. Some count dissenters' "street politics" as *Physiocracy* that tends to turn the wheel of current economic development backward.[30]

Table 1.4 India: employment and unemployment (on a "current daily status" basis)[(a)]

	1983	*1993–94*	*1999–2000*	*2004–05*	*Growth per annum (%)*		
					1983 to 1993–94	*1993–94 to 1999–2000*	*1999–2000 to 2004–05*
Population (million)	718.10	893.68	1005.05	1092.83	2.11	1.98	1.69
Labour force (million)	263.82	334.20	364.88	419.65	2.28	1.47	2.84
Workforce (million)	239.49	313.93	338.19	384.91	2.61	1.25	2.62
Unemployment rate (%)	9.22	6.06	7.31	8.28			
No. of unemployed (million)	24.34	20.27	26.68	34.74			

Source and notes: GoI, *Economic Survey 2007–08*, Table 10.9. (a) Current daily status basis of estimation of employment and unemployment gives the average level of unemployment on a day during the survey year. It captures the unemployed days of the chronically unemployed, the unemployed days of the usually employed who become intermittently unemployed during the reference week, and unemployed days of those classified as employed according to the criterion of current weekly status.

The body of economic theory known as physiocracy developed in France in the eighteenth century. With the physiocrats we enter the era of schools and systems in economic thought. There has been some misunderstanding about the essential qualities of physiocratic thought. Adam Smith criticized their 'emphasis on agriculture and to this day the merits of the physiocrats are often depreciated by the same criticism' (Roll 1961: 128).

According to William Petty (1623–87), the more accomplished pre-classical English economist, only agricultural surplus is the true source of wealth of the country. This theory received criticism from Adam Smith (1723–90), but it was a clear step towards an alternative principle of economic growth with respect to the mercantilist notion of "balance of trade". Petty did not deny the importance of foreign trade as a source of national wealth, but at least exchange was seen as no longer the only economic activity capable of increasing the wealth of nations (Stathakis and Vaggi 2006).

Following Petty, François Quesnay (1694–1774) – of the physiocrat school in the mid-eighteenth century – considered agriculture as the core of society, but only those agricultural activities whose output was considerably higher than their input. That is, the technique of production capable of yielding a large net product over the inputs of cultivators was the source of surplus and hence of economic growth. According to Quesnay, economic development depended on the amount of capital employed in cultivation, because this would transform the poor French agriculture into a productive sector. For the physiocrats, the modernization of French agriculture would have to be the aim of all policies. To meet this end, radical changes in the way the corn prices were determined were considered necessary as incentives for continuing the cultivation of land and reinvesting their saving (Stathakis and Vaggi 2006). Quesnay in fact stressed the potentialities of an agricultural revolution. But he thought the potentialities were stunted by the expansion of capitalism in trade (Roncaglia 2005).

As with Petty and Quesnay, the social division of labour – which causes the greatest improvement in the productive powers of labour, according to Adam Smith – requires a surplus of food, of agricultural products; hence the improvement of agriculture is a necessary prerequisite to secure a surplus produce to the country and to achieve economic growth. This explains why Smith ascribed priority to agriculture in what he considered to be a sort of natural order of investment, according to which capital accumulation followed a precise sequence in society. Therefore, physiocracy essentially set the *precondition* for the progress of social division of labour.

With the social division of labour, output per head rose, wages were slow to adjust, capital was accumulated, extra labour was demanded, wages increased, and in response the population increased. The larger population, receiving increased wages, increased the extent of the market. As such, employment generation did not appear as a critical problem to Adam Smith in the late eighteenth century or to other classical political economists in the nineteenth century. It was presumed that in the course of capitalist development through the division of labour the productive power of labour would increase uninterruptedly; unemployment was just a frictional problem. So, capital investment would increase to utilize the growing labour productivity. Labour from the less productive economic activities (like traditional agriculture) would move to more productive sectors (like modern industry), resulting in wage increases and improvement in the workers' livelihood.

Smith's agriculture, then, was on the way to a radical transformation. There was plenty of agricultural land but a scarcity of agricultural hands. The problem was further aggravated by low national average expectation of life at birth – less than 40 years – which began to rise only around the mid-nineteenth century (Szreter and Mooney 1998; see also Bengtsson *et al.* 2004). It was the northern industrial towns, and particularly the two giants of Manchester and Liverpool, which consistently exhibited the lowest life expectancies. Expectation of life at birth in these two cities was only around 30 or 31 years in both the 1850s and the 1860s, at a time when the national average was fully 10 years higher. Furthermore, by the end of the nineteenth century neither of these two cities had improved much, relative to the higher national average life expectancy then obtaining. One of the principal reasons for the introduction of the Factories Act, prohibiting use of child labour and restricting use of women labour as early as in 1787 in Austria and in 1802 in England, was the objective to increase the size of the adult population, as the latter was still inadequate to fuel the engine for full-steam industrialization.

The Enclosure Movement or the agricultural revolution (1750–1880) in England had displaced a large rural population and converted them into a proletariat who, however, found jobs in the mines, the textile cities and the railways. Still there were gaps between demand and supply, which needed to be plugged by slaves from Africa. Although the slave trade was banned in Britain in 1837, the use of slave labour continued until the 1870s, around which time the Industrial Revolution had lost much of its initial steam and the expectation of life at birth had shown definite and substantial rises, thereby releasing pressure on the labour market and in due course leading to the Long Depression (1873–96). By then, Germany and Russia were coming up with heavy industries. In these crosscurrents, more than 15 per cent of the European population of 320 million (Maddison 2003), or about 50 million people (Lewis 1978), migrated from Europe to mainly North America, Australia and New Zealand in the second half of the nineteenth century. Further, during the time, capital employed per unit of labour was astonishingly low as compared to the contemporary world.

Classical economist Ricardo (1772–1823), however, by a numerical exercise, hinted that unemployment was not temporary, because of the introduction of machinery. Most other classical writers were not convinced: it was obvious from recent economic history that employment had increased hugely in parallel with the employment of machinery (O'Brien 2003). Karl Marx (1818–83) too had a disagreement with Ricardo. To Marx, the size of the industrial reserve army has a cyclical movement – its growing size halts wage increase in the first round. Meanwhile, the productivity growth obtained with mechanization decreases the unit labour costs, resulting in rise in profit, which in turn induces firms to expand again and hire new workers; the industrial reserve army shrinks in the second round – a nineteenth-century formulation of the so-called Phillips curve

(Phillips 1958) that depicts an inverse relationship between rate of change of money wages and level of unemployment.[31]

Contemporary problems of transition: lessons from China and India

The cotton textiles that had acted as the vehicle of industrial revolution in Britain in the nineteenth century later became an increasingly labour-displacing industry with speedy mechanization and automation, providing much less employment than it used to. The same is true for the auto industry that constituted, along with the development of railways, one of the most important vehicles of industrial revolution in America. The number of people employed per unit of capital invested in, say, the Ford motor car factory in the early twentieth century was much higher – or, the capital to labour ratio was lower – than it is now, one hundred years later. At the same time, the scope of free movement of the labour force across countries, unlike in previous times, has become severely restricted in the contemporary globalization, which is unusually liberal toward capital mobility. In brief, the tight labour market conditions in some parts of the nineteenth-century European economy – e.g. in agriculture all through, and in industry during at least the first three-quarters – resulted in the improvement of labour standards and, simultaneously, technological development. Let us consider Indian experience – Chinese, too, for her many similarities with India – in this perspective of economic development in the West.

In China, on the one hand, the average annual growth rate was 9.8 per cent between 2000 and 2006, perhaps requiring a matching labour supply. However, as rural–urban migration was restricted by the *hukou* (household registration system) the industrial labour market in the growth centres seemed to remain tight, raising hopes for increased hourly wage rate. But the hopes were belied.

Industrialization in China has proceeded at a faster pace than in India during the last 20 years. In both India and China, industrial development or, for that matter, the services sector grew at the cost of agriculture. The share of agriculture in China's GDP declined from 33 per cent to 15 per cent in just 20 years between 1985 and 2004. In India, a similar trend, notwithstanding the decline of agriculture to GDP, was slower than in China.

The size of the rural population has drastically reduced in China, unlike in India, since the beginning of the 1990s. The explanation could be: (a) a push due to high rural unemployment; (b) growing urbanization, which has reshaped the boundaries of the rural; or (c) the pull of a tight urban labour market. In fact, the economically active population (EAP) in agriculture itself declined in China between 1979 and 2004, in spite of the fact that more than 40.2 million hectares of arable land were added during the period (FAO, *Statistical Yearbook*, various issues). China's massive net imports of agricultural commodities have had their impact felt in the form of a massive labour surplus in Chinese agriculture. So there has been a shift of the labour force from agriculture to non-agriculture. The displaced have had little choice but to migrate to industrial cities and towns in China, or even to places abroad in a more critical situation.

China – like Bangladesh, Indonesia, Nepal, Philippines, Sri Lanka and Vietnam – is a labour-sending country (Tullao and Cortez 2003). India, incidentally, is both a labour-sending and -receiving country. Usually labour-sending countries are those experiencing high population growth but slow economic growth. Thus the phenomenon of large-scale migration from countries like Bangladesh and Nepal can be understood. However, the Chinese phenomenon is exceptional since her average annual population growth rate was 1 per cent (during the period from 1990 to 2001) and the economy has been growing at an extraordinary rate. It is thus perhaps difficult to deny the negative impact on the rural labour market of the large-scale *net* imports of agricultural products. Despite a positive rate of growth of population (1 per cent in China as compared to 1.8 per cent in India), since 1990–91 – when both the countries initiated trade deregulation in a big way – and up till 2004 more than 804,000 of the EAP in Chinese agriculture were displaced, while Indian agriculture continued to provide additional jobs for the growing population, though at a declining rate.

The large displaced agrarian population in China is mostly forced to seek jobs elsewhere. By official count, China has 114 million migrant workers who have left rural areas, temporarily or for good, to work in cities. And government experts predict the number will rise to 300 million by the year 2020, eventually to 500 million. Shanghai alone has 3 million migrant workers; by comparison, the entire Irish migration to America from 1820 to 1930 is thought to have involved perhaps 4.5 million people (Yardley 2004). This large mass of floating population, not having the rights of residency, is easily fleeced by capital, and this puts downward pressure not only on the wages but on the employment opportunities of the "officially resident" workforce in the Chinese industrial towns and cities. The Chinese urban unemployment rate was 14 per cent in 2002. However, this was not uniform for all the urban labour force. The unemployment rate of urban *permanent* residents increased from 6.1 to 11.1 per cent between January 1996 and September 2002, while that of all urban residents – including temporary residents, i.e. migrants – increased at a slower rate, i.e. from 4.0 to 7.3 per cent.[32]

The preference of urban – industrial or services – capital for those workers who do not have entitlements to welfare benefits and rights like those enjoyed by the urban permanent residents is thus very apparent from the fact that unemployment among the temporary residents is lower than among the permanent residents of the cities. Moreover, the Chinese urban labour market is actually not as tight as it was thought to be. Despite very high growth in manufacturing by the standard of the developing economies, aggregate manufacturing employment in China declined from 86.24 million in 1990 to 80.83 million in 2001. Manufacturing employment in the urban units alone declined from 54.92 million in 1994 (data not available before that year) to 30.70 million in 2001.[33] Data for at least two years, i.e. 1995 and 1996, show that the number of surplus laid-off workers were 2.13 and 3.23 million, respectively; such data have not been available since 1997.

This experience from the neighbouring high-growth economy provides conflicting lessons for India. Many scholars as well as politicians in India argue that agriculture is no longer profitable, so greater allocation of public investments or subsidies in that sector would in fact enhance inefficiency in the aggregate economy. First, they perhaps fail to notice that, unlike the economics of a modern business organization, the economics of small and marginal farming – as in small and micro enterprises – is generally founded on self-exploitation, and the profit calculation itself is different from that of corporate business. Profit is not the driving force in a small peasant economy. Perhaps one finds here the relevance of the ongoing research on the "happiness index", beyond the maximizing behaviour.

On the basis of empirical studies of the peasant farms in Russia and other countries, Chayanov (1966) argued that the degree of self-exploitation was determined by a peculiar equilibrium between family demand satisfaction and *tyagostnost* (the drudgery) of labour itself. Chayanov suggests that the family labour farm has to make use of the market situation and natural conditions in a way that enables it to provide an internal equilibrium for the family, together with the highest possible standard of well-being. This is achieved by introducing into the farm's organizational plan such labour investment as promises the highest possible labour payment per labour unit. Thus,

> [t]he objective arithmetic calculation of highest possible net profit in the given market situation *does not determine* whether or not to accept any economic action, nor does it determine the whole activity of the family economic unit; this is done by the internal economic confrontation of subjective evaluations.
>
> (Chayanov 1966: 7, emphasis added)

"Rational choice" in the postmodern

The urban elites identify themselves with the obsessive development paradigm of the state, ignoring the changing global political economy. To them, it is "contradictory consciousness of the peasantry": with the spread of school education and widespread exposure to modern communications media such as the cinema, television and advertising, there is a strong and widespread desire among younger members, both male and female, of peasant families not to live the life of a peasant in the village but instead to move to town or the city (see e.g. Gupta 2005; Chatterjee 2008). A convincing vision of course it is; but any critical thinker would expect to find a massive exodus of farmers from the countryside. Instead, what we find is mounting resistance mostly from the small and marginal landholders – with property rights or economic rights – across the country, despite inflated compensation packages for land acquisition from the government and despite frequent state violence on the unwilling peasants. The recurring violence has compelled the central government to bring several amendments to the *modus operandi* of land acquisition and utilization under the SEZ Act since it was enacted in 2005.

From fiction to fact: by the turn of the century, as the debate on "uneconomic cultivation" and "social respectability of farming" turned hot, the National Sample Survey Organization (NSSO, GoI) conducted a survey at the instance of the Union Ministry of Agriculture. In India as a whole, the survey reveals – contrary to the ideas of the postmodernists – that 60 per cent of the farmer households reported that they *liked* farming as a profession. Those who did not like farming were asked the reason for their disaffection. The 40 per cent who disliked farming included 27 per cent who did not find it profitable primarily because of their dependence on private moneylenders (who charge exorbitantly high rates of interest on small borrowings). Note that *only 2 per cent* of all farmers disliked farming because of its lack of social status (NSSO 2005a, Report no. 496). Further, the elitist reading of the "consciousness of the peasantry" was also proved wrong by the peasants and allied workforce themselves: in particular, they voted massively in the latest PRI election held in 2008 against the government in West Bengal where forcible and violent acquisition of fertile agricultural land for SEZ or similar other crony capital ventures antagonized the farmers and allied services workforce. Hardly any logic exists within the paradigm of collective well-being that disfavours the voices of the "losers" in the development process (see Box 1.2).

The "trade off" is not easy going. On the one hand, about 20 million agricultural producers in the North – or, taking into account their family members together, at least 50 million people – by dint of large-scale farming with highly mechanized implements have raised output to an astounding height of 10–20 thousand quintals per unit of labour. By contrast, in the LDC where the Green Revolution took place labour productivity is around 200–500 quintals, and, it is around 10 quintals only where traditional agriculture still dominates. Thus the productivity gap between the average EDC and the LDC is around 50:1, whereas 60 years ago it was only 10:1 (FAO, *Statistical Yearbook*, various issues). The central problem that haunts

Box 1.2 Governance at the micro-level: referendum against SEZ

In the first-ever referendum in the country involving farmers, more than 6,000 landowners from 22 Raigad villages made their views on a special economic zone known on Sunday [21/09/08]. Judging by the mood of the farmers in the command area of the Hetwane irrigation dam, it appears that the Reliance group will have its task cut out to acquire land for its multi-billion SEZ project in the Konkan area. Of the 10,000 hectares of land required for one of the biggest SEZs in the country, nearly 3,000 hectares of land lie in 22 villages in the Hetwane dam area.

There are 131 SEZs in Maharashtra which are slated to attract multi-billion investments and generate six million jobs. Although Mukesh Ambani's Reliance group claims to have offered a lucrative compensation package to the Raigad landowners, resentment runs deep in the local communities. Whether it is Sadashiv Mhatre from Mothe Bhal village, former sarpanch Ranjana Mhatre or Arun Mhatre from the neighbouring Vashi village, their views are identical. 'Don't ever make an attempt to bribe us. Even if Reliance offers us one crore rupees per hectare, we will not part with our land for the SEZ project. We are determined to ensure that the SEZ project does not come up in the Konkan belt. Our motto is "SEZ hatao,

Konkan bachao",' Sadashiv Mhatre said immediately after submitting his opinion in the Mothe Bhal zilla parishad school.

Following directives of the state government, Raigad collector Nipun Vinayak had asked the farmers in the 22 villages to submit their opinion in writing on whether they wished to sell their land for the SEZ project. The opinion basically comprised four lines saying, 'The farmer does not want to part with his land for the project ... and the government should forthwith withdraw the notices issued under the Land Acquisition Act for acquisition of land.'

Surprisingly, even those farmers who had surrendered part of their land for the SEZ project have now changed their mind and submitted anti-SEZ opinions. On Sunday, when more than 100 representatives of the media toured the 22 villages, they found that most farmers were dead set against the SEZ project.

It was a month ago that Vilasrao Deshmukh, the chief minister of Maharashtra had promised the anti-SEZ committee led by N D Patil, former tehsildar Subhash Mhatre and activist Vaishali Patil that his government would consider their demand to cry halt to the acquisition of land. It was then proposed that the government hold a referendum for the purpose. The chief minister quickly accepted the proposal and asked the forest department and the Raigad collector to prepare an action plan.

Source: Marpakwar (2008).

development economics nowadays is how to make room for the huge displaced population in the mainframe modern sector once agriculture in the developing countries is mechanized, agricultural land is converted into private estates to augment its profitability, or free trade of agricultural commodities is allowed following negotiations under the umbrella of WTO. One also has to take into account distributive justice.

Issue of distribution

The transition from an agrarian to an industrial economy in the EDCs was accompanied by narrowing gaps in income distribution; consequently, there have been improvements in aspects of human development. However, what we find in India is quite different (more on this in Chapters 6 and 7). In general, *Gini* inequality in consumption is much higher in the urban areas than in the rural, and higher in the relatively industrialized states than in the laggard states. Punjab, for instance, still had the distinction of achieving the highest per capita net state domestic product (NSDP) among the states in India until recently, despite her primary sector contributing more than one-third to the NSDP (Table 1.5). Further, on the basis of NSSO data on monthly per capita consumer expenditure (MPCE) (and in the absence of data on income distribution), Punjab, with the high weightage of agriculture in her aggregate economy, had the least consumption (*Gini*) inequality,

Table 1.5 Economic transitions of varying degree in different states in India: components (%) of net state domestic product (NSDP) at factor cost by industry of origin (at constant prices), during 1980 to 2006

States	*1980–81*			*1990–91*			*2000–01*			*2006–07*		
	Agr	*Ind*	*Ser*	*Agr*	*Ind*	*Ser*	*Agr*	*Ind*	*Ser*	*Agr*	*Ind*	*Ser*
Andhra Pradesh	46.6	16.6	36.8	34.6	22.3	43.1	33.1	18.9	48.0	26.1	14.7	59.2
Bihar	55.2	17.3	27.4	46.6	23.1	30.3	46.3	8.6 [a]	45.1	33.9	5.9	60.2
Gujarat	40.8	27.2	32.0	27.4	34.8	37.8	18.3	33.7	48.0	20.3	29.2	50.6
Haryana	54.6	19.0	26.4	45.7	23.5	30.8	33.0	25.4	41.6	22.8	18.2	59.0
Karnataka	46.1	20.8	33.2	34.8	23.8	41.4	32.3	22.1	45.6	20.3	15.7	64.1
Kerala	39.2	24.4	36.4	36.0	23.9	40.1	20.2	20.7	59.2	17.4	7.9	74.7
Madhya Pradesh	55.6	18.4	26.0	48.5	20.9	30.6	31.4	27.0	41.5	27.4	13.0	59.6
Maharashtra	28.1	35.1	36.8	22.7	34.9	42.4	17.7	25.8	56.5	13.6	17.6	68.9
Orissa	55.3	54.5	43.3	29.2	31.2	37.6	39.0	14.6	46.4	24.5	21.6	53.9
Punjab	49.5	18.5	32.0	48.3	22.5	29.1	42.0	21.4	36.7	34.3	14.8	50.9
Rajasthan	52.3	18.0	29.7	48.6	18.5	32.9	28.2	26.2	45.5	31.7	12.6	55.7
Tamil Nadu	25.9	59.4	40.6	23.4	56.5	43.5	19.0	30.8	50.2	13.6	25.2	61.2
Uttar Pradesh	52.3	15.3	32.4	43.3	19.8	36.9	39.3	19.1	41.6	30.6	14.8	54.6
West Bengal	32.6	29.3	38.1	31.3	27.3	41.4	28.7	20.5	50.8	25.8	11.6	62.6

Source and notes: Based on RBI, *Handbook of Statistics*, various issues. Agr = Agriculture and allied activities (agriculture; forestry and logging; fishing); Ind = Industry (mining and quarrying; manufacturing – registered and unregistered; electricity, gas and water supply); and Ser = Services (construction; transport, storage and communication; trade, hotels and restaurants; banking and insurance; real estate, ownership of dwelling and business services; public administration; and other services). [a] Largely because of the separation of the Jharkhand region from the state, the primary industrial region of Bihar, the share of industry dropped drastically.

in both the rural and urban, as compared to such relatively advanced industrial states as Gujarat, Maharashtra, Tamil Nadu, Andhra Pradesh and Karnataka.

The fact that should not be lost sight of – especially when composite human development is assigned a greater value than per capita income alone in measuring development – is that the distribution of income/consumption in the agrarian economy is much more equitable than it is in the industrial economy *per se*. This is important to recognize since more than half of the labour force is dependent on agriculture in India. In a developing economy like India's, unless the inequality question is addressed at the stage of primary sector development, the problem is very likely to spill over to its later stages of development and aggravate further, especially if the primary sector development is aborted and if the economic plan were to skip the *stages* that classical capitalist development has experienced, historically, across countries. (More on this topic is discussed in Chapter 4.)

Gains versus pains: "street politics"

"Development" has almost declared war upon indigenous peoples, tribals, subsistence farmers and other minorities in India, China and everywhere, and upon all ancient but sustainable lifeways. The killing of protesters at Kalinganagar (in the Jajpur district of Orissa) on the site of a proposed Tata steel plant in January 2006; the killing of farmers resisting the acquisition of land for a very large-scale petrochemical hub in *Nandigram* (West Bengal), in March 2007 and again in November in the same year; the countryside emptied of peasants for the sake of grandiose infrastructural projects; landless peasants turned into perpetual migrants; these are the victims of the model of "development with displacement". But why *are* the poor farmers not friendly to industry?

This would not have been the case had there been productive and efficient utilization of those agricultural lands already acquired for non-agriculture during the last couple of decades, thereby generating employment. A large part of the agricultural land forcibly acquired against the "free choice" of the cultivators and farmers and subsequently handed over to the promoters of commerce and industries remained unutilized – a loss in both ways: neither agricultural nor industrial value had been added. So there is no guarantee that a fresh spell of land acquisitions would set in motion all-round development, with the older institutions and organizations remaining intact. The self-styled agents of development say that development would be stalled without further land acquisition – be it fertile agricultural or not – while the counter-argument is: how much productivity was gained from the previous rounds of land acquisitions that displaced thousands of cultivators and the allied services workforce – engaged in transporting agricultural outputs, cold storage, retail shops, producing and repairing agricultural implements, etc. – from their gainful employment? Note that the ratio of allied (to agriculture) services workers to those who have some entitlement to land is not less than 3. The smaller the land size or higher the crop intensity, still higher is the ratio. Finally, the employment of women, more than men, gets a jolt owing to displacement from agriculture. Altogether, to fuel the engines of industrialization and urbanization, over a million people have been ousted from their land and homes in the last ten years, mostly in the industrially advanced states such as Maharashtra and Tamil Nadu, agricultural states such as Andhra Pradesh, and in states dominated by tribal and backward communities such as Chhattisgarh, Orissa and Jharkhand.[34]

City and industry claim two different kinds of land as such. First, land is targeted precisely in areas of fertile and settled agriculture because that is where infrastructure items such as power, roads and irrigation are relatively developed. In principle, there is no reason why industrial parks could not be situated in deserts in the western part of India, ravines (like Chambal in central India), or at least on plenty of uncultivable land. As such, the corporate sector is inclined to using the existing infrastructure – assiduously created for agriculture by public investment over decades – in order to minimize its initial investment in infrastructure development. This mode of reducing unit costs of production and becoming internationally competitive shows the corporate sector's inaptitude for exploring the frontiers of technological possibilities.

The second kinds of land that have received the attention of the land grabbers are those that have been in either private or community possession so far but without having unambiguous property rights. Estimates show that of the total 1.4 million displaced, 79 per cent are STs from the four states of Andhra Pradesh, Chhattisgarh, Orissa and Jharkhand. The total area acquired for setting up industries in these states was found to be 10.2 million acres (Patranobis 2007)[35] – i.e. almost as if 28 new cities each of the size of Delhi have arisen in the recent past. There is a correlation between attempts to exploit minerals, forests and rivers on an industrial scale and the increasing impoverishment and growing number of cases of human rights violation among those displaced. The "human cost" of a project perhaps does not appear to come into consideration because it is irrelevant when the "opportunity cost" of poor labour is assumed to be *zero* in a labour surplus economy.

Land (of the common people) as private property has mutated to "public good" in the neoliberal era. The process is easier within the ambit of the common law. There came a distinct preference for private ordering over public regulation and for common law over statute law as a system for the ordering of private affairs. Common law is characterized by the importance of decision-making by juries, independent judges, and by emphasis on judicial discretion as opposed to codes. Civil law, on the other hand, is characterized by less independent judiciaries, the relative unimportance of juries, and a greater role of both substantive and procedural codes as opposed to judicial discretion. Common law countries, as in India, tend to rely more on markets and contracts, while civil law countries rely on regulation. The practice of land acquisition that was "unlawful" in the eyes of the judiciary a decade before has somehow become "lawful" in the changed circumstances; however, one often finds conflicting judgments made by various courts of law, state as well as federal.[36]

Empowered with the colonial legal instrument of 1894, the acquisition spree of the state on behalf of corporate aggressive capital is especially noticeable in areas of tribal habitations. The draft National Tribal Policy circulated by the union ministry of Tribal Affairs in 2006 provides answers on why companies seek excess land to set up industries especially in tribal areas:

> [S]ince tribal land is generally non-transferable, the land markets are under-developed and the cost of acquiring land in tribal areas is extremely low. The rate of compensation is, therefore, inadequate, usually based on notional market value. ... The difference in the cost of acquisition of the lands and the subsequent value of the land in the zone of influence after the implementation of the project is enormous. The value of the property goes up substantially due to direct/indirect downstream benefits from the project. This encourages the tendency to acquire land in excess of the requirement.
>
> (GoI, Ministry of Tribal Affairs 2006: 8)

This is not all! In Jharkhand (in the district of Saraikela-Rajkharaswan), for instance, the Tatas – the czar of the Indian corporate sector – wanted to set up their third steel plant in the country on 10,000 acres of land. The tribal cultivators opposed to the land acquisition do not have legal rights to the land, because land reforms were never undertaken in the state. The *Rajas* of Saraikela *de jure* still own all land in the project area; the farmers simply hold unregistered partial economic rights.

Of course, one cannot deny the income multiplier effect of industrial investment. A country or region's income growth *per se* does not, however, automatically ensure improved livelihood of the vast majority of the affected people. Wealth perhaps trickles down, but at varying rates, depending on factor endowments – be it education, skills or physical assets – of the affected people. For the land- and forest-based people holding assets such as land, hut and livestock, and endowed with basic skills of cultivation, yet displaced and proletarianized, finding "decent space" for them is extremely difficult, if not impossible, in the subsequent growth process. During the last six decades, these indigenous people have become the major victims of development projects such as extraction industries, dams and hydel-power projects, and have been turned into paupers. Large dams have been built, displacing the tribal people, but the projects provide irrigation to faraway villages, thus depriving the local tribal villages; large power projects have been implemented but the local tribal villages quite often have no electricity.

One hundred years have gone by since the first Tata steel plant (TISCO) was set up in one of India's most backward regions (i.e. Jamshedpur, Bihar), displacing the indigenous communities. As it stands, the indigenous communities settled around the steel city have even lost their *de facto* political rights, never mind their wretched and inhuman conditions of living in the hinterland of growth. Those of them who can find jobs of domestic help or in the tail-end of the job market most often get paid abysmally low wages even compared with those in other cities in the vicinity. Moreover, these indigenous people in and around the steel city are subjected to gross violations of the government-stipulated minimum wages. Further, their access to health and sanitation is even worse than for people of the same income group in other areas of the region.

The *feasibility* of this kind of growth, which relies heavily on the upper 15 per cent of the consumers, perhaps cannot be contested, since the effective demand problem is no longer confined to the narrow boundaries of the country with the production system converging to the global value chains and the output market access now wide open. However, the *viability* and also the *sustainability* of this type of growth model are still ambiguous. The cities or growth centres could well be fortified by pushing the marginalized people further to the margins. Unfortunately, borderless are such diseases as *kala-azar*, avian flu, tuberculosis, malaria, dengue, and several other vector-borne diseases, which find haven for incubation in the vast ghettos in the peripheries. Because of poor sanitation, they would continue to contaminate the water sources for the fortified cities and towns.

Take for instance the case of vector-borne malaria. How many people really come down with the disease in India every year? Nobody has the exact answer, but the laboratory scientists agree that there is huge under-reporting. Very tentatively, malaria cases in India have remained around two million each year in the last 10 years and have taken the lives of about 1,000 people each year since 1994 (GoI, Ministry of Health and Family Welfare). The disease is relatively severe in states such as Orissa, Madhya Pradesh (MP), Chhattisgarh, Jharkhand and the north-eastern states. Areas of MP and Chattisgarh populated largely by tribal people are badly affected; tribals are only 19 per cent of the population but account for 50 per cent of the malaria cases. Seventy per cent of the malaria cases among them in this region are caused by the *Plasmodium falciparum* parasite, which is responsible for more than 90 per cent of malarial deaths in the world.[37] Although scientists are still in search of understanding the reasons behind the susceptibility of the regions toward the disease, one of the reasons is found to be the fact that the tribals wear scanty clothes — or rather, can't afford better – which makes them susceptible to malaria. And the neighbouring affluent cities and towns can't put up effective barriers against the possible transmission of malarial parasites. Another vector-borne disease, *kala-azar*, is endemic in 48 districts in backward states such as Bihar, Jharkhand and Uttar Pradesh, and also in West Bengal. An estimated 165.4 million population are at risk in these four states. Mostly poor socio-economic groups of the population primarily living in the rural areas are affected (GoI, National Vector Borne Disease Control Programme).

To conclude, the issue is not "anti-industry". Let private industrial investments take the right kind of signals from the market and allocate accordingly. When the government seeks to intrude on the market with special incentive schemes, the chances of getting the wrong signals are high. Besides, this section has tended to highlight the rationale of "disagreement" with the prioritization of big industry over agriculture through various subsidy and incentive schemes.

"Catching up": an elusive milestone

Let us look at the global distribution of wealth before making an assessment of the proximity of India to the status of superpower, or that as a development goal. Wealth can be defined as a sum of real property, financial assets *less* debts.

An estimate of global wealth distribution for the adult population, compared across countries, reveals that global household wealth was US$20,500 per person using official exchange rates, or PPP$26,000 when adjusted for country price levels, for the year 2000 (Davies *et al.* 2006). The average wealth per capita was $1,100 in India, while it was $144,000 in USA, $181,000 in Japan, $1,400 in Indonesia, and so on. The disparity between India and, say, the United States is such that it seems impossible for India to "catch up" even in the very long run; no matter what the feasible Indian growth rate may be, the current US wealth would continue to breed more wealth. Moreover, so far as the composition of household wealth is concerned, real property – particularly land and farm assets – is more important in LDCs, whereas financial assets are more important in the rich countries. In the United States, for instance, real property constituted more than 50 per cent of gross household assets, while financial assets constituted 40 per cent and debts 10 per cent. By contrast, in India, real property alone constituted about 95 per cent of gross household assets (ibid.). Given the fact that the rate of return on real property is generally lower than that on financial assets, "catching up" is yet more elusive as an agenda worth pursuing.

So far as the geographical spread of wealth is concerned, it is heavily concentrated in North America, Europe and high-income Asia–Pacific countries. They collectively own nearly 90 per cent of world wealth. North America has 6 per cent of the world adult population, but 34 per cent of household wealth. Europe and high-income Asia–Pacific countries also own disproportionate amounts of wealth. For Africa, China, India, and lower income Asian countries, the share of wealth is considerably less than the population share, sometimes by a factor greater than 10.

Wealth is certainly more unequally distributed than income, across countries. High-income countries have a bigger share of world wealth than of world GDP. The reverse is true of middle- and low-income economies. Exceptions include Nordic and Eastern Europe transition countries. Let us consider the North Atlantic economies (NAEs) as the reference, corresponding to which the magnitude of income inequality can be measured.

By the end of the Second World War there had emerged a group of countries – i.e. "the rest" – who settled in between the North Atlantic and no-industry poor countries. More broadly, manufacturing-related trade was then limited to the industrialized North and "the rest" in the South – comprising China, India, Indonesia, South Korea, Malaysia, Taiwan and Thailand, in Asia; Argentina, Brazil, Chile and Mexico in Latin America; and Turkey in the Middle East – i.e. those who had acquired enough manufacturing experience in the production of silk, cotton, textiles, foodstuffs and light consumer goods to move into mid-technology sectors and later into relatively high-technology sectors. However, since around the middle of the 1980s, many of the tail-end jobs from "the rest" that were created by internationally mobile capital began to flow to "the remainder",[38] which comprises countries that had been less exposed to modern factory life in the pre-war period. These countries failed thereafter to reach anywhere near the industrial diversification of "the rest" and had less developed labour market institutions. Over time, "the remainder" increasingly established direct trade with the North, however insignificant the volumes might be, and became locations of outsourcing from the North. These countries' low wages and poor labour standards largely compensated for their low productivity and skills gaps.

Against this background, the ratio of per capita GDP (PPP estimate) of different countries in "the rest" to NAE shows that while some countries such as Brazil, South Korea and Taiwan have been able to reduce their income *gaps* with the NAE during the golden age of capitalism and prior to the oil crisis of the mid-1970s, countries such as Argentina, Chile, India, Indonesia, Thailand and Turkey have slipped down further from their initial positions in the income scale (Table 1.6). Brazil's per capita GDP was 29 per cent of that of NAE in 1950, increasing to 32 per cent in 1973. By contrast, India's per capita GDP was 11 per cent of NAE in 1950 and dropped to a mere 7 per cent in 1973. Thereafter, India recovered some of its losses in terms of relative per capita GDP, and South Korea as well as Taiwan roared up, while the Latin American countries progressively lagged behind until 2006. In Asia, countries such as Indonesia, Malaysia and Thailand also experienced increasing gaps with the NAE, especially since the "Asian crisis".

So, very few countries of "the rest" could actually manage to lessen the per capita income divergence with the developed North, despite radical changes in the economy and economic policies. As such, the share of the middle-income third world to world income has increased, while that of the low-income third world has declined. The rising income share of the middle-income countries, however, is due largely to their rising share of world population (Table 1.7).

Initially, in the post-Second World War period, it was thought that the dichotomy between the developed and developing countries was largely because of the low saving rate in the latter. This in turn was the outcome of the existing dualism within the economy of the developing country between traditional and modern sectors. The growth rate in countries such as India and China is now much higher than in the countries of the North, despite agricultural productivity in either India or China being much lower than in the North; i.e. the trend has reversed. However, notwithstanding that the North–South dualism persists, the saving rate over the last 50 years has more than doubled in many of the countries of the South. In the 1950s, the South was overwhelmingly agricultural while the North was industrial. In the contemporary world, the weight of agriculture in GDP has decreased substantially in both the South and the North, though the rate of decline in the North is much greater than in the South.

Two issues of "catching up" are: (a) economic prosperity; and (b) human development (HD). Economic prosperity (as measured by per capita income) is dependent on HD, but HD may or may not correspond to economic development; rather, it depends strongly on the governance. Differential rates of growth of different sectors across countries explain the future trend in global income distribution.[39] In many of the LDCs, the route to industrialization has taken a detour since the inception of current globalization: "digital capitalism" is unfolding

Table 1.6 Trends in North–South convergence: per capita GDP (PPP estimate) of the respective country as a proportion of that in the average North Atlantic economy

Year	*Argentina*	*Brazil*	*Chile*	*Mexico*	*India*	*Indonesia*	*South Korea*	*Taiwan*	*Thailand*	*Malaysia*	*Turkey*
1950	0.88	0.29	0.67	0.37	0.11	0.15	0.15	0.16	0.15		0.23
1973	0.64	0.32	0.41	0.34	0.07	0.12	0.23	0.30	0.14		0.22
1995	0.47	0.30	0.54	0.36	0.08	0.21	0.67	0.73	0.37	0.44	0.31
2006	0.41	0.23	0.30	0.30	0.10	0.11	0.63		0.24	0.30	0.24

Sources and notes: For the years 1950 and 1973, see Maddison (1995); for 1995 and 2006, see World Bank, WDR. The 'North Atlantic economy' is a simple average of 14 European countries plus Australia, New Zealand, Canada and the United States.

Table 1.7 Regional distribution of world income, 1993 and 2006

Region	*Population (million)*		*Share of world population (%)*		*Per capita income (in US$)*		*Share of world income (%)*	
	1993	*2006*	*1993*	*2006*	*1993*	*2006*	*1993*	*2006*
Low-income Third World (a)	3,078	2,403	**56.0**	**36.9**	379	650	**4.9**	**3.2**
Sub-Saharan Africa	599	770	10.9	11.8	520	842	1.3	1.3
South Asia	1,194	1,493	**21.7**	**22.9**	310	766	**1.5**	**2.4**
China	1,178	1,312	21.4	20.1	490	2,010	2.4	5.4
Middle-income Third World	1,219	3,086	**22.2**	**47.3**	2,397	3,051	**12.2**	**19.4**
Total Third World	**4,297**		**78.1**		**951**		**17.1**	
Eastern Europe and ex-USSR	392		7.1		2,665		4.4	
Total poor countries (b)	4,689		85.2		1,095		21.5	
OECD countries (c)	812		14.7		22,924		77.9	
Total rich countries	**812**	**1,029**	**14.8**	**15.8**	**23,090**	**36,487**	**78.5**	**77.4**
World total	5,501	6,518	100.0	100.0	4,343.0		100.0	100.0

Sources and notes: Chossudovsky (1997: Table 1.1); World Bank, WDR, various issues. In 1993, (a) excludes low-income countries of the ex-USSR. (b) Total of poor countries is the sum of the total Third World and Eastern Europe and ex-USSR. (c) Excluding Iceland, Mexico and Turkey.

very strongly without there being capitalism in agriculture or high agricultural productivity. But, "catching up" is perhaps largely due to the labour productivity growth in agriculture. Those who argue, following the classical "West" model, that industrialization at any cost is the ultimate solution to economic development of India and, in turn, to convergence with the West, simply overlook the contemporary central global issues.

The average per capita GDP (at constant 1995 dollar prices) of the 23 countries with high-productive agriculture was five times more than the LDC average during 1979–81; this rose to six times in 2002. This has been accompanied by increasing disparity in agricultural labour productivity. The latter gap between LDC and the 23 countries increased from 1:60 during 1979–81 to 1:94 in 2002. The 23-country average agricultural GDP per EAP in agriculture was US$ 43,510 in 2002 (at 1995 prices).[40] By contrast, the average agricultural productivity in the LDCs was $461. India, in particular, is lagging behind even farther: the productivity difference between India and, say, the US is 1:134, and with Canada it is 1:107 (FAO 2004).

Population-wise, EAP in agriculture in the high-productive 23 countries was 10 million (or 0.75 per cent of the world total EAP) as compared to 666 million in the LDCs (or 49.4 per cent) in 2004. Assuming four dependents per EAP, about 2.66 billion people in the LDCs are dependent on an agriculture that is far less productive than in the developed countries. More than one-fifth of the EAP in agriculture in the world are in India (Table 1.8). The weight of Indian

Table 1.8 World agriculture: regional distribution of economically active population (EAP), 1979 to 2004

Variable	*EAP in agriculture*				
	1979–1981	*1989–1991*	*1999–2001*	*2003*	*2004*
India as a ratio of World (%)	19.5	18.9	20.0	20.4	20.5
Low-income countries as a ratio of World	43.9	44.7	48.0	49.1	49.4
	Share in total EAP in the economy (%)				
India	69.4	64.1	59.6	58.3	57.8
OECD (30 countries)	15.0	11.4	8.4	7.6	7.4
OECD (20 countries) (a)	8.0	5.8	4.2	3.7	3.6
Low-income countries	75.5	71.7	62.9	61.3	60.8

Source and notes: FAO (2004). (a) OECD (20 countries) excludes Turkey (whose 43 per cent of EAP is in agriculture), Poland (20 per cent), Portugal (11 per cent), Mexico (19 per cent), Greece (15 per cent), Hungary (10 per cent), Ireland (9 per cent), South Korea (8 per cent), New Zealand (9 per cent) and Slovakia (8 per cent).

agriculture – in terms of the population dependent on agricultural activities – in its national economy has reduced by more than 12 percentage points between 1980 and 2004. Even so, about 277 million people are still economically active in Indian agriculture. If the family members are included, not less than 800 million people are still dependent on agriculture. This much of a productivity gap, *weighted* by EAP in agriculture, exists between India and the developed economies, the closing down of which largely depends on the performance of agriculture in India, whereas industrial development, by displacing millions of farmers, would only be contributing a fraction, if at all, to the dynamics of convergence.

The problem is compounded as capitalism is not the characteristic feature in that sphere of manufacturing which provides employment to 93 per cent of the country's manufacturing workforce. Yet, while China, Indonesia, Thailand and Malaysia are industrializing, India is on the fast track to tertiarization (Tables 1.9a and 1.9b). It is indeed intriguing to examine whether tertiarization is the emerging instrument of "catching up" in the new world economic order, as the nature of world distribution is largely ingrained to the *nature* of wealth creation across countries. We will discuss this more in Chapter 4.

The plan

In this background of the duality in development – often the fallout of obsession for certain archaic ideas of development and entrepreneurship – the focus of this book is on the structural deficiencies of a positive relationship between national economic prosperity and human development. This has to be read as an outline

Table 1.9a Structural disparity between selected EDCs and developing countries in Asia, in 1985 (% share in GDP)

Developed country	*Agriculture*	*Industry*	*Services*	*Developing country*	*Agriculture*	*Industry*	*Services*
United Kingdom	2	36	62	China	33	47	20
United States	2	31	67	Indonesia	24	36	41
France	4	34	62	Thailand	17	30	53
Japan	3	41	56	Philippines	27	32	41
Germany, Fed. Rep.	2	40	58	Malaysia	—	—	—
Italy	5	39	56	South Korea	14	41	45
Australia	4	33	63	Pakistan	25	28	47
Canada	3	30	67	India	31	27	41

Sources: World Bank, WDR, various issues; for India, see CSO, NAS.

Table 1.9b Structural disparity between selected EDCs and developing countries in Asia, in 2004 (% share in GDP)

Developed country	*Agriculture*	*Industry*	*Services*	*Developing country*	*Agriculture*	*Industry*	*Services*
United Kingdom	1	27	72	China	15	51	34
United States	—	—	—	Indonesia	17	46	38
France	3	24	73	Thailand	10	44	46
Japan	1	30	68	Philippines	14	32	54
Germany	1	29	69	Malaysia	10	48	42
Italy	3	28	70	South Korea	3	35	62
Australia	3	26	71	Pakistan	23	24	54
Canada	—	—	—	India	22	26	52

Sources: World Bank, WDR, various issues; for India, see CSO, NAS.

for how best to make growth "inclusive". It begins with, in Chapter 2, an inquiry into the degree of India's integration with the global economy, as globalization has had many hopes for the well-being of the Indian people in general, and the working population in particular. But, why, despite ample opportunities created by the export markets for the late-developing countries, India lags behind many others, has been chosen as the starting point for a comprehensive analysis of the "fragility" of South Asia's first giant. What transpires without further ado is India's institutional and organizational limitations in research and development (R&D). In Chapter 3, the problems affecting R&D – and thereby, industrial capabilities – are analysed with factors both from the supply side and the demand side. The study leads us to the blind alley of stunted social division of labour as the cause of many "diseases". The driving force behind progressive social division of labour – or maybe, the other way round – is the structural transformation of the economy. The characteristics of economic restructuring in India *vis-à-vis* other developing and developed countries are analysed in Chapter 4. The specific nature of structural changes in India seems to be the derivative of failed agrarian transformation. Chapter 5 makes an in-depth analysis of the growing vulnerabilities of Indian agriculture – especially at a time when the world food crisis is looming large. These various trends in the structural parameters show up in the wage and earnings distributions in the economy that are having a cumulative effect. Chapter 6 is an attempt to measure and explain the distribution. "Crony capitalism" and/or the "nanny state" appear in a big way, with a distortional effect on earnings distribution.

"Governance" ultimately is about creating positive externalities. At the microeconomic level, the market as well as government failure in, say, Singur or Raigad is rectified by a people's referendum. At the other end, at the macroeconomic level, the stability failure is frequently rectified by the government through its stabilization policy. Nevertheless, at the meso-level, the government is uncertain on the distribution failure – in health, education, social security and "power". The uncertainty is not so much about its capabilities – the institutional – as it is about the (organizational) aptitude for supplying collective goods. Chapter 7 analyses governance at the meso-level, and suggests two critical answers to degenerating governance; of course, "political closure" of the earlier South-East Asian type is not any of those. Finally, the central "thread" through the chapters is reeled off in Chapter 8.

2 Global trade and investments

Opportunities and challenges for India

India's exports: an overview

At its peak, the ratio of non-oil Indian exports (at current prices) to GDP at market prices was 11.8 per cent in 2006–07, rising from 6.6 per cent in the initial year of reforms, i.e. in 1991–92 (RBI, *Handbook of Statistics* 2008–09). Therefore, although the relations between trade and poverty should not be overemphasized, there are important dimensions of trade and income effect to explore. First of all, India is losing up-market despite efforts by her industries to peg the unit labour costs to the international order. Since the early 1960s, the share of the OECD countries taken together in India's total exports has declined. And, contrary to expectations, the export market in Europe and Japan has been shrinking, in relative terms, at a faster rate ever since trade deregulation. India is progressively becoming dependent on LDCs in Africa, Asia, Latin America and the Caribbean for her exports (Table 2.1).

The OECD, in absolute terms, still receives considerable exports from India, but that follows the logic of the industrial divide: India is the world's biggest diamond and gemstone cutting centre; polishes 90 per cent of the world's small and 50 per cent of the big diamonds. The gems and jewellery industry is now India's single largest export earner and constitutes 24 per cent of exports of manufactured goods. The US is the single largest importer of gems and jewellery from India, and there are significant imports by Belgium, Japan and Switzerland. Ready-made garments occupy the second place in India's export basket, constituting more than 10 per cent of aggregate manufactured exports, the bulk of which is directed to OECD. Leather and leather products also constitute major exportables to OECD. These are all produced extensively by labour-intensive methods and mostly in the unorganized sector.

It is therefore not surprising to find that exports of manufactures based on labour and natural resources (including gems and jewellery) as a proportion of total non-oil Indian exports, which constituted 40 per cent in 1980, steadily increased to nearly 60 per cent in 2005 (Table 2.2). Ghana, India, Morocco and Turkey, among other developing economies, experienced the largest increase in the share of labour- and resource-intensive manufactures, whereas countries like Taiwan and South Korea managed to pull down the relative importance of this

Table 2.1 Destination of Indian exports (% of total), 1990 to 2005

Year	*Developed countries*			*Developing countries*
	Europe	*USA*	*Japan*	
1990	57.3	15.1	9.3	21.5
2000	54.6	21.3	4.1	39.4
2005	45.1	16.7	2.4	53.2

Source: RBI, *Handbook of Statistics*, various years.

Table 2.2 Changing composition of Indian exports, 1980 to 2005

	1980	*2005*
Exports of labour-, and natural resources intensive manufactures as percentage of total non-oil Indian exports	40	60

Source: RBI, *Handbook of Statistics*, various years.

product group along with the primary commodities (UNCTAD, TDR, various issues).

There are complementary problems for an economy like India's with this kind of over-dependence on exports that are labour- and natural-resources-intensive. Take the case of diamonds. India imported rough diamonds worth about $10 billion in 2007–08 and exported finished diamonds worth $14 billion, engaging about one million workers. However, India's supremacy – currently sharing more than 60 per cent of world production in value terms and 80 per cent by volume – is under threat from recent international developments: diamond-producing countries such as South Africa and Congo are setting up a downstream diamond industry; China has become active in the past decade, especially in small diamonds; Israel is taking away the big diamonds; and countries like Malaysia, Mauritius, Thailand and Sri Lanka are regularly updating technologies. India's imports of rough diamonds have already gone down by 30 per cent in the past three years (Aron 2008).[1] As a result, 10 per cent of the merchants have diversified to other business and 20 per cent of the work force is jobless (ibid.). The only factor that decelerates India losing business to others is Indian skills in cutting and polishing. Once other countries adopt the skills, India may have to get processed diamonds from them to make value-added jewellery.

Given the composition of India's exports, one might expect some positive impact on wage and employment of low-skilled and/or semi-skilled workers in the unorganized sector. However, since this sector finds an unlimited supply of labour at the prevailing wage rate, the net effect of trade on the income of the workers remains ambiguous. On the question of how far the income-effect of India's trade pattern is cumulative, the new international division of labour alone can guide us.

Global trends in merchandise flows

The integration of the economies in the world system is at once visible in the approximately six-fold increase in world exports (in US dollars) between 1980 and 2006. Aggregate exports from the developing countries increased more than seven times, while exports of the developed countries increased rather more slowly, i.e. by 5.3 times.[2] Imports into the developing countries increased at a still higher rate; there was about eight-fold increase. In comparison, the rate of growth of imports into the developed countries was slower, increasing 5.4 times.[3]

This trend shows, among other things, that the import-substitution strategy, which occupied the centre stage in the development agenda of most of the post-colonial developing countries, is fast being replaced by trade liberalization. The emerging global pattern can be characterized as *ultra-pro-trade-biased* where the growth in trade value is greater than the income growth; the rate of annual change in volume of total exports has been greater than that of world GDP.[4]

One of the explanations for the radical growth in trade is that the global trade network now covers a greater number of countries than before. Second, the declining rate of population growth is coupled with changes in consumption behaviour in the contemporary world, following rising per capita income and the changing demographic profile in the EDCs – unlike during 1875–1913, when the rising ratio of foreign trade to world output was associated with rapid growth of population. Third, there has been increased trade in intermediate goods or semi-manufactures.[5] Fourth, the rising prices of fuels and mining products, since 2003, explain a large part of the growth in the trade value. Finally, the policy of promoting production and restricting consumption, and generating excess foreign exchange reserves in one part of the globe and excess liquidity-funded consumption in the other part, mainly in the United States, is also behind the global imbalance between trade growth and income growth. All these factors together have resulted in the rising share of the developing countries in world trade since the 1980s (Table 2.3).

Despite very major growth in the movements of merchandise across national boundaries, the North–South integration is under the microscope – a fact that

Table 2.3 Share (%) of the developed and the developing countries in world exports and imports

Region	*1980*	*1990*	*2000*	*2006*
		Exports		
Developed	65.3	72.0	65.6	59.1
Developing	29.4	24.2	31.7	36.8
Others	5.3	3.8	2.7	4.1
		Imports		
Developed	71.1	73.4	69.5	64.8
Developing	23.8	22.3	28.7	32.1

Source: UNCTAD, TDR, various issues.

Table 2.4 Trend in trade integration of the developed and developing countries, 1965 to 2003 (% share of the exporter's total)

Importer → *Exporter ↓*	*1965*		*1985*		*2003*	
	Developed	*Developing*	*Developed*	*Developing*	*Developed*	*Developing*
Developed countries						
All merchandise	67.2	22.6	67.5	22.1	74.7	21.7
Manufactures	64.5	26.4	67.0	24.0	74.0	22.6
Primary commodities	75.2	15.2	71.6	16.9	78.0	17.3
Developing countries						
All merchandise	68.9	25.1	60.3	26.9	53.8	43.4
Manufactures	53.4	43.8	58.3	33.7	54.4	44.2
Primary commodities	71.7	21.8	59.4	18.2	52.6	40.8

Source and notes: UNCTAD, TDR (2005). The share of South-East Europe and the CIS countries respectively are not included in this table, which explains why the shares do not add up to 100.

contradicts the understanding of globalization, but perhaps not without economic reasons (Table 2.4).[6] Precisely, the destinations of 57 per cent of aggregate exports from North America and Europe were the latter two regions themselves in 2006 (WTO, ITS 2007). Similarly, the destinations of about three-quarters of Europe's exports are countries in Europe. The parochial *trend* is visible in exports as well as imports of both the manufactured and primary commodities. Consequently, it appears as if the developing countries have formed a "trade block". In 1965, the developing countries together used to import about one-quarter of their own aggregate exports. This proportion jumped to more than 43 per cent by the turn of the century. More significantly, the share of the South's exports of manufactures to the North declined by about 4 percentage points – despite the much-hyped Global Production Network (GPN) – between 1985 (at the beginning of globalization) and 2003, when almost all of the major barriers to free trade in merchandise were abolished by the developing countries in order to be part of the GPN. Perhaps the observed *decline* is due to the fact that GPN as of now does not embrace even one-third of the countries in the world, while many more countries have stepped into industrialization.

Yet another great departure from the century-old pattern is the global trade in primary goods. Over a long historical period, the South used to export primary goods to the North in lieu of manufactures from there. The theoretical justification of the latter pattern is found in, say, the Heckscher–Ohlin model: trade results from the fact that different countries have different factor endowments. Besides, some of the "centre–periphery" theories of unequal trade (and "drain of surplus") were developed on the premises of the North–South dichotomy. As late as in the 1960s, about three-quarters of the aggregate exports of primary commodities from the developing countries were being imported by the developed countries. However, four decades later, the same ratio has declined to 53 per cent (Table 2.4). A substantial rise in agricultural productivity in the North, at a rate much higher than that in the South, and the demographic transition in the North have largely reversed earlier international trade relations.

Agricultural products and minerals, ores and metals together constituted about 18 per cent of the total merchandise exports from the South to the North in 1980 (Table 2.5). By 2003, the ratio had declined to less than 12 per cent. Most significant is the diminishing relative dependence of the developed countries on mineral fuels and lubricants from the developing countries. The reasons are mainly thus: in the 1990s the relative price of oil had a downward swing, but since the beginning of 2002, because of the discipline established by the Organization of the Petroleum Exporting Countries (OPEC), the trend reversed. As crude prices rise relentlessly, it is increasingly substituted by ethanol in the US and Europe. In the transportation sector, ethanol is the most widely used liquid biofuel in the world.[7] In Europe, France is the second largest EU producer of biodiesel after Germany, and the second largest EU producer of bioethanol after Spain.[8]

The combined imports of primary commodities by the North from the South were US$15.6 billion in 1965. In the following four decades there has been an almost 17-fold increase in the value of primary goods exported from the South to the North. However, the reverse process appears to have gathered steam. Although the North is still a *net* importer of primary goods from the South, the North's exports of primary goods to the South increased, too, by about 22 times, from $6.2 billion to $136.2 billion between 1965 and 2003. Among other factors, the fall in prices of other commodities *vis-à-vis* manufactures was critical to the changes in the relative value composition of trade between the developing and the developed countries, beginning from 1980 and at least up to 2000, but definitely not beyond that.

Table 2.5 Percentage composition of exports from the South to the North, 1980 to 2003

Exporting economies (all developing)	*1980*	*1990*	*2000*	*2003*
Agricultural products	13.2	15.1	8.9	9.2
Minerals, ores and metals	4.7	4.6	2.7	2.5
Mineral fuels, lubricants and related materials	65.0	23.7	14.2	12.2
Labour-, and resource-intensive manufactures	9.4	24.6	20.3	20.7
Low-skill and technology-intensive manufactures	1.6	5.1	5.3	5.6
Medium-skill and technology-intensive manufactures	1.0	7.4	14.1	15.6
High-skill and technology-intensive manufactures	1.7	5.0	6.3	6.9
Electronics, excluding parts and components	1.4	7.7	11.2	12.9
Parts and components of electrical and electronic goods	1.9	6.8	17.0	14.4
Total merchandise exports	100.0	100.0	100.0	100.0

Source: UNCTAD, TDR (2005).

The new international division of labour

Primary goods

The productivity growth in agriculture in most of the developed countries is way above that of the developing countries. Yet, when it comes down to the issue of unit costs of production the competitive advantage of the North remains ambiguous, so long as we exclude state subsidies. Agricultural subsidy in the North plays a significant role in international trade in agricultural commodities, which is why it has become the most contentious issue in global trade negotiations. Industrial and urbanized countries, in general, are protecting agriculture more than most of the developing countries. The US agricultural department, for instance, is required by law to subsidize over two dozen commodities. Between 1996 and 2002, an average of $16 billion was paid per annum by programmes authorized by various US farm bills dating back to the Agricultural Adjustment Act (1933), the Agricultural Act (1949) and the Commodity Credit Corporation (created in 1993), among others. In the OECD as a whole, in the mid-1980s, overall protection (total support) for agricultural producers, including border protection and direct subsidies, was about 63 per cent of gross agricultural output at world prices.[9]

Rising agricultural protection in developed countries and concerns about its impact on poorer developing countries brought about international efforts in the 1980s to reduce price distortions in the world markets. At the start of the Uruguay Round of trade negotiations in 1986, some agricultural exporting countries formed the Cairns Group and ensured that members of the General Agreement on Tariffs and Trade (GATT) put agricultural trade and subsidy reform high on the Uruguay Round agenda. Thereafter, the EU and the US reduced their overall support marginally to 45 per cent during 2000–02, while the contribution of border barriers to total protection came down from 77 per cent to about 63 per cent. However, if the 1960s and 1970s are taken as the reference base, protection went up in most of the OECD countries between 1986 and 2002 (Aksoy 2005).

In the EU, the prices received by farmers were 65 per cent higher than international prices during 1986–88, becoming 30 per cent higher during 2000–02. Similarly, in the US, domestic prices declined from what was 16 per cent higher than international prices to 9.3 per cent higher (Aksoy 2005). To the dismay of the globalized South, during the 1990s, as the borders opened up, the direct production-related payments to farmers were increased. Thus the Uruguay Round failed to have much impact on the levels of agricultural support in the large industrial countries. The overall support given to agricultural producers in OECD countries through higher domestic prices and direct production-related subsidies was $228 billion during 2000–02. Of these, 37 per cent went to farmers as direct subsidies. More than 90 per cent support in the EU went directly to the producers, while in the US almost half of the total amount of support went to the producers and the rest was distributed among the general services and the consumers (OECD 2003). In brief, the subsidies in the OECD have distorted the open international markets in rice, wheat, milk, beef and pork, sugar and cotton.

To elaborate, textiles production has shifted to the South, but the US still remains the world's leading cotton exporter (accounting for more than 40 per cent of global exports) and the second-largest grower after China.[10] About 25,000 American cotton growers annually harvest $3–5 billion worth of cotton. What is more, they collect government subsidies of about $4 billion a year, in some years topping the value of their crop. Without these and other subsidies, the US perhaps would not be competitive worldwide. Various US administrations and many trade-theorists have attacked export subsidies and their "trade-distorting" payouts to farmers in other countries, whereas they come forward to rescue US farm support policy by saying such payments do the least damage to farmers and prices in other countries. Ironically, the US subsidies for cotton have depressed cotton prices, harming the interests of four West African cotton-producing countries: Benin, Chad, Burkina Faso and Mali (Devarakonda 2007). Further, US subsidies for corn, rice and sorghum (a type of grain grown in hot countries) are pushing down global prices for these commodities, thereby affecting farmers in such countries as Argentina, Haiti, Ghana, Guyana, Kenya, South Africa and Zambia.[11] Similarly, Brussels' largesse on tomatoes, peaches and citrus fruits was denying commercial opportunities in the EU or elsewhere to producers in countries including Brazil, Chile and China. Further, today, the EU accounts for one-fifth of world sugar exports, about 30 per cent of world dairy exports, and one-tenth of world wheat exports. Despite production costs – with rare exceptions – being considerably higher in Europe than in many other countries, the EU has maintained its large market share through the complex range of subsidies under the Common Agricultural Policy.

Surplus production (over-consumption) (see Table 2.6) in the OECD, backed up by the huge price support from the government, inflicts enormous damage upon the developing countries.[12] Any subsidy that promotes over-production and increases exports to the world market at prices below the costs of production encourages dumping. Take the case of sugar dumping and its impact: Mozambique is one of the world's poorest nations with roughly 80 per cent of its people living in rural areas, and where agriculture is almost the only source of employment. Sugar is a high-potential export crop, facilitating livelihood diversification and stabilizing household incomes. Production costs are less than €286 per tonne, making the country one of the world's most cost-effective producers. However, the subsidized European surplus reduces Mozambique's share in the export market, with consequent impact on domestic employment and wages. Further, take for instance Jamaica's dairy industry: until the early 1990s, Jamaican farmers were largely protected from subsidized imports. But when the government was made to liberalize imports as part of World Bank-led adjustment policies, dairy farmers began to suffer. Subsidized European milk powder is cheaper than Jamaica's local milk, so there is no market for Jamaican fresh milk.

Subsequently, the developing countries formed the G-20 group at the time of the Cancun Ministerial conference in the Doha Round in 2003 to secure reductions in protection in the developed countries. Brazil launched a WTO case in 2007[13] against the legality of a broad range of US farm support programmes,

Table 2.6 Production and consumption of selected articles in OECD countries, as percentage of world respective total, in 2005

Article	*OECD as % of world*	
	Production	*Consumption*
Beef	41.1	41.5
Butter	42.2	36.1
Cheese	78.1	76.1
Coarse grains	52.8	49.3
Milk	46.6	—
Oilseed meal	40.8	55.0
Oilseeds	42.2	40.2
Pig meat	36.0	34.7
Poultry meat	45.1	42.8
Rice	5.5	5.2
Skim milk powder	78.8	58.0
Sugar	28.6	27.5
Vegetable oils	27.1	34.1
Wheat	40.9	32.6
Whole milk powder	51.8	23.5

Source: OECD (2006).

following an earlier complaint in this regard by Canada. Many of the developing countries, including India, have joined the campaigns against rich nations distorting the global market for farm products with their state subsidies. The Indian government would perhaps like to protect her farmers, but given the size of her annual state revenues, supporting producers at a level comparable to the OECD countries is difficult, if not impossible (see Table 2.7). The instrument of "deficit spending" – to the extent it is non-hyperinflationary – is too weak to raise the Indian subsidy level to the OECD standard. Thus, allowing free access of the OECD agricultural commodities to the Indian domestic market by eliminating customs duties and trade barriers would simply kill millions of jobs.

Manufactured goods

The crucial economic factor that explains the changing international division of labour in industry and services is the intensity of research and development (R&D) and the corresponding life-cycle of the product. The higher the R&D-to-sales ratio, the shorter is the product life and vice versa, e.g. in information technology or food processing (see Figure 2.1 as an indication).

The annual trends in international patent applications, filed by technical fields under the Patent Cooperation Treaty (PCT)[14] of 1978, distinctly show that the greatest numbers of PCT international applications are in the fields of telecommunications, information technology and pharmaceuticals, while the fastest growing technology areas are nuclear engineering (see WIPO, *Yearly Review*, various issues) – i.e. these are the areas of rapidly changing technology.

Table 2.7 Agricultural subsidies (producers' support estimates) in selected OECD countries and India (in US$)

Country	*1986–88 (Base year)*		*1997*		*1998*		*1999*	
	Per farmer	*Per hectare*	*Per farmer*	*Per hectare*	*Per farmer*	*Per hectare*	*Per farmer*	*Per hectare*
Canada	12,000	75	7,000	42	8,000	48	9,000	52
EC	11,000	707	16,000	815	18,000	890	17,000	831
Japan	15,000	10,048	21,000	10,211	22,000	10,005	26,000	11,792
USA	17,000	98	12,000	73	19,000	116	21,000	129
OECD	11,000	187	10,000	189	11,000	209	11,000	218
India	11	8	55	43	61	46	66	53

Source: GoI, Ministry of Agriculture, Department of Agriculture and Co-operation (2005).

Notes: Precise comparison of subsidies between India and OECD countries is not possible on account of differences in the composition of PSE and subsidies as computed in India. Agricultural subsidies in India include fertilizer, electricity for irrigation, and imputed subsidies on irrigation. Values in rupees are converted into US dollars at the exchange rate prevailing in 1999, namely Rs 43.3 per dollar.

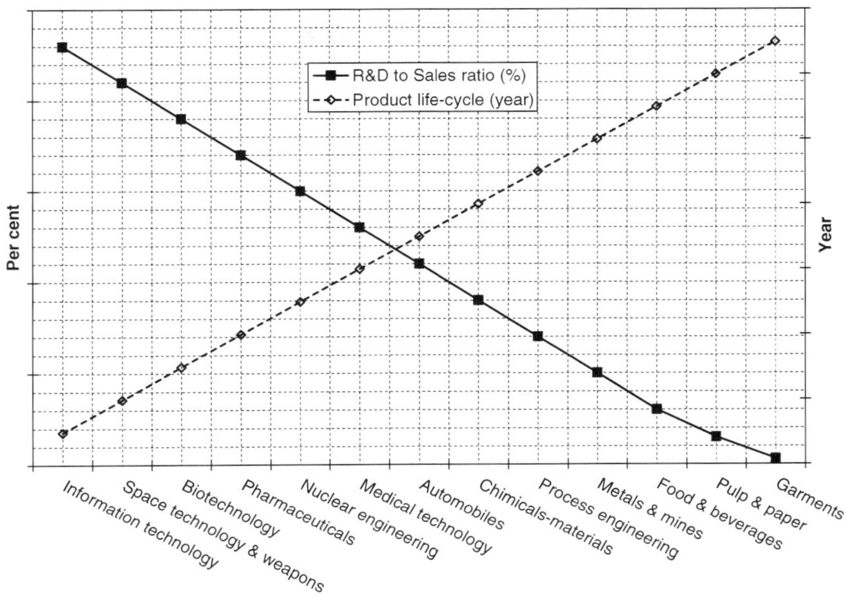

Figure 2.1 R&D costs and the length of product life cycle: defining the North–South divide.

The latter group of products constitutes the core competence of the North, while the South generally has to concentrate on the rest in the globalized trade regime. The outliers in the South are countries that have managed to hold a greater share of outsourced R&D by the TNCs as part of the GPN.[15]

The net result is that the North and the South compete in different segments of manufacture in the global market.[16] Boeing and Airbus Industries are competing with each other in markets where the South is not a competitor whatsoever. France exports Renaults to Italy and buys Fiats from there. Bangladesh and Vietnam garment manufacturers are in competition with each other in markets where producers from the North are virtually absent.

In capital-intensive as well as R&D-intensive production lines, there is a clear advantage to the North as against the South. Following the UNIDO definition of "high-technology exports",[17] one-half of the world's exports of high-technology products originated from Europe and North America in 2007.[18] Moreover, the same database shows that high-technology products such as "parts and accessories for machines" (SITC code 759), "thermionic, microcircuits, transistors, valves" (code 776), "optical instruments and apparatus" (code 871) and "photographic apparatus and equipment" (code 881) have been gradually losing their respective weights in the high-technology exports from Europe and North America – thus highlighting the relevance of the factor called "core competence" in the global production network.

In the industries in which the North has competitive advantages the unit wage costs do not usually exceed 5 per cent, whereas in industries in which the South has advantages it is higher. In other words, the knowledge-intensity (of a product) has become the yardstick for a new international division of labour. The North has not completely withdrawn from the lines of production in which she lost competitive advantage but rather continues to exploit the brand names and outsource the production facilities, which constitutes what is now known as GPN. Levi Strauss and company, for instance, which began to outsource its sewing operations overseas in the 1980s, has closed down all the US domestic plant of Levi's brand of denim jeans, one of the most widely recognized brands in the history of the apparel industry, and instead is having them made in the South for exclusive sale in Wal-Mart stores – the total annual sales of which amounted to just over $4 billion in 2007, $3 billion less than during the brand's peak performance in the mid-1990s.

No matter what advantage the South has in terms of wage costs in, say, pharmaceuticals, she is no competitor to the North. Drug discovery and development is a multi-billion-dollar global industry, in which the stake of countries such as India is in decimal points. This gets reflected in the volumes of exports of pharmaceuticals: Europe exported $247.35 billion, North America $35.12 billion, whereas Asia exported $21.17 billion in 2006 (WTO, ITS). Moreover, Indian exports of pharmaceuticals were valued at $3.51 billion in that year – about 4–5 per cent of her aggregate exports (WTO, Statistics database online). Of these, bulk drugs constituted 45 per cent and formulations 55 per cent, a *ratio* that has remained stable since 1999–2000 (source: Bulk Drug Manufacturers' Association of India).

To India's disadvantage, the domestic pharmaceutical industry is engaged in peripheral research, developing new formulations of existing drugs or new routes of drug delivery and getting patents for these. Since 1994, the Trade-Related Aspects of Intellectual Property Rights (TRIPS) agreement under the auspices of WTO has retarded the progress of the industry to a great extent in the late-developing countries. Notwithstanding, India has shown her economic advantages in the generic versions of drugs. For instance, until 2000, anti-retroviral (ARV) drugs were not affordable to the poor the world over. Transnational drug companies priced ARV drugs between US$12,000 and 13,000 annually per person. However, since 2000, prices began falling after Indian manufacturers introduced less expensive generic versions – currently for as low as $140 annually per person, thanks to the absence of a product patent regime in India.[19] The *de facto* non-tariff barrier to pharmaceutical products from India in the North markets is quite apparent as nearly 70 per cent of medicines exported from India go to the developing countries; Indian companies provide approximately 50 per cent of the essential medicines that UNICEF distributes in developing countries (Annam 2008). The transnational drug companies' attempts at successive patenting of mildly variant forms or derivatives of known substances after expiry of the monopoly period – a practice popularly called "evergreening" of patents – is part of a strategy of the TNCs from the EDCs to prevent WTO-member countries from invoking the flexibilities available within the TRIPS agreement.

India has also been able to develop the R&D-intensive biopharmaceuticals sector in the last couple of years.[20] However, it is basically the emergence of (contract) research organizations to undertake clinical trials involving numerous patients on behalf of the global drug research giants including Eli Lilly, Merck, Novartis, Aventis, Bayer and GSK that dominates the scene. One of the major explanatory factors is, of course, the availability of a huge number of patients. But no less important is the availability of a large pool of specialized medical practitioners in India. On the whole, India is still at the receiving end of one of the most thriving GPNs, i.e. in biotechnology.

In brief, if the United States has lost its domestic market of labour-intensive garment making to the South, the domestic enterprises in capital-intensive and R&D-intensive lines of production in the South are fast losing their markets to the North. The trends in the composition of Indian imports following deregulation of foreign trade since the early 1990s amply show the areas where she has been losing or gaining advantages (Table 2.8). As it happened, if production of television sets shifted to the South, TV serial production remained in the North, for export to the South as well. If computer assembly has gone to the South, software designing has remained in the effective control of the North. While the North has specialized in developing software packages, the South has emerged significantly in software services.

Not the least, there has also been an increase in the volume of transfer of sophisticated R&D-dependent arms and ammunition from the developed to the developing countries. During 2001–05, of the total volume of US$93.5 billion (at 1990 prices) of transfers of major conventional weapons, Asia (excluding Middle East countries) received about 40 per cent and the Middle East 19 per cent (SIPRI 2006). Russia and the USA each accounted for roughly 30 per cent of global deliveries of major weapons. One has to address the concerns of the developed countries about outsourcing in this perspective.

Table 2.8 India: trend in volume of imports of different commodities (index numbers with base 1978–79 = 100)

Group	*Commodity*	*1990–91*	*1999–00*	*2005–06*
I.	Food and food articles	297	629	734
II.	Beverages and tobacco	321	780	5019
III.	Crude materials, inedible, except fuels	228	417	649
IV.	Mineral fuels, lubricants etc.	182	464	689
V.	Animal and vegetable oils, fats and waxes	52	219	451
VI.	Chemicals and related products	240	604	951
VII.	Manufactured goods classified chiefly by material (paper etc.)	187	463	730
VIII.	Machinery and transport equipment	441	1039	5174
IX.	Miscellaneous manufactured articles	328	4072	2856
General index		238	705	1649

Source: RBI, *Handbook of Statistics* (2006–07).

Offshore outsourcing

Although there are various ways of defining "outsourcing", purchasing a significant percentage of intermediate components or services from outside suppliers is central. It can also be defined as the process of subcontracting network operations and support to an organization outside one's own company. In manufacturing, offshore subcontracting from the North has assumed growing significance since the early 1970s. Imports of "other semi-manufactures" – according to trade statistics – into the country largely account for outsourcing in manufacturing; these imports have been on the rise in global trade since about the mid-1970s. The US is far behind the EU (15 countries) or Western Europe as a whole in terms of respective values of these imports (WTO, ITS, various issues). What is more significant is that outsourcing operations in the EU are mostly confined within the member countries; they seldom go out to high-wage North America, or to low-wage Asia.

For the United States, outsourcing to high-wage countries in North America and Western Europe put together far exceeded that to low-wage Asia. Within Asia, China alone constituted more than 90 per cent of the value of outsourced jobs. To note, low-wage Africa has no role to play in the subcontracting network operations, and Latin America is far less important than North America, Western Europe, or even Asia in the network. In other words, the GPN is built more upon technological capabilities of countries than on relative wage costs. It has also opened up the possibilities of upgrading technological capabilities in the South and shifting from labour-intensive to more technology-intensive areas of production. Those countries that have successfully developed an appropriate incentive structure for outsourced R&D facilities in the economy are emerging as key sources at the supply end of the GPN.

Beyond "core competence": middle-range industries

The GPN has also reorganized itself following the growing vigilance of the citizens regarding the environment, and the covertly or overtly anti-union attitudes of a section of the employers in the EDCs. Until very recently, there was limited technology diffusion from the North to the South. However, the emerging trend is to export the entire production operation of certain industries, unlike in the past, to developing countries, not only because of cost advantages but, more importantly, to bypass various pollution control rules at home.

So far as the cost advantage is concerned, cheap labour in the developing countries of course comes first, as in the apparels. Most of the high-end industrial jobs that are outsourced to the developing countries are jobs which were relatively unionized in the North and had low direct supervision costs. Studies show that unionized workplaces are being disproportionately affected by US production shifts. Nearly 29 per cent of the companies shifting production out of the US were unionized and 39 per cent of all jobs being shifted out of the US are from unionized facilities. Almost 53 per cent of jobs shifting out of the US to Mexico and 34 per cent of jobs shifting to China are unionized. It is not the small, relatively new and otherwise unprofitable firms that are shifting out the unionized production lines to take advantage of the WTO regime. The companies shifting jobs from the US to China tend to be large (i.e. enjoying economies to scale and thereby having a dynamic comparative advantage in international trade), publicly held (in other words, equity holders still have confidence in the firms), highly profitable and well established (Bronfenbrenner and Luce 2004). These critical aspects are often ignored in the literature on GPN.

In order to get into the latter production network, India needs de-unionization. She has certain disadvantages in this respect *vis-à-vis* China, because in a multiparty democratic system it is difficult to arbitrarily violate or withdraw the rights that were once conferred to workers by formal laws, and to have perfect labour market flexibility – i.e. there are institutional as well as organizational hurdles. Notwithstanding, the Indian government has been engaged in finding ways, craftily bypassing the democratic rights of the workers, to make such changes in the labour market that would facilitate integration to this type of GPN. One such bypass is the SEZ programme, as discussed in a later section.

As to the second critical aspect of GPN, trade was never before so tightly intertwined with environment issues as it is in the current globalization. The Pollution Prevention Act and the Registration, Evaluation, Authorization and Restriction of Chemical substances (in short, REACH) in Europe are virtually compelling companies there to export their entire production lines to countries in the South where pollution control mechanisms are either poor or ineffective because of poor governance. In fact, the intellectual underpinning for further migration of the "dirty" industries to the LDCs was strongly favoured within the World Bank in the early 1990s (see Box 2.1) (Johnson *et al.* 2007).

A recent survey indicates that half of all companies in Europe's energy-intensive industries regard the EU's Emissions Trading Scheme (EU ETS) as one of the primary factors affecting their long-term investment decisions (Enkvist *et al.* 2007). Industries such as steel, cement and, most importantly, petrochemicals are thus increasingly being shifted out to those developing countries which having a standard supply of power (because these industries are also highly power intensive).[21]

Indeed, the issue of sustainable development in the developing countries has become more important in the context of current GPN. Take for instance, the proposed petrochemical complex – to be promoted by the Indonesian Salim business group and later occupied by such TNCs as Dow Chemicals, Du Pont and Monsanto – in a very densely populated and agriculturally fertile region in Nandigram (West Bengal). About 90 per cent of the industrial raw material would be imported, processed in the SEZ and exported. Value addition would surely be there but the proportion of it is unknown. On the other hand, the project required 20,000 acres of contiguous land. The area originally identified (by the government) for the project is having as high a population density as 700 per square kilometre, 112 temples, 44 mosques, 4 high schools, apart from many primary schools, *madrasas*, playgrounds and settled villages.[22] Ultimately, protracted (lasting for more than a year) and often violent conflicts between the government

Box 2.1 Memo (dated 12 December 1991) to the World Bank by Lawrence Summers, Chief Economist

"Dirty" Industries: Just between you and me, shouldn't the World Bank be encouraging MORE migration of the dirty industries to the LDCs [Less Developed Countries]? I can think of three reasons:

1) The measurements of the costs of health impairing pollution depend on the foregone earnings from increased morbidity and mortality. From this point of view a given amount of health impairing pollution should be done in the country with the lowest cost, which will be the country with the lowest wages. I think the economic logic behind dumping a load of toxic waste in the lowest wage country is impeccable and we should face up to that.
2) The costs of pollution are likely to be non-linear as the initial increments of pollution probably have very low cost. I've always thought that under-populated countries in Africa are vastly UNDER-polluted; their air quality is probably vastly inefficiently low compared to Los Angeles or Mexico City. Only the lamentable facts that so much pollution is generated by non-tradable industries (transport, electrical generation) and that the unit transport costs of solid waste are so high prevent world welfare enhancing trade in air pollution and waste.
3) The demand for a clean environment for aesthetic and health reasons is likely to have very high income elasticity. The concern over an agent that causes a one in a million change in the odds of prostrate [*sic*] cancer is obviously going to be much higher in a country where people survive to get prostrate cancer than in a country where under-5 mortality is 200 per thousand. Also, much of the concern over industrial atmosphere discharge is about visibility impairing particulates. These discharges may have very little direct health impact. Clearly trade in goods that embody aesthetic pollution concerns could be welfare enhancing. While production is mobile the consumption of pretty air is a non-tradable.

The problem with the arguments against all of these proposals for more pollution in LDCs (intrinsic rights to certain goods, moral reasons, social concerns, lack of adequate markets, etc.) could be turned around and used more or less effectively against every Bank proposal for liberalization.

Postscript

After the memo became public in February 1992, Brazil's then-Secretary of the Environment Jose Lutzenburger wrote back to Summers: 'Your reasoning is perfectly logical but totally insane. . . . Your thoughts [provide] a concrete example of the unbelievable alienation, reductionist thinking, social ruthlessness and the arrogant ignorance of many conventional 'economists' concerning the nature of the world we live in. . . . If the World Bank keeps you as vice president it will lose all credibility. To me it would confirm what I often said . . . the best thing that could happen would be for the Bank to disappear'. Sadly, Mr Lutzenburger was fired shortly after writing this letter.

Source: The Whirled Bank Group, 'Our Words: The Lawrence Summers Memo'. Available at: http://www.whirledbank.org/ourwords/summers.html; accessed 8 October 2007.

forces and the would-be land-losers, joined by other farm-related workforce and local retail traders, forced the project to be abandoned in that location.[23] However, it is planned to set up the enterprise in a place just offshore of the original location across the river Hooghly and near the confluence of the Haldi river and the Bay of Bengal, on an ephemeral island (Nayachar) made up of unconsolidated alluvium that rose just three metres above the sea in the early 1930s.[24]

So far as the employment consequences are concerned, hardly a fraction of the people facing the threat of displacement is likely to find jobs in the proposed chemical hub; not only because they do not have the skills endowment for the chemical plants but also because the capital–labour ratio itself is unusually high in petrochemicals. For instance, the chemical hub in the Jurong Islands off Singapore, considered as the beacon of the chemical world, would provide at the most 1,800 jobs when completed in 2010.[25] Incidentally, Jurong Consultants (linked to Indonesia's Salim business group) has endorsed the Nayachar location.

Singapore has no such vulnerable alluvial basin or river network that can pollute vast tracts. However, the human ecology effect of the project is far reaching. The enormous amount of hazardous wastes, including carcinogenic, mutagenic and toxic components of the project, have to be released to two adjacent rivers, Hooghly and Haldi. Also, the seasonal offshore currents in the zone will carry the pollutants along the coast into the world-famous Sunderbans delta. Tidal currents will push them inland through the massive Indo-Bangladesh deltaic river network (Sinha 2009). This would affect the lifelines of people in a vast area, including numerous fishermen, the aquatic chain, cultivation, and the entire food chain. This kind of consequence of petro-projects is nothing new, and has happened in the past, e.g. in the rich Kubatao Valley in Brazil, which later turned into a "death valley" in the mid-1980s: the transnational chemical firms left a devastating effect on environment, green cover, water and the people there. The "trade fetish" ought not to ignore also the growing scarcity of fresh water in the world, which is most likely to have a negative impact – against the positive effect of trade – on human well-being as the access of the people in the lower income groups to fresh water becomes more and more restricted.

Further, GPN has undoubtedly turned an obscure hamlet, i.e. Tiruppur in Tamil Nadu, into one of Asia's largest knitwear clusters. Dyeing and bleaching – both chemical and water intensive – are integral parts of the knitwear industry. With increased exports, the quantum of effluents from the dyeing and bleaching factories discharging into the Noyyal river (a tributary of the Cauvery river, flowing through three major southern agricultural districts) has also multiplied. The discharge into the river was allowed to accumulate into a dam – i.e. the Orathupalayam dam that was built on the river for irrigation purposes. The dam was completed in 1992 but could be used for irrigation purposes only for a short period, i.e. till 1996. Thereafter, the polluted water accumulating in the dam became the source of degradation of cultivable land, decline in yield and contamination of ground water, which in turn enhanced health risks of the villagers and livestock. Acting on a writ petition filed before the High Court of Madras (Chennai), the Court constituted an expert committee in 2005 to investigate and suggest ways and means (for details, see Swaminathan 2007). The matter of environmental pollution affecting the livelihood in a broader area than the knitwear cluster, as such, is yet to be amicably settled, because the governance has considerably weakened *vis-à-vis* the "free riders", and because of the colossal problem of "moral hazards" once the government insures entrepreneurs against misfortune.

To further elaborate, at one stroke the Apex Court of India has legalized the felling of 280,000 trees in the interest of the South Korean steel major Posco's project in Orissa (India). This was preceded by the recommendation of the Central Empowered Committee to diversify 1,253 hectares of forest land in the area for the purpose of the project. This fact – despite the new conservation policy of the central government adopted in 2006 that vows in so many words to protect the forest cover of the country – indicates the extent to which the national governance has become vulnerable to corporate capital and GPN (see also Box 2.2).

From North–South to intra-South trade

Another emerging feature of global economy is the faster growth in the South–South trade, which has steadily increased as a proportion of the total exports from developing countries.[26] However, the bulk of this increased trade constitutes agricultural products and fuels, minerals and metals. The rate of growth of trade in manufactures is lagging far behind in intra-South trade.[27]

Within the South, the relative position of Latin America is fast being replaced by the fast developing Asia. The intra-developing Asian trade has increased at a faster rate than the South–South trade as a whole.[28] About 37 per cent of the aggregate commodity exports of developing Asia remained confined within developing Asia in 1990,[29] but it had crossed the half-way mark by the turn of the century.[30] Earlier, e.g. in 1990, Japan was the destination of 33 per cent of developing Asia's exports. In the changed circumstances, China has become the prime destination of developing Asia's exports with a 20 per cent share, replacing Japan whose share reduced to 18 per cent in 2003 (UNCTAD 2006). China's emergence is very much associated with the value chains she has established with the US, in particular, which in turn has reoriented the trade channel from the South to the North, and the global trade balances.

The OECD countries together – known for comparatively far higher labour standards than in most of the South – accounted for more than half of the US aggregate trade deficits until 2003. The US trade deficit in manufactured goods (i.e. SITC code 6) with the OECD, which was about 63 per cent of the manufactured total in 1996, steadily declined to 42 per cent in 2005, although there was a faster increase in US imports of manufactured goods from the OECD than in exports to the latter (see USITC, online). It was the phenomenal growth of the US–China trade, primarily through the value chain of Wal-Mart and others, that shifted the US trade balance away from the OECD countries. Many countries in the developing Asia are thereafter hooked to the China–North value chains, resulting in the growing intra-South trade, especially in intermediate goods and raw materials.

Box 2.2 State fails to curb sponge iron pollution: people's health at stake [excerpts from a report published in *Hindustan Times*, Kolkata Live, 10 April 2009].

Heavy toxic metals like chromium, cadmium, carbon monoxide, carbon dioxide, nitrogen, nickel, arsenic and manganese coming out from the chimneys of sponge iron industries located in Purulia, Birbhum, Jhargram, Bankura and Durgapore in the state of West Bengal are taking a toll on the local people's health. Not only 7,000 labourers employed in 42 large sponge iron units, almost 50,000 people living in and around these units are suffering from life-threatening diseases caused by pollution emitted by the units.

The state-run West Bengal Pollution Control Board (WBPCB) in 2005 in its effort to put a final check on these polluting units issued a directive to all the 42 sponge iron units for installing a pollution control device made by Tata. This low cost device, if installed, would not only help the units maintaining the pollution level, but at the same time, would stop production if the unit starts emitting more pollutants than the permitted level. It automatically disconnects power supply to the kiln if the pollution control equipment (i.e. electrostatic precipitating device, ESP) is off. Once the ESP is locked, the owner of the polluting unit has to apply again to the WBPCB for a fresh locking code, without which restoration of production would not be possible.

A highly placed official with the state environment department on the basis of anonymity confirmed that when governments in Karnataka, Orissa and Madhya Pradesh successfully compelled the existing sponge iron industries installing the ESP, surprisingly West Bengal failed to do so.

As compared to the nature of production shifts from the US to China, the shifts from other Asian countries to China tended to be more specialized, both in areas of capital and in R&D-intensive areas such as electronics. A large proportion of shifts from Europe, Australia and Canada to China consist of such environmentally hazardous production lines as chemicals and petroleum (Table 2.9). Latin American countries are fast losing their labour-intensive industries such as textiles and metal fabrication and production to China. The latter meanwhile has expanded technology-intensive production capabilities through its own R&D growth as well as outsourced R&D facilities by TNCs to China. Moreover, China also deliberately kept – by using her political manoeuvrability – skilled wages at a much lower level than in the OECD, most of the Latin American countries, or in other NIEs, which gave her the double-edged advantages.

Relative labour costs synchronized

Wage as well as exchange rate variation in the late-developing countries has never before been as critical in international trade as it is now, especially since the emergence of China in a big way. The very wide *wage gap* between the North and an average developing country earlier granted flexibility to the latter to raise the

Table 2.9 Distribution (%) of non-US production shifts into China, by source country and industry (during January–March 2004)

Product	*From:*			
	Asia	*Europe*	*Latin America*	*Australia and Canada*
Apparel and footwear	0	2	0	60
Appliances	6	6	0	20
Auto parts	6	6	0	0
Automobiles	3	0	0	0
Chemicals and petroleum	3	18	0	20
Communication/information technology	0	2	0	0
Electronics/electrical equipment	52	33	0	0
Finance, insurance and real estate	0	2	0	0
Household goods	0	2	0	0
Industrial equipment and machinery	0	7	33	0
Metal fabrication and production	12	6	33	0
Plastics, glass and rubber	3	7	0	0
Sporting goods and toys	0	2	0	0
Textiles	12	7	33	0
Wood and paper products	3	2	0	0
	100	100	100	100

Source: Bronfenbrenner and Luce (2004).

wage level, the technology remaining the same, without much negative effects on the import elasticity in the North for commodities from the South. However, the world has changed a great deal since then. An important compilation of international comparisons of hourly compensation costs in manufacturing is done periodically by the Bureau of Labour Statistics, US Department of Labour.[31] As such, the wage gaps between the developed and the developing countries are still high. If $100 was the hourly compensation costs of the production workers in US manufacturing, it was $12 in Mexico, $21 in Brazil, $4 in the Philippines, $62 in South Korea, $2 in Sri Lanka, $27 in Taiwan, in 2006; and it was $3 in China in the last couple of years, and even lower in India (see USDOL, BLS 2008).[32] However, the average hourly compensation costs expressed in national currencies show an exemplary shift: The annual *rate of change* across countries in the world tended to converge with the deepening of free trade (Table 2.10). In other words, it appears that employer labour costs across countries are now pegged to each other.

The large differences in exchange rate between the North and the South was also an added advantage to the South by which the latter could have neutralized the *negative* effect of wage rise on exports. This remained valid till the developing country had a certain degree of autonomy in fixing the currency rate. Now, because of the growing interdependence between the developing countries – as reflected in the rising intra-South trade – exchange rate variations have to follow one another in the South. Once exchange rate manoeuvrability is lost, unit labour costs management has become the focus in developing Asia. Either there ought

Table 2.10 Production workers across regions: annual percentage change in hourly compensation costs in national currency in manufacturing, 1975 to 2006 (trade-weighted measure)

Region	*1975–1980*	*1980–1985*	*1985–1990*	*1990–1995*	*1995–2000*	*2000–2006*
OECD	13.9	15.8	15.8	7.5	4.6	3.8
Europe	12.2	8.8	5.7	4.5	3.5	3.4
Euro area	11.8	9.1	5.2	4.5	3.0	3.2
Asian NIEs	21.6	11.8	13.6	11.8	6.2	3.5

Source and notes: USDOL, BLS (2008). *Trade-weighted measure*: The trade weights used to compute the average compensation cost measures are weights based on the relative dollar value of US trade in manufactured commodities (exports plus imports) with each country or area in 2004; the Asian NIEs are Hong Kong SAR, the Republic of Korea, Singapore and Taiwan.

to be technological progress that raises labour productivity, or else the worker in the export sector has to keep working for longer hours without compensation and make compromises on real wage increases. Generally, the varying factor endowments along with uneven technological progress determine the factor intensities of products across countries. If that is so, keeping the domestic wage internationally competitive is illustrative of increased capital gains – the larger the relative size of the export sector in the domestic economy, the greater would be the profit share in the national income. In the process, ultimately the EDCs gain disproportionately.

If a country with relatively high international trade density (e.g. China) could hold the labour compensation rate down, a *cascading effect* would be felt across countries, irrespective of whether there is different specialization in different countries, or whether factor endowments of countries are different. China's economic surge, based on low labour costs, sends shock waves across the developing world. The conventional wisdom is that a rising relative wage induces entrepreneurs to substitute labour with capital of a higher order. Currently, the race to the bottom, so far as the wage is concerned, has forced the countries having comparatively higher labour standards to develop comparative advantages in high technology, biotechnology or nanotechnology, and in product design, coordinating global production networks, as Italy did after it lost its competitive advantage in the textile and apparel industry to countries with low wage costs. Since 2000, Mexicans have lost assembly jobs, hundreds of factories have closed their doors, and Mexico's trade deficit with China has grown to more than $5 billion. As such, middle-income countries like Brazil and South Korea find it difficult to pull their wages down to compete as a low-wage producer. They are thus rather compelled to focus on higher value-added products, which require higher R&D capabilities.

The problem however is with the low-wage goods producers and exporters like India whose flexibility in the manufacturing as well as the services sector is limited by R&D capacity. Briefly, in terms of the number of patents applied for, India is not even among the top 30 countries, while China is fifth after Japan, the US, South Korea and Germany. On the basis of WIPO Industrial Property Statistics, countries such as Brazil, South Africa and Israel are far ahead of a retreating India (more on this in the following chapter). India is thus fast losing many of its production lines to cheaper imports from China, which combines higher productivity with lower wage. However, India's poor performance in R&D, in products as well as process innovation, as compared to other developing countries like China or Brazil, explains her retreat from catching up with the North through industrialization.

Trade in services

World trade in services nearly tripled in value terms between 1990 and 2005. This trend has been consistent with the undergoing radical structural transformation in many countries. The share of services in GDP has grown from 65 to 72 per cent in the developed countries and from 45 to 52 per cent in the developing countries between 1990 and 2005. In terms of employment, services today account for over 70 per cent in developed countries and about 35 per cent in the developing countries. Faster growth of the sector in the developed countries has led to the declining share of the developing countries in aggregate world trade in services (Table 2.11).

The faster growth of the services trade in the North is strongly associated with the growth of financial services there – the latter has been higher than either industry or agricultural production, which is a direct outcome of the international distribution of financial assets favouring the developed countries. The share of financial assets in gross household assets (GHA) varies across countries, as noted earlier, but it is quite substantial in, say, Canada, Germany, Japan and the United States, contributing 25–45 per cent. By contrast, GHA in the developing countries such as India and Indonesia overwhelmingly comprise real property, while financial assets constitute less than 5 per cent, which again, unlike in the North, are largely made up of savings accounts instead of shares and equities (see Davies *et al.* 2006). Relative returns on different forms of assets determine

Table 2.11 Global exports of services: share (%) in aggregate trade in goods and services in respective economies, 2001 to 2005

Economy	*2001*	*2002*	*2003*	*2004*	*2005*
World	20.3	20.6	20.3	20.1	19.7
Developed	22.4	23.1	23.0	23.0	23.0
Economies in transition	15.3	16.4	16.1	15.0	14.1
Developing	15.9	15.4	14.8	14.5	14.0
Africa	19.2	19.8	19.6	18.4	16.1
Latin America and the Caribbean	14.5	14.3	14.0	13.1	12.7
Asia	15.8	15.2	14.4	14.3	14.0
Oceania	27.8	26.5	26.1	24.8	24.8

Source: UNCTAD (2008: Table II.2).

the directions of flow of services as well as the gains from trade in services, in both North and South.

Second, the offshore outsourcing of white-collar jobs from the North, which began with simple services like call centres and tele-marketing, later included jobs such as finance, accounting, medical services, research and development in the offshore centres. The value additions are more at the upper ends than the tail-end of the global value chains. Third, the more the knowledge/information intensity of the service is, the less is the proportion of low-skilled workers to the total in the particular sub-sector of services (see Figure 2.2 as an indication). The North thus has a clear advantage over the South in the skill-based high value added services and, in turn, is able to increase her share in both global trade and income.

The North–South dualism manifests itself in the fact that the largest profit-making enterprise in the world (until 2005), i.e. Wal-Mart – with sales over $300 billion a year, and having revenues larger than those of Switzerland – has set up more than 3,000 sweatshops in China, which are, however, powerless price

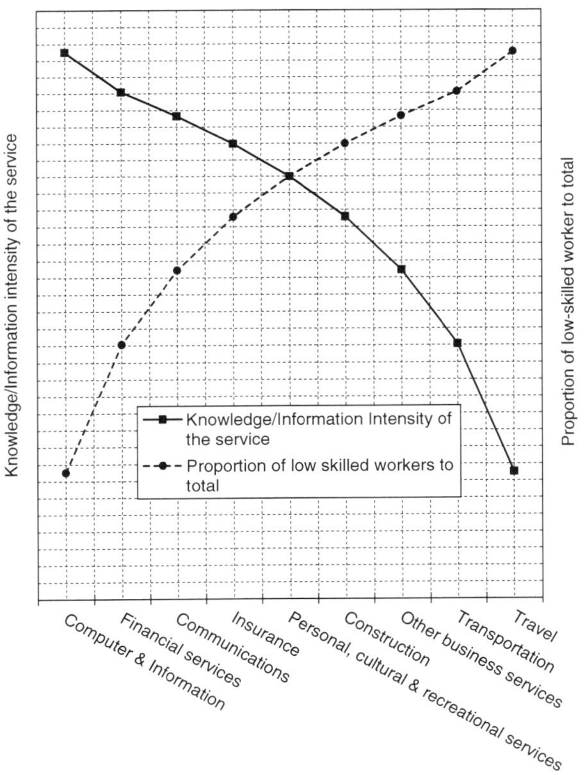

Figure 2.2 Services: composition of skilled labour in different sectors.

takers rather than partners, deal makers or oligopolistic price administrators.[33] Without ignoring the relevant political forces, it is perhaps more important to recognize that Wal-Mart has achieved a monopoly status in retail business owing initially to its pioneering the IT-based logistics revolution.

Generally, services, while currently accounting for over 60 per cent of global production and employment, represent not more than 20 per cent of total trade (BoP basis). Although many services at home are simply not tradable with other countries, the situation has been changing due to the introduction of new transmission technologies (electronic banking, tele-health or tele-education services), the opening up in many countries of long-entrenched monopolies (e.g. voice telephony and postal services), and regulatory reforms in hitherto tightly regulated sectors such as transport. Many services that have long been considered genuine domestic activities have increasingly become internationally mobile, and their tradability has enhanced thanks to the achievements of the Uruguay Round of negotiations among countries, which led to the General Agreement on Trade in Services (GATS) in January 1995. The GATS was inspired by essentially the same objectives as its counterpart in merchandise trade. All WTO members, some 140 countries, are at the same time members of the GATS and, to varying degrees, have assumed commitments in individual service sectors.

The GATS distinguishes between four major modes of supplying services: (a) cross-border supply (Mode 1 under GATS); (b) consumption abroad (Mode 2); (c) foreign direct investment (FDI) or commercial presence (Mode 3); and (d) migration (Mode 4) – as when a self-employed worker who is paid directly by customers or as an employee receives wages while abroad, which the GATS refers to as the temporary movement of "natural persons" over borders. Mode 4 movements of service providers can be substitutes or complements for other modes of services trade. For example, accountancy services can be provided online (Mode 1) rather than by sending an accountant abroad (Mode 4), or the client can travel to the country where the service provider is located (Mode 2). Modes 3 and 4 involve the international movement of factors of production: Mode 3 commercial presence involves the movement of capital and is almost always accompanied by some Mode 4 movements, as key personnel accompany investments in subsidiaries; and Mode 4 is labour migration to provide services (for a summary, see Martin 2006). Roughly, Mode 1 (cross-border supply) accounts for 30 per cent, Mode 2 (consumption abroad) 15 per cent, Mode 3 (commercial presence) 52 per cent, and Mode 4 (migration-compensation) 2 to 3 per cent of global trade in services. While other modes of supplying services are heavily concentrated in the developed countries, the weightage of Mode 4 is quite high in the populated developing countries like India, Pakistan, Nepal or Bangladesh.

Within the developing countries, the volume of services trade is heavily concentrated in a few, depending largely on their factor endowments – i.e. physical capital, knowledge capital, natural resources, cultural diversities etc. Not more than 20 countries accounted for 75 per cent of the total developing-country services trade in 2005, six of which accounted for 50 per cent (UNCTAD 2008). An increasing number of developing countries have become successful exporters of tourism, transportation and construction services, audiovisual, computer and information technology (IT) services, and business and professional services. However, they lag far behind the developed countries in exports of "financial services, royalties and licence fees" and "personal, cultural and recreational services". Countries in the North desperately invite globalization of Mode 3 trade in services, since their comparative advantages are in investing capital in the form of subsidiaries to provide banking, insurance and other services in the South, but not Mode 4 services. This is revealed in the standard analyses of 'requests and offers'.[34]

Consequently, the developing countries had a *negative* balance of trade in services with the developed countries, while their combined merchandise trade balance has been *positive* (Table 2.12). Though India does not have a positive merchandise trade balance, the exports of "software services" reduce her current account trade deficit to a great extent. For instance, while the merchandise deficit was US$63.2 billion in 2006–07, *net* exports of software services were $29 billion, reducing that much of deficit in the current account (RBI, *Handbook of Statistics* 2007–08).

However, the Indian software sector has certain limitations which, if they remain unattended, might reduce its importance in India's BoP in future. The export volume of "software services" from India is indeed large, but grossly missing from the basket are software products or packages, which compares badly with Ireland or Israel's software export profile (D'Costa and Sridharan [eds] 2004). A narrow specialization of customized software service exports is a gross weakness of Indian industry. "Custom application development" is where the software exporter designs the customer firm's IT software and IT system for specific functions, e.g. for a bank or an airline company. This segment occupies not more than 4 per cent of global IT services. In the higher-wage IT "consulting services", "managed services" or "system integration", India's global market share is less than 1 per cent (Table 2.13). In "application development" – where wage rate per hour is comparatively lower than in other IT segments in the US – India's share in the global market is more than 16 per cent (Banerjee 2007a).

Table 2.12 Trade balances in merchandise and services: developed and developing economies, 1980 to 2006 (US$ billion)

Year	*Trade balance (Merchandise)*		*Trade balance (Services)*	
	Developed	*Developing*	*Developed*	*Developing*
1980	–146.1	104.6	16.1	–61.1
1990	–129.2	42.8	8.7	–29.8
2000	–387.9	140.2	58.9	–44.6
2003	–420.0	178.3	81.8	–48.3
2004	–548.5	213.1	117.8	–54.2
2005	–743.8	391.5	152.0	–48.4
2006	–828.8	493.6	179.1	–49.0

Source: Computed from UNCTAD, *Handbook of Statistics*, various issues.

Table 2.13 Software services: India in the global market, 2003

Services	*Global software services spending (US$ billion)*	*India's global market share (%)*	*US wage rate ($/hour)*
	(1)	*(2)*	*(3)*
Consulting	41.5	< 1	80–120
Applications development	18.4	16.4	25
System integration: hardware and software deployment and support	91.7	< 1	18–25
System integration: applications, tools and O/S	62.4	< 1	40
IT education and training	18.5	0	40
Managed services	124.9	1.6	60–120
Total	357.6		

Sources: For cols (1) and (2), see Nasscom, *Strategic Review* (2004); for col. (3), USDOL.

In other words, India is competing with the tail-end of US jobs in software services, while the high-end jobs – those associated with high-end R&D – largely remain the exclusive domain of the US and some other developed countries.

Like software exports, net exports of Mode 4 services also have been significant in reducing India's current account trade deficit, thereby reducing short-term capital inflows. Interestingly, foreign investments (FDI plus portfolio) in India were US$15.5 billion in 2006–07, while private foreign remittances by Indian migrants abroad amounted to a staggering $27.9 billion – i.e. 1.8 times more than net foreign investments in that year (RBI, *Handbook of Statistics* 2007–08). While huge merchandise trade deficits have negative effects on jobs at home, jobs (both skilled and low-skilled) are created abroad for Indian migrants to compensate for some of the aggregate losses. However, remittances strengthening the BoP situation might at the same time fuel inflation, in the absence of additional job creation in the domestic economy.

Mode 3 movement of services

The pattern of global movements of foreign direct investments (FDI) is reinforcing the new international division of labour. During 1986–1990, developed countries shared 82.4 per cent of the total while the developing countries in Africa, Latin America, the Caribbean, Asia and the Pacific together accounted for only 17.5 per cent. Ironically, after more than a decade of liberalization and structural reforms in most of the developing South, the global distribution pattern of FDI remained almost unchanged, with the South attracting only 17.9 per cent, a mere 0.4 percentage point gain (UNCTAD, *World Investment Report*, WIR, various issues). If China is excluded, the picture for the rest of the South is even gloomier. The least developed countries, offering the cheapest labour in the world, had a share of 0.4 per cent in the total FDI inflows during 1986–1990. Global capital did not flow much into these countries thereafter, thus their share in world FDI inflows remained the same as before – 0.4 per cent in 1999–2000. Global FDI inflows then declined until 2003, but the United States remained the largest recipient, ahead of the UK, China and Luxemburg.

After four consecutive years of increase, global FDI inflows became $1,833 billion in 2007. Of these, inflows into the developed countries were $1,248 billion. The US maintained its position as the largest recipient country, followed by the UK, France, Canada and the Netherlands. The EU was the largest host region, attracting almost two-thirds of total FDI inflows into developed countries. In fact, the share of the developed countries to total FDI inflows has progressively increased since 2005 – from 63.8 per cent to 66.7 per cent, further to 68.1 per cent in consecutive years. As a result, the share of the developing countries has gradually declined (UNCTAD, WIR 2008).

Relatively low FDI inflows from the North perhaps explain the slower R&D progress in most of the developing countries including India, especially after the emergence of the new international division of labour. There are two paths of R&D transfer by the EDCs from home country to foreign country. First, there is *captive offshoring*, i.e. transfer done internally by moving services from a parent company to its foreign affiliates. It involves complementary FDI. This is different from *outsourcing* R&D, which always involves a third-party provider abroad, be it a local company or a foreign affiliate of another TNC. When put to the scale of spillover effect of different kinds of R&D activities in the host country, captive offshoring of course comes last (Cantwell and Janne 2000). After all, the share of R&D by foreign affiliates varies considerably across countries, while the offshoring of R&D by European TNCs to developing countries is still in a nascent stage. In 2003, foreign affiliates accounted for more than half of all business R&D in Hungary, Ireland and Singapore – mostly in the services sector – and about 40 per cent in Australia, Brazil, the Czech Republic, Sweden and the UK. By contrast, it remained under 10 per cent in countries such as Chile, Greece, Japan, South Korea and India (UNCTAD 2005).

Foreign capital and labour market

As FDI dependence of the developing country becomes overwhelming, the *power* of capitalist ownership gets accumulated in the grand *metropolitan*, becoming more and more centralized. As one finds in China, this power has enabled foreign capital to easily flout the national labour laws. FDI found China the most attractive destination since the state is omnipotent there, and thereby could assure the foreign investors of long-run stability in unit labour costs. Only one trade union is allowed in China – and it is controlled by the government and designed to suppress labour, not represent it. Nonetheless, the Chinese workers are kicking back: there are 87,000 workplace protests a year. Last year, there was a tumult in Chinese factories after a string of workers died of organ failure while doing 50-hour shifts. The panicked Chinese government was poised to make a major concession: they were going to allow the formation of elected trade unions in the factories. Organized workers can ask for more safety measures and better wages. But it didn't happen – because there was panic from rich-world investors. Microsoft, Nike, Ford, Dell and others – acting through the American Chamber of Commerce – swiftly announced the laws were "unaffordable" and "dangerous", and muttered they might look elsewhere. European and American governments parroted the corporate line. Far from lobbying for freedom, they enthusiastically lobbied against it. So the Chinese government watered down the proposals (Hari 2008).

On the other hand, portfolio capital plays an influential role in the real sector via the stock markets, as one finds in India. Comparatively greater inflows of portfolio investments or hot money into India than to China (Table 2.14) made the entire economy vulnerable to the powers of international finance capital. The fiscal and monetary policies of the government need to comply with the interests of the financial markets. That is why successive Indian governments have willingly accepted the Fiscal Responsibility and Budget Management Act (2003), which restricts deficit spending (Bhaduri 2008). The government is more inclined to raise resources through privatization and so-called public–private partnership, but not by imposing a significant turnover tax on transactions of securities. The latter, note, is conducive to the growing *richness* in the country.

Table 2.14 China and India: distinctive trends in inflows of FDI and portfolio capital (values in US$ million), 1990 to 2005

Year	*China*		*India*			
	Actual FDI	*% of total capital inflows*[(a)]	*FDI*[(b)]	*Portfolio*	*FDI as % of total capital inflows*	*Portfolio (%)*
1990	3487	33.9	97	6	94.2	5.8
1991	4366	37.8	129	4	97.0	3.0
1992	11007	57.3	315	244	56.4	43.6
1993	27515	70.6	586	3567	14.1	85.9
1994	33767	78.1	1314	3824	25.6	74.4
1995	37521	78.0	2144	2748	43.8	56.2
1996	41726	76.1	2821	3312	46.0	54.0
1997	45257	77.0	3557	1828	66.1	33.9
1998	45463	78.5	2462	–61	102.5	–2.5
1999	40319	76.6	2155	3026	41.6	58.4
2000	40710	68.5	4029	2760	59.3	40.7
2001	46880	94.4	6130	2021	75.2	24.8
2002	52740	96.0	5035	979	83.7	16.3
2003			4322	11377	27.5	72.5
2004			5652	9315	37.8	62.2
2005			7751	12492	38.3	61.7

Sources: For China, see Huang (2003: Table 1); for India, RBI, *Handbook of Statistics* (2006).
Notes: [(a)]This includes, beside FDI, foreign loans and contractual alliances. [(b)]Until 1999–2000, the coverage of FDI flows in India was confined only to equity capital. Apart from equity capital, reinvested earnings and inter-corporate debt transactions, China includes short-term and long-term loans, trade credits, bonds, grants, financial leasing, investment by foreign venture capital funds, earnings of indirectly held enterprises, non-cash equity transactions, control premium and non-competition fees within FDI. It also includes project imports as FDI flows, whereas they are recorded as imports in India.

In the case of FDI, the flouting of the country's labour laws could be more direct – as one finds in the Chinese SEZs – than pressure exercised by capital on the management of the firm through the stock markets, as in India. Unlike FDI, as the capital market appropriates more power over other institutions, corporations often try to send manipulative signals to that market; the lay-off is often part of the game to improve their stocks trading prices. They believe, or the market has led them to believe, that the investors' mood is: downsizing is the ultimate in the profitability of a company. Moreover, though portfolio capital is inflationary, requiring continuous revisions of real wage, the stock market sentiments encourage the corporate not to act in tune.

Special economic zones: the rise of political entrepreneurs

In order to bypass many of the structural deficiencies in boosting exports from India the central government floated the SEZ policy. The main objectives of the SEZ Act and policy were (a) generation of additional economic activities; (b) promotion of exports of goods and services; (c) promotion of investment from domestic and foreign sources; (d) creation of employment opportunities; and (e) development of infrastructure facilities. The SEZ Act (2005), supported by the SEZ Rules, came into effect from 10 February 2006, providing for simplification of procedures and for single-window clearance on matters relating to central as well as state governments.

The incentives and facilities offered to the SEZ units include (a) duty-free import and domestic procurement of goods for development, operation and maintenance of SEZ units; (b) 100 per cent income tax exemption on export income for SEZ units for the first five years, 50 per cent for next five years thereafter and 50 per cent of the ploughed-back export profit for the next five years; (c) exemption from minimum alternative income tax; (d) external commercial borrowing by SEZ units up to US$500 million in a year without any maturity restriction through recognized banking channels; (e) exemption from central sales tax; (f) exemption from service tax; (g) single-window clearance for central and state level approvals; and (h) exemption from state sales tax and other levies as extended by the respective state governments.

In brief, under section 26 of the SEZ Act, 2005, every developer and entrepreneur shall be entitled to exemptions from any duty of customs on goods imported into and exported from the zones, from duty of excise, from service tax, from the securities transaction tax leviable, have entitlements to drawbacks, and so on. Besides, like the Chinese Residency permit system, under section 46 'every person, whether employed or residing or required to be present in a SEZ, shall be provided an identity card', thus restricting free mobility of labour within India. Under section 51 of the SEZ Act (2005):

> the provisions of this Act shall have effect notwithstanding anything inconsistent therewith contained in any other law for the time being in force or in any instrument having effect by virtue of any law other than this Act.

Although it is not explicitly stated, the implication of the latter provision for the labour market is that the existing laws would not be applicable in the SEZ. In other words, job security, work security, income security, social security and rights to association could easily be denied to the workers inside the SEZs. This almost looks like a sovereign colony within a country, in the model of nineteenth-century "Shanghai Concessions" or *extraterritoriality*.[35]

In addition, all the import/export operations of the SEZ units are on a self-certification basis. The units in the zones are required to be a net foreign exchange (NFE) earner, calculated cumulatively for a period of five years from the commencement of production. These units have to execute a legal undertaking with the development commissioner to achieve *positive* NFE. For any violation of the SEZ scheme, the Director General of Foreign Trade (DGFT) or the authorities empowered under the Act are required to initiate action under the Foreign Trade (Development and Regulation) Act (1992), which includes the issue of a 'show cause' notice, levy of penalty, suspension/cancellation of the importer–exporter code, licences etc. The applicable customs duty foregone is required to be recovered by the revenue department.

Briefly, SEZ is a specifically delineated duty-free enclave and is a deemed foreign territory for the purpose of trade operations, duties and tariffs. Accordingly, goods and services from the domestic tariff area (DTA) to SEZ are to be treated as exports and goods coming from SEZ into DTA are to be treated as imports.

There are 222 SEZs in private and joint sectors which have been notified since the SEZ Act (2005) came into force, in addition to the 19 SEZs that had existed prior to the implementation of the Act. In terms of industry type, although more than half of the SEZs are IT or ITes (information technology enabled services), there is a wide gap between the trends in the global market in other sunrise industries and their production in India (Table 2.15). The total of direct employment proposed in these SEZs (notified after the 2005 Act) is 2.45 million. Incidentally, the current direct employment is 98,000, i.e. just 4 per cent of the suggested employment (GoI, Ministry of Commerce and Industry, Department of Commerce 2008, *Special Economic Zones in India*).

Duty foregone by the government on the SEZ scheme was about US$1.915 billion (i.e. Rs 88,420 million) between 2000–01 and 2005–06. The budget estimate of the duty foregone was $474 million (i.e. Rs 21,460 million) for the year 2006–07 (CAG 2008a). After allowing such huge export subsidies the economy legitimately expected to earn considerable NFE; unless of course the foreign inelasticity of demand for Indian products stood in between.

Performance evaluation, SEZs

The Comptroller and Auditor General of India (CAG) conducted an audit between July 2006 and May 2007 with the limited objective of verifying that the units in the SEZs had complied with the applicable Customs Act, Rules, notification etc. and had functioned appropriately under the provisions of the export–import

Table 2.15 India: industry type-wise number of special economic zones (SEZs) (as on 15 May 2008)

Type of SEZ	*Number*	*Type of SEZ*	*Number*
IT/ITes	136	Services sector (basically, real estate)	4
Electronic hardware	13	Power	2
Pharmaceuticals	12	Aluminium and related industry	2
Biotechnology	4	Stainless steel and ancillary/downstream industry	1
Textiles and apparel	8	Automobile and components	1
Gems and jewellery	3	Paper	1
Engineering products	11	Petrochemical and petroleum	1
Leather and footwear	4	Chemicals	1
Multi-product	10	Port-based	2
Food processing	5	Handicraft	1

Source: Based on the detailed list published by GoI, Ministry of Commerce and Industry, Department of Commerce (2008).

policy (CAG 2008a). The CAG reviewed the performance of 370 functional units and another 180 closed units, and has come out with revealing facts. The audit observed that 22 SEZ units had been achieving the prescribed (positive) NFE mainly through *domestic sales*, which obviously violates the basic objective of the SEZ scheme. Of the overall export earnings of the SEZ units, 72 per cent came from domestic sales, and actual export earnings were only 28 per cent. The *range* of domestic earnings as a percentage of total export earning across these units was 59 to 100. Customs duty of about $230 million (i.e. Rs 10,433 million) was foregone on imports of goods by these units.

This certainly highlights the degree of overestimation of India's foreign exports. Audit scrutiny records of, say, Nokia India Pvt Ltd, a unit in Chennai SEZ, revealed that the unit cleared mobile phones with a value of US$1.08 billion during 2005–07 in DTA (instead of exporting to abroad) at a "nil" rate of duty. In the absence of enabling provisions in the Rules, duty of more than $150 million foregone on the inputs used in the manufacture of these mobile phones could not be recovered. Since the SEZ scheme relies mainly on self-certification and does not require the quarterly or annual performance reports to be supported by other statutory documents such as annual accounts, customs records, income tax returns and bank realization certificates, quite often the data on NFE earned by the SEZ units turn out to be unreliable. The CAG report has documented several cases where the SEZ units have reported positive NFEs while actually these were *negative*: more *cif* value of imports than *fob* value of exports.

However, unlike in China, the types and sizes of units coming up in the SEZs in India, coupled with their mode of operation so far, do not give a bright impression of radical changes in her export capabilities. However, India could still push forward the handicapped baby called SEZ so long as her external reserves remain at a fairly high level.

External reserves and imbalances

Thanks to globalization, and in the course of (a) goods trade and finance expansion and (b) growing economic migration, most of the developing countries have accumulated huge foreign exchange (FE). The most spectacular increase in FE reserves is recorded in Asia – especially in India and China – and Africa, rather than in South or Other America. Between 1990 and 2004, accumulated external reserves of the developing countries grew by 572 per cent. Country-wise, there has been an increase of 1,468 per cent in China's FE reserves, while in India it was 660 per cent (Table 2.16).

The FE reserves in these countries and regions swelled as the volume of the US trade deficits increased. The *necessity* for increased reserves grows with the increasing volumes of trade. Every country would like to keep at least as much of reserves as would be required for her expected import bills for the coming couple of months – that is the adequacy norm of international liquidity, although it is true that a country can hardly face a situation where she can export nothing but will import at the usual rate.

In 1980, an average developing economy used to maintain external reserves equivalent to 4 months of imports. In 2004, that had increased to 9.3 months' import-bill equivalent. The *equivalence* was still greater in the faster growing import regions, namely in East and South-East Asia, but most strikingly in Africa, which has been experiencing a much slower rate of trade expansion than the other regions (Table 2.16). Holding foreign exchange reserves that support longer months of imports than usual is most pronounced in China and India, though theoretically the volume of reserves need not grow as fast as the volume of trade. It is also important to recognize that in India the ratio of "external liabilities to external reserves" has declined in recent years (see RBI, *Handbook of Statistics*, various years).

Apparently a crisis of confidence is brewing; confidence in the dollar is decreasing; yet everyone is trying to prevent a global financial crisis from occurring. In fact, the poorer countries are providing a great service to the global finance market: their dollar reserves are keeping the market stable. In the past, the main surplus countries receiving dollars from the US deficits were the members of the European Economic Community (EEC) and Japan. The US continues to play the role of world banker, and the economic benefits are accruing to the world banker in the form of *seigniorage*, or simply the profits from banking. The phenomenon of seigniorage is one of the main sources of transfer of real resources from the poorer to the richest nation of the world.

The International Monetary Fund (IMF), set up at Bretton Woods just before the end of the Second World War, was essentially designed to deal with the problems that had haunted international economic relations during the 1930s: competitive devaluations, discrimination in foreign exchange dealings and tariffs, lack of convertibility and disorderly capital flows. However, IMF's provision of international reserves remained totally inadequate in the context of the current trade explosion; it remained only a small part of the total international reserves. An inbuilt mechanism meanwhile has developed out of the stupendous growth in global trade and the new international division of labour, and subsequently the

Table 2.16 Growing external reserves (total reserves *minus* gold) of India and other developing countries, 1980 to 2004

Region/Country	*Change in external reserves (US$ billion)*							*Number of months of imports (a)*				
	Annual average (1980 to 1990)	*Annual average (1990 to 2000)*	*2001*	*2002*	*2003*	*2004*	*Growth (1990 to 2004) (%)*	*1980*	*1990*	*2000*	*2002*	*2004*
Developing economies	15.8	72.1	92.0	208.2	347.3	428.7	572.3	4.0	4.7	6.8	7.9	9.3
South America	0.3	7.4	(–)9.9	(–)3.5	25.5	16.9	223.7	5.6	6.7	8.7	9.1	9.6
Other America	0.6	3.5	12.1	5.6	9.2	8.3	220.4	1.6	2.3	2.5	3.5	3.9
Africa	(–)0.8	5.4	12.4	7.4	23.9	42.1	796.1	4.0	3.2	7.2	7.8	10.3
Asia	15.7	55.8	77.3	198.8	288.5	361.1	618.8	4.1	5.0	7.3	8.4	9.8
East and South Asia	16.8	50.8	79.6	182.2	272.3	349.3	654.5	2.8	5.0	7.4	8.8	10.5
China	2.7	13.9	47.3	75.5	117.0	206.3	1468.3	1.5	6.1	8.6	9.9	13.1
China, Hong Kong		8.3	3.6	0.7	6.5	5.2	–37.6		3.2	6.2	6.1	5.5
India	(b)	3.6	8.0	21.8	31.3	27.7	660.2	5.5	0.8	8.9	12.7	16.2

Source and notes: Based on UNCTAD, *Handbook of Statistics* (2005). (a) Reserve stock of the year divided by the average monthly imports of the current and following year, as calculated in the *source*. (b) In India, total reserve was $6.9 billion in 1980, dropping to $1.5 billion in 1990.

role of IMF has shifted to something other than managing international financial relations, such as imposing a structural adjustments programme on to a selective FE reserves-hungry country, and so on.

The critical dilemma of the developing economies is that the exchange rate appreciation is assumed by many as having a negative impact on the so-called "competitiveness of nations", especially since trade among the relatively low-wage developing countries assumed importance in the South's trade-basket, and since the exchange rate differentials among them are little. All of the major trading partners in the South, who have more-than-adequate reserves, should simultaneously appreciate their respective currencies. As that turns out to be a non-starter, the activism of the country's central bank in the currency markets – i.e. purchasing more foreign currency to prevent a rise in the domestic currency value – leads to a further accumulation of FE.

The irony is that to facilitate foreign capital inflows into the developing economy, *ceteris paribus*, the exchange rate needs to appreciate. Being unable to accomplish that, the developing countries instead attempt to insure increased return on foreign capital (a) through labour market reforms (e.g. wage depression, lengthening working hours without compensation); (b) by building the required infrastructure for private investments with public revenue; and (c) through other organizational and institutional reforms (e.g. bending the laws of the country in favour of foreign investors, adopting policies towards forming SEZs). These render the exports cheaper, with a steady currency rate. Thus the developing countries are beaten twice in the new international economic order.

To corroborate further, China's FE reserves were about US$14 billion in 1994. So China at that time certainly did not need to devalue her currency. Yet China devalued the yuan by 40 per cent at one stroke in January 1994, and then pegged that devalued yuan to the US dollar. Thus the Chinese effectively cut the price of the products they export by 40 per cent, a cut so deep that no other country in the region could compete with them in labour-intensive industries. Factory owners had to find ways to cut costs or go broke. Wages and workers' basic rights became prime targets. Failing to compete with the working conditions in China, factories closed in South Korea, Taiwan and Singapore. Next, factories in Indonesia, the Philippines and Thailand were lost to China, aggravating the Asian crisis of 1997–98.

China – perhaps to strengthen her export-led strategy – opted for devaluation and pegging currencies to the US dollar. China's negligible dependence on imported fuels – about 4 per cent of aggregate imports as against 26 per cent in India in 1994–95 – was an advantage which no other country in this region had. India, despite heavy dependence on imported petroleum, continues to purchase billions of dollars on the currency mart in order to stabilize her currency rate. In other words, currency appreciation would have eased out (a) the balance of payments (BoP) to a great extent by forcing her import bills down at a time when the marginal propensity to import in the economy has increased with growing income inequality, and (b) fiscal problems.

It seems difficult for India to achieve both external and internal equilibrium. The current account deficit in the BoP is modest because of strong invisibles, and could be comfortably met by the anticipated net capital inflows provided the government policies are bent in favour of the financial markets. Thus a relatively greater inflow of portfolio investments would have profound influences on the fundamentals. As a result, the country's price level is going out of control, since the employment effect of the capital inflows is not commensurate. Countries that allowed exchange rates to be determined by markets could not then use the currency as a policy tool to fight inflation. Therefore, the government has limited options other than to put an embargo on fiscal deficit or deficit spending by the government, which otherwise was an effective instrument of stabilization. Instead of increasing the interest rate to attract foreign capital – which would have kept the domestic investment rate steady – the government shifts the burden to the labour market, resulting in depressed wage, poor education, poor health, failing public distribution, and vanishing social security.

In brief, the massive trade deficits of the United States hang in the balance the stability of the world economic system as such. The stability is largely earned at the cost of the huge external reserves of the developing countries as well as wage depression. While the dollar is artificially depressed, the developing country can neither appreciate the currency rates, for obvious reasons, nor be capable of strengthening the monetary authority to address basic macro policy issues other than putting pressure on the labour markets. This has given rise to the race-to-the-bottom. Consequently, the new paradigmatic shift in the development discourse toward *human development* as the key is facing a crisis of incompatibility.

The export-led growth in the large developing countries such as India and China, in the globalized economic system, itself is to blame, unlike in countries like South Korea. The strategy ignores distributive justice – as the "trickle down" effect does not work for many structural reasons – by restricting consumption at home and promoting production for accumulating dollars. The accumulated dollar reserves of India or China are recycled back to the US largely in the form of – instead of private investment – purchases of US dollar assets by RBI or the People's Bank of China. The rising US trade deficit as a ratio of GDP and the consequent surge of liquidity inflow have boosted asset prices in the US. As real estate and stocks surged, substantially raising US household wealth, households diverted a rising share of their income to consumption. Apart from a further rise in the US demand for imports, this resulted in more inequality in the Mode 3 (commercial presence) movements in services between the United States – or, for that matter, the developed North – and the developing countries such as India.

Concluding remarks

The trade policy of a nation state – together with most of the conventional trade theories – has lost its past significance as international finance capital has achieved a domineering position, with WTO deciding the *terms* of trade between countries and the GATS setting four major modes of supplying services, especially globalization of Mode 3 trade in services. The labour laws and environmental regulations of a developing country are easily bent to accommodate foreign capital. How much sovereignty is left for the nation state to decide on an autonomous trade policy, apart from fixing the magnitude of state incentives for private capital and enforcing flexibilization in the labour market?

As a result, increased volumes of trade, its composition, directions and increased foreign reserves, have prompted unevenness in development across countries and lopsided international distribution of income. One has to do some research to find out the contemporary relevance of the canonical Stolper–Samuelson effect (Stolper and Samuelson 1941). In the industries in which the North has comparative advantage wage costs do not usually exceed 5 per cent of the costs of production, whereas in industries where the South has comparative advantage the wage costs are much higher. Thus the factoral terms-of-trade of the South are likely to experience a secular decline unless it undertakes major steps to improve its R&D capabilities. There are indications that the prices of manufactured exports from the South are falling relative to the prices of the manufactures they are importing from the developed countries (UNCTAD, TDR, various issues). The rising export volume can compensate for a terms-of-trade deterioration. The possibility for this to happen is much greater if exports consist of manufactures for which the foreign elasticity of demand is comparatively higher, than if they consist of primary commodities. The nature and composition of South–South trade are likely to have a favourable terms-of-trade effect for China, but most of the other developing countries have already begun to feel the pinch. Higher export earnings, despite lower export prices, have enabled Asian developing countries to pay higher prices for imported inputs. However, countries in South America and Africa are handicapped in this respect.

Some countries, including India, despite running perhaps unfavourable terms-of-trade in primary-manufacture as well as manufacture–manufacture trade, have been able to neutralize, to some extent, the adverse income effect by exporting relatively high unit-value IT services. The composition of trade in services varies across countries in the South. Of the country's aggregate exports of services, low-unit value[36] transport services, for example, exported from South Korea, Singapore, Chile, Kuwait or Panama constituted more than 40 per cent. On the other hand, high-unit-value computer and information services exported from India constitute about 50 per cent of her aggregate service exports; other countries in the South are nowhere near India in terms of the value of these service exports. If the government incentive structure is the necessary condition for dynamic comparative advantage, India perhaps needs to readjust the structure in favour of "services" instead of the conservative *mix* of exportable manufacture, following the changing global political economy. Ironically, the official database on trade and outputs of various sub-sectors of services are extremely poor – unlike on agriculture and industry – and often non-existent. To illustrate, although the Indian IT sector has emerged very strongly in the global market, the scholars and planners have to do a lot of guesswork simply on the basis of the private source of data, i.e. Nasscom.[37] There is a similar state of affairs in tourism. This situation is not apprehensible, especially when put in the light of the history of the evolution of statistical systems in the EDCs as well as in many late-developed countries; unless "development" is rudderless.

3 Industrial capabilities

Research and development as the indicator

Introduction

To recapitulate, from the previous chapter:

- Low unit labour costs alone do not fetch competitive advantage in the world market. After-sales service as well as quality carries more weight than nominal price of the product in international competition.
- The value of supply chains originating from different countries in the South varies depending on the variation in the individual country's R&D capabilities. High-technology exports as a proportion of India's total manufactured exports constituted a mere 5 per cent in 2005, whereas, to mention a few developing countries, it was 71 per cent in Philippines, 39 per cent in Papua New Guinea, 20 per cent in Mexico and 6 per cent in Vietnam (World Bank, WDR 2008: Table 5).
- India is almost invisible in the supply chain of products like computer hardware, but her significant presence is found in labour-intensive and low-value-added manufacturing such as textiles, garments, leather, gems and jewellery, and in the tail-end IT/ITes products.
- Generally, as the domestic wage level rises, the tendency is to shift to higher value-added products. But, India has hardly the flexibility – unlike the middle-income countries such as Mexico – owing to her poor technological capabilities. So, what explains the latter?

Much of the economic growth in the EDCs is attributed to technological progress. The benefits of technical change are accumulated at the cost of high investments in education and training, building up of scientific institutions, in R&D, and in capital equipment embodying the results of R&D. New knowledge has no autonomous mechanism by which it could generate economic growth. Neither could an invention generated by scientific or technical advances automatically augment growth. Only when the knowledge or the invention gets transmuted efficiently into the production system does economic growth follow. There are two factors integrating science and technology in economic growth: (a) production of technical knowledge through R&D; and (b) a continuous innovative chain linking scientific research, invention, development, design, tooling, first production, and marketing of the new product (Jones 1971). The latter factor is driven by the economics of production and competition at the enterprise level, which takes into consideration current unit labour costs, the demand elasticity, advantages and disadvantages of the pioneering venture, and market pre-emption capacity. However, as disorder arises in the autonomous decision-making by the numerous firms, a proactive government comes forward with incentive schemes for newer products and processes.

There is the hypothesis that the weakness of scientific institutions is one of the main elements which have been responsible for the limited impact of science and technology in the developing countries (see e.g. Singer 1975). However, the limitations of this theory become obvious as one tries to analyse the association between science, technology and industrialization in India. In the immediate postcolonial India, there were eight universities that offered postgraduate courses in science and 38 engineering colleges with nearly 3,000 students. There were three government agencies for promoting scientific research, namely the Indian Council of Medical Research (formerly, Indian Research Fund Association, founded in 1911), the Indian Council of Agricultural Research (1929) and the Council of Scientific and Industrial Research (1942). Under these bodies there were 22 research organizations. The total number of scientific societies at that time was 59. These included such centres of excellence as the Indian Association for the Cultivation of Sciences (1876), Indian Institute of Science (1911), Bose Institute (1917), Tata Institute of Fundamental Research (1945), Bhabha Atomic Research Centre (1948), to name a selective few that specialized in advanced scientific education and research. Nine men of science had become Fellows of the Royal Society, and one of them had won the Nobel Prize. The strength of the scientific institutions is further evident from the fact that it was decided to build an atomic reactor of the swimming pool type as early as 1955. The entire reactor was designed and built by the Indian scientists and engineers in just over a year, with only the fuel elements which contain enriched uranium being supplied by the United Kingdom Atomic Energy Authority. The reactor became critical in August 1956, and was the first reactor in Asia apart from any that Soviet Russia may have had in its Asian territories. This reactor was designed and built by India at a time when most European countries, except the UK and France, were buying the first reactors from the US (Bhabha 1966). Thereafter there has been a rapid growth in the numbers of scientists as well as engineers and technicians, and also of research organizations, public and private.

The latest most noteworthy scientific – or, technological, according to some – achievement is India's maiden lunar mission on 22 October 2008. India has become the sixth nation, after the US, Russia, the European Space Agency (ESA), China and Japan, to send a mission to the moon. The Indian Space Research Organization's (ISRO) home-grown rocket PSLV-C11 put the Chandrayaan-1 spacecraft in a transfer orbit. Chandrayaan-1 was built at ISRO's Satellite Centre, Bangalore, with contributions from various wings of the space agency, including the Vikram Sarabhai Space Centre in Thiruvananthapuram (Kerala). The eleven payloads, five designed and developed in India, three from ESA, one from

Bulgaria and two from NASA, were designed to expand various facets of scientific knowledge about the moon. The Indian payloads included Terrain Mapping Camera, Hyperspectral Imager, Lunar Laser Ranging Instrument, High Energy X-ray Spectrometer and Moon Impact Probe. The ground facilities of Chandrayaan-1 performed the highly important task of receiving the microwave communication containing the health information of the spacecraft as well as the valuable scientific information sent by it. Ultimately, on 14 November 2008, the Indian footprint fell on the lunar surface. It is primarily a "high" technological feat, but the mission has many scientific values. With this, India's space commerce – building satellites for foreign customers – got a big boost. It is important to recognize that ISRO has perhaps been able to keep itself outside the orbit of "low politics" of the administration, which has caused degeneration of many of the centres of excellence so far.

The growth of national capability to create *science* notwithstanding technological backwardness haunts the country. The weakness becomes prominent not so much when technology is developed in a non-competitive space – e.g. where both the producer and user are public sector enterprises – as when it comes to the development of commercially viable as well as competitive technology. In other words, the transmutation of scientific knowledge into field-level practices is often found to be ruptured.

In neoclassical trade theory, technology is treated as being freely available to all countries and, within countries, to all firms; countries simply settle on appropriate levels of capital/labour intensity in accordance with their factor price ratios, which are determined by their factor endowments. Even the literature on "appropriate technology" assumes that efficiency would reign in all firms if only the relevant techniques were discovered and factor price distortions removed. This sort of assumption induces the literature on transfer of technology to focus attention on the *terms* of the transfer and *imperfections* in international technology markets, rather than on the efficiency with which the technology is assimilated or adapted by the importing firm or economy.

Endogenous growth theories try to overcome this shortcoming by building macroeconomic models on a microeconomic foundation (see e.g. Lucas 1988; Romer 1990; Aghion and Howitt 1992). Critical importance is usually ascribed to the production of new technologies and human capital. The engine for growth can be as simple as a constant return to scale production function or more complicated setups with spillover effects, increasing numbers of goods, increasing qualities, etc. (see the review by Parente 2001). The endogenous growth theory demonstrates that policy measures can have an impact on the long-run growth rate of an economy. For example, in some endogenous growth models, subsidies on R&D or education increase the growth rate by increasing the incentive to innovate. The government therefore has great potential to influence the long-term rate of growth through steering the underlying amount of inventive activity.

One wonders why India, despite having a considerable wealth of human capital (i.e. scientists, engineers and technicians) that compares well with many of the developed countries, still lags them in technological capabilities, as is explicitly reflected in her composition and directions of exports. On the one hand, manufactures based

Table 3.1 Changes in wage and unit labour cost in India and other selected developing countries

Country	*Index numbers for the year 2000 (with 1980 = 100)*	
	Unit labour cost (W/Y)	*Real wage (w)*
Chile	82.1	148.0
India	52.8	145.9
Indonesia (1980–99)	81.7	188.0
Malaysia	84.9	216.5
Mexico (1984–2000)	90.2	100.7
South Korea	72.1	329.8
Turkey	54.5	107.8
Uruguay (1980–99)	68.0	98.5

Source and notes: UNCTAD, TDR (2003). Lower 'W/Y' implies higher productivity per unit of labour (i.e. $W/Y = wL/Y$) with rising w, where Y is output, W the wage-bill, and w is the wage rate.

on labour and natural resources as a percentage of total non-oil Indian exports increased from 40 to 60 per cent between 1980 and 2005 (see Table 2.10). On the other hand, India's exports to Europe, Japan and the US have to some extent declined relatively (see Table 2.9). This is notwithstanding the so-called increase in India's international competitiveness; major credit goes to comparative decline in unit labour costs (Table 3.1).

The supply-side factors

Between 1950–51 and 2004–05, the number of colleges for general education (including science) and professional education (engineering, technology, architecture, medical and education) increased by 28 and 15 times, respectively. Numbers of universities increased nearly 15 times. The growth has accelerated since 2001–02 owing to increased private participation in the education services: in higher education, colleges for general education increased by 1.2 times, and colleges for professional education increased by 1.3 times while universities or deemed universities increased by 1.5 times since then (GoI, Ministry of Human Resource Development 2007). The pass-outs of science and engineering graduates from these universities/colleges have laid down the bottom line of the country's technological capability. By this indicator, India stands close to or even above many of the developed countries, and certainly has no competitor nearby within the developing world, excepting China (Table 3.2).

The supply of science and engineering graduates does not appear a problem for higher R&D activities in the 3,960-odd R&D establishments that include a significant number of private initiatives (Table 3.3). Of these, 436 scientific and industrial research organizations (recognized by GoI, Department of Scientific and Industrial Research, DSIR) are engaged in scientific research in the areas of agriculture, medical, natural and applied sciences. In fact, the huge pool of R&D personnel and researchers (full-time equivalent) in India is comparable

Table 3.2 Science and technology graduates (pass-outs in 2004) in India and selected countries

Country	*Science and engineering/technology graduates (in number)*
Brazil	64,688
France	169,606
Germany	86,343
India	456,000 (202,000)[a]
Japan	231,278
South Korea	236,966
United Kingdom	136,997
United States	296,796

Sources and notes: UNESCO Institute for Statistics (2006); for India, see GoI, Ministry of Human Resource Development (2007). [a] The figures are for the year 2003 (September). The figure within parentheses indicates the number of science graduates only.

Table 3.3 Number of R&D establishments – public and private – in India, in 2006

Central government	707
Public sector (includes only in-house R&D units of central public sector undertakings)	115
State government institutions	834
Universities, deemed universities and institutions of national importance	284
Private sector (includes in-house R&D units, and scientific and industrial research organizations recognized by DSIR)	2,020
Total	3,960

Source: GoI, Ministry of Science and Technology (2007).

worldwide only to China, France, Germany, Japan and the Russian Federation (UNESCO Institute for Statistics, S&T database).

As regards the distribution of the country's aggregate R&D investments, the share of the private sector is around 20 per cent (Table 3.4). This is certainly disappointing since more than half of the R&D organizations are in the private sector. One of the reasons for the low proportion of private investments in aggregate R&D is that about 80 per cent of the R&D expenditure of the government goes to exclusive defence-related R&D in a few organizations. As such, India's R&D expenditure constitutes 0.86 per cent of GDP. Moreover, the latest official estimate shows that industry spent a mere 0.47 per cent of its sales turnover on R&D in 2002–03 (GoI, Ministry of Science and Technology, DSIR 2007). Market leaders (in different product groups) themselves within the Indian corporate manufacturing sector are found to have been spending less than 1 per cent of their sales revenue on R&D (Banerjee 2003). Besides, the R&D intensity is lowest in the capital-intensive and high-technology industries, while the asking rate in these areas is 10–12 per cent or even more of sales revenue in order to remain internationally competitive (*cf.* Figure 2.1).

R&D usually involves 5–10 per cent of the *total costs* in successful product innovations. Engineering and designing the product and tooling the manufacturing

Table 3.4 India: distribution of R&D investments by type of organization – private and public – in 2002–03

R&D investments by	*Per cent*
Central government	62.6
State governments	8.5
Public sector industry	4.5
Private sector industry	20.3
Higher education sector	4.1
Total	100.0

Source: GoI, Ministry of Science and Technology (2007).

engineering (i.e. getting ready for manufacture) involves another 50–70 per cent of the total costs. Given the high initial capital required, only a *potentially* profitable innovation stimulates investment. Thus, often when the investment cycle is upwardly moving, the innovation cycle follows the same direction – though this has not happened in India during the last 15 years or so. However, it would be wrong to relate R&D expenditure entirely to short-run economic growth; R&D is not a stop-and-go phenomenon. Innovation depends, among other things, on the accumulated stocks of technical knowledge, which can be augmented only by a continuous process of R&D effort – this can best be captured in an intergeneration model, and thus would suggest India's lapses as a pre-1990 phenomenon. In the end, so far as R&D expenditure as a ratio of GDP is concerned, India lags far behind not only the EDCs but also such developing countries as China and Brazil (Table 3.5).

Table 3.5 R&D expenditure as a proportion of GDP, in selected countries

Country	*R&D expenditure as % of GDP*
Australia	1.55
Brazil	1.04
Canada	2.00
China	1.23
France	2.27
Germany	2.64
India	0.80
Israel	5.11
Japan	3.11
Pakistan	0.27
South Korea	2.91
Sweden	4.27
UK	1.88
USA	2.67

Source: GoI, Department of Science and Technology (2006).

Fiscal incentives and support measures

There are a number of fiscal incentives and other support measures aimed at promoting R&D in industry as well as encouraging the adoption of locally available R&D to industry. For example:

a incentives based on direct taxes: 100 per cent write-off of revenue and also capital expenditure on R&D; income tax exemption at the rate of 150 per cent on the R&D expenditure for companies engaged in the business of biotechnology or the manufacture of drugs, pharmaceuticals, electronic equipment, computers, telecommunication equipment, aircraft and helicopters, automobiles including automobile components in government-approved in-house R&D centres. Expenditure on scientific research in relation to drugs and pharmaceuticals includes expenditure incurred on clinical drug trials, obtaining approvals from any regulatory authority and filing an application for a patent.

b Incentives based on indirect taxes: customs duty exemption for publicly funded R&D institutions and privately funded scientific and industrial research organizations, both for capital equipment and consumables needed for R&D. Similar are excise duty exemptions.

c Other incentives include support in the form of grants for industrial R&D projects; associations of industry with the national R&D programmes in areas of atomic energy, space and defence research; promotion of technology transfer from national laboratories; and nationally funded R&D programmes to industry through public sector organizations.

Since 1996, the Technology Development Board (of GoI) invests either in equity capital or gives soft loans to industrial concerns and other agencies, as applicable, attempting development and commercial applications of indigenous technology or adapting imported technology to the "new" domestic operating systems. Further, the Department of Science and Technology (DST) has initiated a separate programme for the drugs and pharmaceuticals sector for promoting collaborative research. The objectives of the programmes are: (a) to synergize the strengths of publicly funded R&D institutions and the Indian pharmaceutical industry; (b) to create an enabling infrastructure, mechanisms and linkages so as to facilitate new drug development; (c) to stimulate skill development of human resources in R&D for drugs and pharmaceuticals; and (d) to enhance the nation's self-reliance in the drugs and pharmaceuticals sector, especially in areas critical to national health requirements.

The outcome: patent statistics as summary indicator

A patent is a document issued by an authorized governmental agency granting the right to exclude anyone else from the production or use of a specific new device, apparatus or process for a stated number of years (that varies across countries).

The patent statistics[1] is a surrogate of detailed R&D data and the inventiveness of a country – i.e. what has happened to the underlying rate of technical and scientific progress and the competitive position of firms in the global market.[2] Two things are crucial for a good index of inventive activity: (a) human resources for R&D; and (b) R&D expenditure. While the former is generally a supply-side factor, the *causation* of the latter is to be ascertained under specific conditions.

It is worth asking, what aspects of economic activity do patent statistics actually capture? It gives us a better understanding of the economic processes that lead to reductions in the costs of producing existing products – i.e. a better measure of the outward shifts in the production possibilities frontier, when all the patents are aggregated in an economy – and the development of new products and services (see Griliches 1990). However, what determines the allocation of resources to such "technology changing" activities – is it private or social returns to knowledge?

In fact, with increasing trade deregulation and exports of knowledge-intensive goods, the patenting ratio of foreign (the North) to domestic (the South) is generally expected to rise. The Patent Cooperation Treaty (PCT) is an international treaty, administered by the World Intellectual Property Organization (WIPO), which makes it possible to seek patent protection for an invention simultaneously in each of a large number of countries (who are Contracting States to the PCT) by first filing a single "international" patent application. India incidentally is the third largest PCT international applicant among the leading developing countries in this respect (Table 3.6).

On the other hand, in terms of the increase in value of exports (in US dollars), India is way behind such countries as Brazil, China, Mexico, Singapore and South Korea (Table 3.7). Taking these two factors together, India perhaps has failed to commercialize all of her international patents; perhaps also, many of the patented inventions are peripheral to her export sector.

First, so far as the trend in the domestic patent applications in India is concerned, chemical and mechanical fields of invention taken together dominate,

Table 3.6 Number of PCT international applications[a] filed by applicants from the developing countries (having at least 100 applications in each of the years)

Country of origin	*2003*	*2004*	*2005*	*2006*	*2007*
Brazil	219	278	271	333	394
China	1,295	1,706	2,503	3,949	5,470
India	764	724	679	834	880
Mexico	131	118	141	167	182
Singapore	282	431	443	472	533
South Africa	357	411	358	424	405
South Korea	2,949	3,558	4,688	5,945	7,066
Turkey	111	115	174	269	355

Source and note: WIPO, The International Patent System (2007). [a] An application for the protection of an invention filed under the Patent Cooperation Treaty (PCT).

Table 3.7 Values (fob, US$ billion) of exports from selected developing countries, 1980 to 2006

Country	*1980*	*1990*	*2000*	*2006*
Brazil	20.1	31.4	55.1	137.5
China (ex. Hong Kong, Macao)	18.1	62.1	249.2	969.1
India	8.6	18.0	42.4	120.9
Mexico	18.0	40.7	166.4	250.3
Singapore	19.4	52.7	137.8	270.6
South Africa	25.5	23.6	30.0	53.2
South Korea	17.5	65.0	172.3	326.1
Turkey	2.9	13.0	27.8	82.7

Source: UNCTAD, Handbook of Statistics (2006–07).

while computer/electronics and biotechnology are distant followers. Second, if the proportion of patents granted out of the total number of applications is any indication of the quality of R&D and the information base, India is far away from the knowledge frontier: merely 2.4 per cent of applications in the field of computer/electronics and 4.3 per cent in biotechnology were granted in the 5-year period during 2001–02 to 2005–06. Third, the number of patents granted in India was highest in the field of food, followed by electrical, chemical and mechanical (Table 3.8). Finally, of the 18.5 per cent of the applications granted in total, the ratio of foreign to Indian is 2.09, highlighting the vital role played by foreign companies in India's R&D.

The divergence in R&D trends in India from the rest of the world is apparent from the distribution of domestic patents applied for or granted in different

Table 3.8 India: percentage of patents granted out of the patent applications, by field of invention, during 2001–02 to 2005–06

Field of invention	*Total no. of patent applications filed in 5 years*[(a)]	*Ratio of patents granted to patents applied for (%)*
Biotechnology	2,810	4.3
Chemical	14,232	22.5
Computer/Electronics	8,487	2.4
Drug	8,897	19.1
Electrical	5,899	22.9
Food	643	65.3
General	9,088	19.1
Mechanical	13,186	22.3
Total	63,242	18.5[(b)]

Source and notes: GoI, Ministry of Commerce and Industry, Office of the Controller General of Patents, Designs, Trade Marks and Registrar of Geographical Indications, *Annual Report* 2005–06. [(a)] Includes resident, non-resident and National Phase Applications under PCT. [(b)] The ratio of foreign to Indian (out of the total number of patents granted) is 2.09.

technical fields in India; this is different from the distribution of PCT international applications.[3] The areas where technologies worldwide have been changing rapidly, i.e. biotechnology, information technology and nuclear engineering, are India's relatively weak domains, as is revealed in the applications filed or in terms of the patents granted (Table 3.9).

Role of FDI

The weaker domains of technical change were expected to be plugged by FDI inflows in the aftermath of removal of all sorts of barriers to their entries in the 1990s. India's basic infrastructure in terms of the number of scientific institutions ought to have been an added attraction for FDI. Ironically, about a quarter of the total FDI inflows in the country between 2000 and 2008 got engaged in the financial and non-financial services sector (Table 3.10). Construction activities, housing and real estate sectors together attracted another 10 per cent of the aggregate FDI inflows. Even the sector of industrial infrastructure such as power and ports together had a share of less than 6 per cent. Thus the R&D-intensive and rapidly changing technological fields still remained the least priority areas in India, excepting the "computer software and hardware" which attracted 13 per cent of

Table 3.9 International comparison: technical field-wise PCT international applications published *versus* patent applications (Indian plus foreign) filed in India as well as granted

Technical field	*PCT international applications published, as % of the total (during 2003 to 2007)*	*India: Patents granted, as % of the total (during 2001–02 to 2005–06)*
1. Biotechnology	4.6	1.0
2. Chemicals	13.8	27.4
3. Electrical	9.5	11.6
4. Food	1.2	3.6
5. Mechanical	11.1	25.2
6. Pharmaceuticals	7.1	14.6
7. Telecommunications, information technology and semiconductors[(a)]	19.9	1.8
Sub-total (1–7)	67.2	85.2
8. General[(b)]		14.8
9. Instruments (excl. semiconductors)	16.3	
10. Process engineering	11.5	

Sources and notes: For data on India, see GoI, Ministry of Commerce and Industry, Office of the Controller General of Patents, Designs, Trade Marks and Registrar of Geographical Indications, *Annual Report 2005-06*; for international applications, see WIPO, *The International Patent System* (2007). [(a)]In the Indian data source the category used is 'computer/electronics'. [(b)]This category is used in the Indian patent data.

Table 3.10 India: sector-wise FDI inflows, during April 2000 to March 2008

Sector	*Percentage of total FDI inflows*
Services sector (financial and non-financial)	22.64
Computer software and hardware	13.07
Telecommunications (radio paging, cellular mobile, basic telephone services)	6.81
Construction activities (including roads and highways)	5.44
Housing and real estate (including cineplex, multiplex, integrated townships and commercial complexes, etc.)	4.54
Automobile industry	4.01
Power	3.91
Petroleum and natural gas	3.35
Metallurgical industries	2.99
Chemicals (other than fertilizers)	2.50
Drugs and pharmaceuticals	2.28
Electrical equipment	1.93
Ports	1.77
Cement and gypsum products	1.71
Consultancy services	1.61
Trading	1.52
Hotels and tourism	1.49
Electronics	1.24
Food processing industries	1.22
Information and broadcasting (including print media)	1.01
Sub-total	85.04
Sectors having less than 1% each in total FDI	14.06

Source: GoI, Ministry of Commerce and Industry, Department of Industrial Policy and Promotion (2008).

FDI inflows during the period; the nature of much of these FDIs has already been explained. The sector-wise distribution of FDI raises doubts about the extra mileage that it would provide to India's exportability in the changing international division of labour.

Moreover, the country-wise distribution of the *sources* of the FDI indicates the *mismatch* between the desired and actual sectors of inflows. Mauritius, little known in science and technology, tops the list of investing countries, and Cyprus is now the eighth largest FDI source for India, ahead of countries such as France, Germany, UK and the US (Table 3.11).[4] Actually, countries like Mauritius and Cyprus are tax havens or "grey enclaves".[5] Most of the funds flowing in from these tax havens are in housing and real estate, involving little technology transfer. In fact, although the extent cannot be exactly estimated, a large part of the FDI inflows into India from these sources stems from "round tripping" – referring to investors from India who incorporate firms in Mauritius, Cyprus or the UAE, route money to these firms because tax havens provide opportunities to taxpayers to avoid or evade tax in India, and then invest back to India.

Table 3.11 India: share of top investing countries in FDI equity inflows, during April 2000 to March 2008

Country of recorded origin	*Percentage of cumulative inflows, 2000 to 2008*
Mauritius	41.01
USA	7.25
UK	6.98
Singapore	6.97
Netherlands	4.33
Japan	3.40
Germany	2.47
Cyprus	1.58
France	1.22
Switzerland	1.07
Total FDI inflows = US$62.509 billion	

Source: GoI, Ministry of Commerce and Industry, Department of Industrial Policy and Promotion (2008).

Creativity to innovation and diffusion: the demand-side factors

A patent application is a document submitted by an inventor requesting to be issued a patent for an invention described in the specification that accompanies the application. This is followed by the innovation phase, still primarily a domain of knowledge economy. The *economics* of creativity becomes important at the diffusion phase, i.e. transforming *feasible* innovation into commercial *viability*, where, among other factors, external economies or diseconomies become critical inputs in economic calculations.

Quite often the problem of industries in the late-developing countries is that they cannot meet industrial standards of quality and reliability. They are therefore forced to compensate for their defects by reducing prices. Since the markets in the industrialized world set the standards, the best way of meeting them is perhaps to adopt the production practices of the industrialized world. The labour standards of the industrialized world are consistent with those production practices because they were developed simultaneously (Piore 2000).

In the EDCs, wage pressure from below – often due to the lack of supply of the required category of labour, and to proactive State actions for the improvement of her citizens' conditions of work and social security – had always put the entrepreneurs on tenterhooks. They used to search for labour productivity-augmenting technology, labour-replacing technology and mass-production technology through long, often tortuous and cyclical processes.

Transfer of those technologies from the North to the South was once viewed as a rational choice for a better world. However, the *history* of technology transfer never appeared as straightforward as many scholars have thought it to be (for a detailed discussion, see Banerjee 2005). Besides, the assimilation in the South of technology from the North has often come across problems that are clearly associated with the labour standards in question – the technology–labour standards mismatch, in other words.[6] Indeed, where the importing country's labour standards could not be modified to meet the production practices of the source country, the latter had to make room for the low labour standards, leaving much greater room for low-road development and a new international division of labour: low wage leads to low production practices, thereby to low income, which perpetuate poverty and augment the cheap labour supply. The production practices are thus caught in the low wage trap.

The effect of economizing on labour standards by externalizing labour costs or risks – e.g. by denying a decent wage, casualizing the workforce, outsourcing jobs, or by denying social security benefits – may at first seem an appealing course of action to survive competition. But the short-term benefits of such a strategy may be greatly outweighed by longer-term costs, since the firm that seeks to benefit from a low labour cost strategy may in so doing limit its future strategic options, biasing these toward servicing the lower, less profitable range of the market. Thus one would have short-term savings on labour cost alongside longer-term costs in lost revenue potential. Wal-Mart – America's largest employer, and the largest worldwide retailer – pays wages that deny a fair number of employees the ability to live with dignity and autonomy, yet the business is growing. Here is the dilemma of the scheme.

However, the firm that prefers to save money by under-investing in labour standards – the firm that lays off workers, pays low wages, economizes on safety and health measures, or neglects in-job training of the workers – obtains savings at others' expense, be they the state, firms, or individuals. Ultimately, the state has to undertake the responsibilities of closed and sick firms' employees, raise taxes to provide health services to the workers in the private sector, and provide skill education. It is no surprise that taxpayers annually subsidize Wal-Mart to the tune of US$2,103 per employee in the form of food stamps, school lunches, Medicaid for uninsured workers, housing assistance, low-income energy assistance etc. that amounts to a total taxpayer subsidy for Wal-Mart of nearly US$3 billion a year (Hoopes 2006).

How the pressure from below for improved labour standards acts upon industrial efficiency is explicit in the recent development experiences in some of the developing countries in Asia and Latin America. Beside fears that foreign firms would not sell them advanced technology, the earliest incentives that provoked South Korea and Taiwan to start building institutions and raising finance for R&D were the rapidly rising domestic wages. The sharp differences between wage behaviour in Korea and Taiwan on the one hand and Argentina and Mexico, for example, on the other are striking. Wages (real) in the former countries rose to the extent of 8 per cent per annum between 1969 and 1990. By contrast, those in the latter fell by 0.1 per cent in Argentina and 0.8 per cent in Mexico. The response to rapid real wage increases in Korea and Taiwan – first on the part of the government and then on the part of the private firms – was to increase domestic R&D activity and to globalize production. Argentina and Mexico did not have wage pressure to force them to increase R&D investments; in fact, declining wages contributed to maintaining the status quo (Amsden 2001).

Further, the decline of shares of Argentina and Mexico in total manufacturing value added by the developing countries became immediately noticeable during the following years. The late-industrialized East Asia thus pulled ahead of Latin America towards the end of the twentieth century. In 1975, manufacturing value added in Latin America – mostly in Argentina, Mexico and Brazil – had accounted for 55 per cent of total manufacturing value added by the developing countries. By 1994, Latin America's share had fallen to 35.9 per cent. On the other hand, the share of South and East Asia increased from 26.4 per cent in 1975 to 47.9 per cent in 1994 (Amsden 2001).

Decent work

It is time for us to examine the causal relation between labour standards and economic growth through technical changes that shifted the production possibilities frontier outward over a historical period of time. The earliest factory legislation was enacted perhaps in Russia in 1719, applying to the serf-labour in state factories (Brooke 1898). Thereafter, in Austria factory legislation was made in 1787 to forbid children under nine from working in factories. Beginning with the English Factory Act of 1802, which restricted the daily hours of work of apprentices to 12, forbade night work and included provisions regarding education, the European nations had by the turn of the nineteenth century quite a number of legislations pertaining to improvement of working conditions. Standards were first applied to children and women, with very few provisions regarding hours and wages applied to adult males until the twentieth century (Engerman 2003).

The cotton textiles industry was the largest at the time in Britain and was the leading export industry of the country, also having the largest numbers and proportions of women and children. It was also the first industry that came within the comprehensive purview of labour standards in Britain (Keeling 1914). Mining too was singled out early, often leading to restrictions that meant female and child labourers were not permitted to work in mines, particularly underground.

There were three major causes behind the adoption of labour standards through legislation in several European nations in the nineteenth century. First, workers and unions advocated further reforms as their bargaining strength improved. Second, factory owners – who might otherwise benefit from having lower standards themselves – often, in tight labour markets, sought legislation that regulated standards to improve the labour supply conditions to their factories as compared to others. While the relationship between the legislation and changes in wages, hours and labour force participation may be uncertain, it seems clear that in the period after the introduction of labour standards there was a reduction in hours worked in the affected sectors, increases in wages, reductions in child labour along with substantial increases in education and child literacy, and increases in female labour force participation. Factories became cleaner and safer, and the rate of industrial accidents declined (Engerman 2003). Last, but not least, there was an urgent need for longer reproductive age of women as well as longer survival of children because of the low life-expectancy that prevailed until the middle of the nineteenth century in Europe; this began to rise later, as stated in Chapter 1.

The ILO global estimates on occupational accidents provide some indicators – such as the frequency and nature of industrial accidents – to measuring labour standards. In 2001, on average, 7,609 per 100,000 employees in India had to remain absent for more than 3 days due to industrial accidents. The figure for high-growth China was even greater, i.e. 9,392 persons. As compared to that, the numbers in the developed North were less than one-third, i.e. 3,070 (calculated from ILO 2005).

The history of labour standards is in fact difficult to separate from the history of other social reforms and policy developments. Today Scandinavia must be ranked high on the scale of realized labour standards by any measure. Most other countries have elementary standards such as minimum wages set by law; however, the Scandinavian countries of Denmark, Norway and Sweden do not. One way to view this is that minimum wages regulated by law are simply redundant in societies with strong and encompassing unions (Moene and Wallerstein 2003). Labour standards in Scandinavia were also raised by policies designed for other purposes. The active labour market policy, for example, keeps open unemployment down by sending the unemployed back to school for vocational training. The other part of the social democratic employment strategy was the use of macroeconomic policies to maintain full employment, which put the entrepreneurs on the path of continuous technical change. Unless labour productivity rises proportionate to wages in a tight labour market condition via technological progress – and not by illegally lengthening the working hours – decline in profitability is inevitable.

By contrast, in India, there is much legislation aimed at protecting the wages of the labour force. Yet there are gross abuses and violations of the laws. The Indian constitution accepts the responsibility of the state to create an economic order in which every citizen finds employment and receives a *fair wage*. One of the earliest decisions taken by the government of independent India was to set up a committee (in 1948) to define a fair wage, and to suggest the economic and legal means for ensuring that wage to every employed citizen. Ever since then, there have been many attempts to define the concepts of a fair wage, a minimum wage, a floor wage and a living wage. They can also be traced to the Fundamental Rights and Directive Principles specified in the Indian constitution and the international conventions that India has accepted or ratified. There have been several attempts to identify how far the "capacity to pay" can be allowed to determine the minimum wage, and at what point the capacity to pay should be taken into account and should be regarded as the main determinant. The roundabout progress that India has made in this respect is, however, reflected in the reports of committees, conferences, commissions and judgments of the Apex Court (India's Supreme Court) over the last six decades.

The availability of undervalued labour has negative implications for productive *efficiency*, because (a) it provides a way of compensating for managerial, organizational and other forms of inadequacies; (b) it delays the scrapping of obsolete capital equipment; and (c) it allows for price competition based on lowering wage costs. Moreover, workers with comparable skills and efficiencies are undervalued to varying degrees. This allows individual employers to adjust their wage costs to their ability to pay, either by shifting their demand for labour to a more disadvantaged segment – i.e. unorganized and disadvantaged – or because their workers are trapped in their respective segment as open market job opportunities are low or nil; they thereby have less bargaining power and thus are in a weak position to resist declines in their wages.

The theory of *inverse* relationship between the wage-rate (w) and the profit rate (r), often cited as a counter-argument, is not tenable when the "wage–effort" relationship is introduced. Labour productivity depends on the real wage paid by firms, because workers do have a conception of a "fair wage". Insofar as the actual wage is less than the fair wage, workers supply a corresponding fraction of normal effort (Akerlof and Yellen 1990). If effort supplied is denoted by e, actual wage w, and fair wage by w^*, then $e = w/w^*$. With the introduction of the effort–productivity relationship, we can have $r = e(1/w)$ (where $0 \leq e \leq 1$).[7]

The employer can enhance the average or normal intensity of the worker by (a) simply increasing the number of tools a worker has to operate, or (b) speeding up the conveyor belt on which the worker operates, thus achieving higher output, but only in the short run. One must however distinguish *intensity* from *efficiency*. Efficiency is defined as output per unit of time worked at normal intensity, the technical conditions of production remaining the same.

Standards of "effort" and efficiency: the public sphere parameter

Mastering technological change requires education. Beyond *motivation*, increased aptitudes on the part of the workers for learning the new technology are crucial. As Rosenberg (1970: 555) points out: 'the notion of a production function as a "set of blueprints" comes off very badly ... if it is taken to mean a body of techniques which is available independently of the human inputs who utilize it'. While the country-wise variation in the spread of modern economic growth has depended to a large extent on the diffusion of a body of knowledge concerning new production techniques, the acquisition and application of this knowledge by different countries has been governed largely by whether their populations have acquired traits and motivations associated with formal schooling (Easterlin 1981).

To take lessons from another Asian but developed economy, namely Japan, exposure of the population to formal schooling is critical for acceleration in the rate of technological change. Japan's educational attainment was clearly distinctive even before the Meiji Restoration, though important reforms were introduced in 1872. Many scholars have highlighted the role of education in Japanese economic growth in general. Like India, the Japanese economy has a dual structure. The industrial capabilities of the economy nevertheless increased. In the late 1950s, 30 per cent of the labour force worked in family-owned microenterprises. Compared with the British figure (0.2 per cent), the Japanese percentage was very high. At the time, modern corporations employed only 46 per cent of the total labour force in Japan, compared with 90 per cent in Britain and 80 per cent in the United States (Gao 2001). What is even more worth noting is the proliferation of small firms, which remains a distinctive aspect of Japanese production organization even today but has never been an obstacle to technology diffusion. In fact, job outsourcing by the *Toyotist* corporations relies heavily on the knowledge endowment – through mass education – of the Japanese workers in the small and self-employed enterprises.

In India, the government has taken exceptional measures, politics apart, to maintain a steady flow of "knowledge workers", most of whom get absorbed in the organized sector, and many are considered as R&D personnel. However, the manual workers, the overwhelming majority of whom keep the wheels running in the small or self-employed enterprises in the organized as well as the unorganized sector, are discriminated against, as one finds in the allocation of education expenditure (see also in this respect GoI, Ministry of Human Resources Development 2007–08). It is important to recognize that education up to a standard imparts innovativeness and receptivity to adopt newer technology and changing consumer demand among the manual workers.

The gross enrolment ratio (GER) at primary-level education (class I–V and age group 6–11) in India was 109 per cent in 2005 (see Figure 3.1). However, the distribution of public expenditure per level shows that primary-level education received 36 per cent of the total. At secondary-level education (class VI–XII, age group 11–18) – the level at which one gets introduced to the scientific-technical concepts of reality – the GER drops to 55 per cent. Of course, private household decisions about the payoff to education are crucial in the expansion of schooling at this stage. But that does not explain why the share of secondary education in public expenditure was 43 per cent and less than the proportionate share in GER. By contrast, while GER in tertiary education was 12 per cent, the sector received a disproportionate share of 19 per cent of public expenditure.

The significance of the government spending speaks for itself when private unaided primary schools constitute 7.8 per cent of the total primary schools in the country, and the private unaided secondary schools constitute on an average 27.1 per cent (GoI, Ministry of Human Resources Development, *Educational Statistics* 2008). In brief, 80 per cent of Indian children study in government and government-aided schools (GoI, Ministry of Human Resources Development 2007–08: 13). At a time when access to school is severely restricted by the unusually long distance a rural student has to travel along dusty and muddy tracks from home in a large proportion of the countryside, the teacher-to-pupil ratio is generally unfavourable, and the lack of proper classrooms and teaching equipment is a common phenomenon, the demand for more public expenditure in school education, for minimizing the drop-out rate and for quality education is not unreasonable. This can be said without disagreeing with the fact that per capita costs (especially because of capital expenditure) in higher education are generally higher than in education at the school level.

The mean years-of-schooling of a non-agricultural worker is 5.2 in the countryside and 7.7 in the urban areas (Table 3.12). At a more disaggregated level, an average urban male worker spends 8 years in school, while the female spends 6 years.

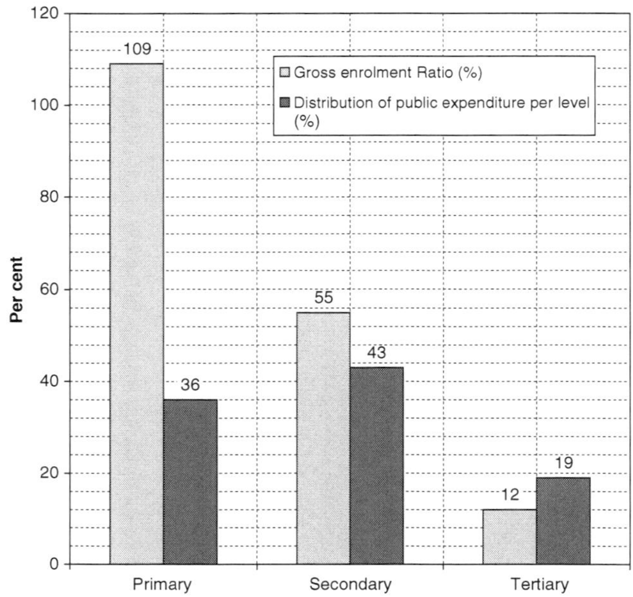

Figure 3.1 India: participation in education at primary, secondary and tertiary levels, and distribution of public resources over different levels of education, 2005–06.

Sources: GoI, Ministry of Human Resources Development, Educational Statistics (2008); UNESCO Institute for Statistics, UIS Statistics in Brief, Education in India (2008).

Notes

(1) Gross enrolment ratio is the total enrolment of a pupil in grade or cycle or level of education, regardless of age, expressed as a percentage of the corresponding eligible official age-group population in a given school or academic year.

(2) Primary enrolment age group is 6–11 (class I–V); secondary enrolment age group is 11–18 (class VI–XII); and tertiary enrolment age group is 18–24.

Table 3.12 Mean years-of-schooling of non-farm workers, by sector of occupation and sex, 2004–05

Sector	*Rural*			*Urban*		
	Male	*Female*	*Total*	*Male*	*Female*	*Total*
Unorganized	5.1	2.9	4.6	7.0	4.7	6.6
Organized	7.6	5.7	7.2	10.1	10.1	10.1
All workers	5.7	3.6	5.2	8.1	6.3	7.7

Source: NCEUS (2007: Appendix A2.2), as computed from NSSO 2006d, Report no. 515.

The educational status of an unorganized sector worker is even more disturbing; mean years-of-schooling is 4.6 in the rural and 6.6 in the urban areas. In other words, for the bulk of the workforce, up to the middle of secondary schooling is all that counts so far as their educational status is concerned. Hence, to the extent that public expenditure on secondary education remains neglected, the industrial capability of the country will lag behind countries which fare better in the latter respect.

Profit–wage relations

The sector-wise trend in labour productivity (with reference to the national average = 100) shows agriculture to be on the downward slope during the last two decades. Labour productivity in the industrial sector increased in the 1980s, but subsequently declined significantly. The relative productivity of the services sector remained much above others all through these decades (see Table 4.5). In brief, there might be technical improvements here and there but not in the industrial economy as a whole as much as has happened in the services sector. Moreover, employment elasticity in organized manufacturing reduced significantly: the number of workers as well as the number of total persons employed in the organized factory sector has tended to decline since 1997–98. Since the mid-1990s, the growth in manufacturing and industrial employment has been the single largest contribution of the unorganized sector, noted for its technological backwardness and much lower productivity.

A comparison of the wages in the Indian factory sector and the trend of the rupee–dollar exchange rate would elucidate how Indian labour over time has not only become cheaper in the global value chains but has dipped below the international poverty line. The real wage (per person-day worked) in US dollar terms tended to converge over time with the international poverty line of US$1. Until 1990–91 the real wage remained at a much higher level than the "one-dollar-a-day" line, but ultimately fell below the poverty line in 1996–97 (Figure 3.2). This happened despite growth in labour productivity at a much faster rate than the rate of increase in wage. Labour productivity in the Indian factory sector – measured in terms of value added per worker (in real terms) – increased by nearly three times between 1980 and 2005. Besides, productivity grew with the reduced number of workers (see Figure 3.3). This would have been a "natural" phenomenon had there been marked technological changes in Indian industries.

As compared to countries like Indonesia, Malaysia, Mexico or South Korea, unit labour costs in India have almost halved in the last two decades, without tangible technological advancement comparable to other developing countries (see Table 3.1). The labour productivity growth has to a great extent been the outcome of lengthened working hours without compensation. So long as productivity rises without simultaneous increase in wages, there is little incentive for the entrepreneurs to upgrade technology.

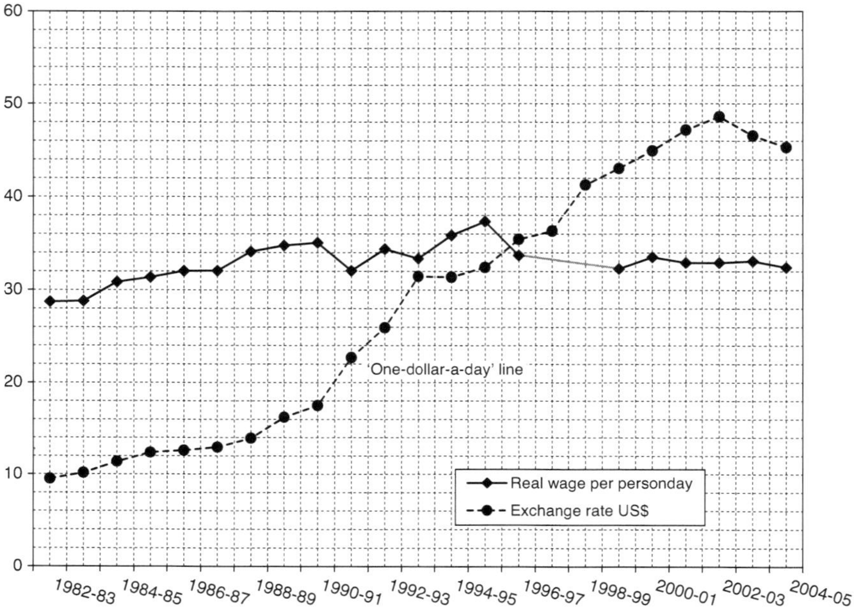

Figure 3.2 Trend in real wage in the Indian factory sector *vis-à-vis* the international poverty line.

Sources and notes: Real wages are computed from CSO, *Annual Survey of Industries*, using the consumer price index (for industrial workers) as available in RBI, *Handbook of Statistics*. Data for 'person-days worked' are not available for 1997–99; hence the discontinuous wage-line.

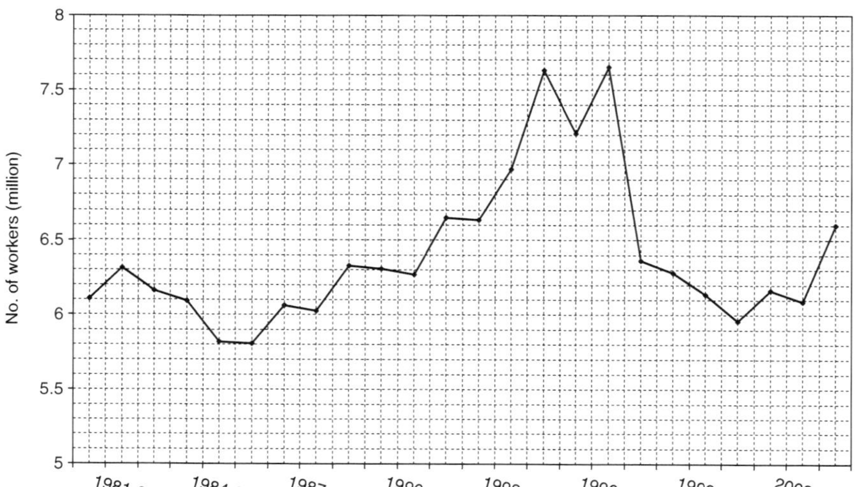

Figure 3.3 Trend in employment of workers in the Indian factory sector, 1981–82 to 2004–05.

Source: Based on CSO, *Annual Survey of Industries*, various issues.

The disorder in the primary labour market spills over to the secondary labour market, which until recently remained completely outside the purview of the central trade unions. In this context, the Minimum Wages Act (1948) is a landmark in the history of social legislation in India as it guarantees the payment of minimum rates of wages to workers in scheduled employments, who are largely unorganized and have therefore weak bargaining power. The state governments are empowered to add any type of employment to the schedule under section 27 of the Act. At present, there are 60 types of employment in the schedule, of which 15 were in the original Act. Besides fixing the minimum wage rates, the state governments are supposed to revise the rates at regular intervals. Although minimum wages were fixed in most of the scheduled unorganized industries long ago, they have not been revised for more than a decade in most of the manufacturing activities (for a detailed account, see Papola 2008: vols 1–10).

Conclusion

A purely technological solution – a cheap "technological fix" – to industrialization is a myth. First of all, 'technical change is not, and never has been, a random phenomenon' (Rosenberg 1970: 551). Second, the learning experiences in the design and use of machinery are vital sources of technological dynamism, flexibility and vitality. Combining these two, the conclusion that follows is that mass school education, at the minimum, is the necessary condition for technical change. Transfer of technology from abroad to circumscribe the problems at home is a palliative, but of short duration in nature.

India is trapped in a low-level equilibrium. She has scores of world-class R&D centres established by foreign TNCs and a few Indian firms, largely pharmaceutical majors. They produce the bulk of the patents filed from and in India. In 2004, of the 1,911 patents granted in India, 1,147 were by foreign entities. On the other hand, there is a network of national laboratories, universities and government institutions that produce publications, file patents but have a terrible record of converting their work into commercial applications. The scientific publications also indicate the scientific progress of a country. Between 1993 and 2004, India was able to produce 2.16 per cent of articles in world scientific publications, while the figure for China was 2.62 per cent.[8] It is very well to say that India punches above its weight in publishing papers on natural sciences, but it reflects poorly on the national innovation system, mostly because of the lack of *effective demand* for better technology and for a symbiotic relation between science and technology.

4 Economic restructuring

Employment and income implications

Structural changes: then and now

In India, the rupture of the interconnectedness between changes in income and structural transformation is explicit in her growth cycle over a long historical period in relation to Western Europe and the US (Table 4.1). During 1873–1913, when per capita income in Western Europe and the US grew at a rate higher than 1 per cent, it was 0.54 per cent in India. Between 1913 and 1950 India even had a *negative* growth rate, while the developed countries with a positive growth rate in per capita income headed for another transition in the economy subsequent to industrialization. During the "golden age" of capitalism India trailed far behind the developed countries so far as growth in per capita income was concerned. It is only during the post-1973 period that India has shown a growth – obviously on a low base – the rate of which is higher than the EDCs'. India's per capita GDP was 1,957 (1990 international Geary-Khamis dollars) in 2001, the level which an average Western European country had reached 130 years ago, i.e. in 1870 (Maddison 2003). However, this did not put the Indian economy on hold from replicating the later stage of the EDCs' economic growth.

Three basic indicators of economic restructuring are: (a) changing relative contribution by different sectors, namely agriculture, industry and services, to the country's GDP (say, y_i/Y); (b) changing sectoral distribution of employment (n_i/N); and (c) changing relative wages in different sectors (say, w_i/w_{agr}).[1] Briefly, the product substitution effect accompanies industrialization: consumer demand shifts away from agricultural products. And, as per capita income rises further, beyond a point, the demand for services goods rises faster than either agricultural or industrial goods. In other words, as per capita income rises, income elasticity of demand changes disproportionately for different goods and services. Mass demand for better health care, higher education of improved standard, nature tourism, better and extended banking and financial services, etc. rises. One would thus witness changes in GDP and the employment shares of various sectors and also in relative wages, in the course of economic development.

The distribution of additional income over different age groups (young, middle, old etc.) of the population is also important in changing the aggregate pattern of consumption in the economy. The population growth rate over a historical period and the corresponding changes in the *age composition* of the

Table 4.1 Rate of growth of per capita GDP: India, Europe and the United States, during 1820 to 2001

Country/Region	*1820–70*	*1870–1913*	*1913–50*	*1950–73*	*1973–2001*
Western Europe	0.98	1.33	0.76	4.05	1.88
United States	1.34	1.82	1.61	2.45	1.86
India		0.54 (a)	–0.22 (a)	1.43 (b)	2.84 (b)

Sources: For Western Europe and the United States, Maddison (2003); for India, (a) Maddison (2003), and (b) computed from CSO, NAS (series with base: 1999–2000).

population thus have a bearing upon the changing demand for different economic sectors – with growing age, for example, demand for health services rises and an inverse relation follows for industrial goods.

The average annual rate of growth for the globe's population peaked in 1963–64, followed by a gradual decline. The absolute increase in global population per annum reached its height in 1989–90 and then started declining (US Census Bureau 2004). However, life expectancy at birth is generally upwardly moving. A low fertility rate and low mortality rate, coupled with longer life expectancy in the EDCs, has led to more of an inverted pyramid (or cylindrical) shape of age-wise distribution of population; the older age groups progressively dominate the population. By contrast, in the LDCs in general, and in India in particular, the proportion of population decreases progressively as age increases, beginning with ages 15 to 19 – i.e. the population graph looks like a pyramid.

The regional or country-wise variation in the trends in population growth, however, gets distorted by the international flow of migrants. An incredible 3 million people – mostly from regions with shorter life expectancy – crossed national boundaries in 2002. Mexico was the largest sender of people, having a net outflow of 280,000 people to other countries, including the US. The next largest sender was China, transferring approximately 230,000 people to other countries. Almost every net sender of migrants was an LDC (US Census Bureau 2004). On the other hand, the US and other developed countries were the top receivers of migrants. However, for the majority of larger countries 'the relative effect of net migration [on population size – D.B.] was small to moderate' (ibid: 28). The impact is greater in the sender countries: migration from the LDCs, besides having an impact on the demographic pattern, leaves its mark on domestic income distribution through foreign remittances. This has become unusually large in countries such as India; remittances from abroad contribute more than 3 per cent to India's GDP, which is incidentally much greater than FDI inflows.

These demographic changes in the contemporary world have in turn a profound impact on the consumer demand pattern. First, the lower population growth rate as a whole has generally prompted the demand for agriculture as well as industrial products to grow, but at a decelerating rate. Second, in the EDCs, the larger proportion of population in the age-group of 65 and above creates comparatively greater demand for services such as domestic medical care, etc., than otherwise would have been the case.

Traditionally, industrialization in the EDCs went hand in hand with the development of capitalism in agriculture. By the end of the eighteenth century, when the industrial revolution had been acquiring a definite shape in Britain, the country achieved the highest agricultural productivity among the European countries. As a result, domestic demand for industrial goods such as clothes, footwear and utensils – which until then used to be produced in disparate small units by craftsmen – prompted mass production of those goods. The industrial revolution did not immediately bring to the market any products that had not been produced until that time. It was the change of *place* – from an agrarian locale to a location dotted with numerous tall and black smoke-billowing chimneys atop large factory sheds.

By contrast, in many of the LDCs, industrialization has taken a detour since the inception of the IT revolution (which incidentally coincided with contemporary globalization): "Digital" capitalism[2] is unfolding very strongly without there being capitalism in agriculture – neither is there high productivity in agriculture – although agriculture still provides a livelihood to most of the country's population. Capitalism is also not the characteristic feature in that part of manufacturing in the LDCs – i.e. in the unorganized sector – which provides employment to the bulk of the country's manufacturing workforce. A comparatively higher proportion of per capita consumer expenditure is still on food articles rather than on industrial goods or services in most of the LDCs.

These facts are generally not captured in the (conventional) processes of capital accumulation. In the information economy 'the sources of productivity lie in the technology of knowledge generation, information processing, and symbol communication' (Castells 2001, vol. 1: 17). The most notable aspect of the new knowledge economy is the rapid and fundamental extension of commodification to areas and aspects of knowledge and information and their production, dissemination and storage not previously seen. This has been possible through the rapid expansion and development of personal computers (PCs) and communication technology. Simultaneously, as the character of labour undergoes a shift from *manual* to *intellectual*, the principal source of productivity change in the information economy becomes *accumulation of knowledge*. Thus, in this economy, growth depends more upon human capital and less on physical capital. In other words, human capital – a convergent mix of *body* and *mind* (i.e. knowledge) – would increasingly substitute physical capital. However, the problem is that, unlike in the previous system, anyone can acquire the means of production, i.e. the knowledge required for the job, but not everyone can win.

At present, the term "knowledge worker" is widely used to portray people with considerable knowledge and learning: doctors, lawyers, teachers, accountants, chemical engineers. However, the most striking growth will be for "knowledge technologists": computer technicians, software designers, analysts in clinical labs, manufacturing technologists, paralegals (Drucker 2001). These people are as much manual workers as they are knowledge workers. In fact, they usually spend far more time working with their hands than with their brains. But their manual work is based on a substantial amount of theoretical knowledge, which can be acquired only through formal education and not through an apprenticeship. They are not, as a rule, much better paid than traditional skilled workers are, but they see themselves as "professionals".

We thus enter into an era where the "manual–knowledge" dichotomy, at an early stage of development in many of the LDCs, has grown to a size and strength which is unprecedented. Historically, EDCs had reached the peak of industrialism in terms of economy, society and polity by the 1950s. Since then, the share of GDP originating in the industrial sector and the share of industrial employment in the country's aggregate moved downward. But, by then, the problems of transition from agrarian to industrial society were resolved. Migration from agriculture to city-based industry was no longer a significant social or economic issue. The knowledge workers gradually replaced the manual/factory workers in the economy, which tended to move towards production and distribution of information instead of physical products. There emerged post-industrial capitalism.

Changes in India: illusions and reality

In the immediate postcolonial India, the GDP share of agriculture and allied activities was 55 per cent, while that of industry was 11 per cent and the services sector 34 per cent (Table 4.2). Following the programme of industrialization based on basic and heavy industries that started with the Second Five-Year Plan (FYP) (1956–61), the share of the industrial sector increased, while during the last five decades the share of agriculture has dwindled to a third of its former value. However, the relative size of the services sector has been unusually large since the early 1950s, and since the 1990s when market-oriented reforms became institutionalized the sector rose to the occasion by contributing more than half of the country's GDP. As it stands now, India has decisively moved onto the path of economic growth of the developed countries without the industrial sector ever employing more than one-fifth of the country's workforce. This is unprecedented!

The Indian economy has undergone modernization with the expansion of the services sector. In Japan, by way of comparison, the steady rise in the manufacturing share, which overtook agriculture in the 1920s, epitomized the notion of the modern Japanese state (Alexander 2008). Perhaps the late-developing countries can skip many of the sequential stages of world technological progress and

Table 4.2 India: changing shares (%) of the different sectors in GDP (at constant 1999–2000 prices), 1950 to 2006

Sector	*1950–51*	*1960–61*	*1980–81*	*1990–91*	*2000–01*	*2004–05*	*2007–08*
Agriculture and allied activities	55.3	50.8	37.9	31.4	23.9	20.2	17.8
Industry	10.6	13.2	17.4	19.8	25.8	26.2	26.6
Services	34.1	36.0	44.6	48.8	50.3	53.6	55.6

Source: Based on CSO, NAS, various issues.

find out appropriate technology without incurring the costs involved in the processes of trial and error.

Yet, if the changing composition of consumer demand was the determining factor of differential growth rate across sectors, the Indian phenomenon stands out against what is a very popular understanding. The per capita consumer expenditure on food articles as a proportion of the total has been declining, while the expenditure on services goods initially increased in the 1990s (see Figure 4.1). Subsequently, disproportionality cropped up: the proportion of per capita consumer expenditure on services declined, despite the reduced weight of, in particular, cheaper public services in health and education and growing costlier private services. Also, note that "Food articles" as a proportion of total consumer expenditure is still much greater than that of either services or durable goods (which are mainly industrial, including construction) in India. But why?

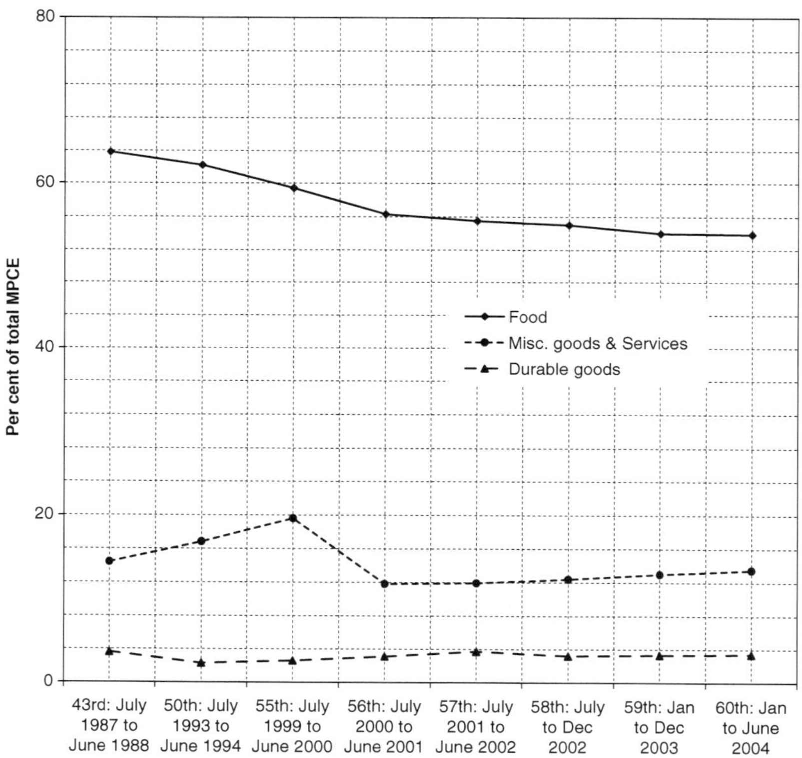

Figure 4.1 All-India: percentage distribution of monthly per capita consumer expenditure (MPCE) on food and others, 43rd to 60th rounds of survey.

Source and notes: Based on NSSO (2005b) Report No. 505. 'Miscellaneous goods and services' is a residual group containing items other than food, pan [betel leaf], tobacco, intoxicants, fuel and light, clothing, footwear, rent, taxes and durable goods.

The dynamics

While the pattern of consumer demand is dependent on per capita income, the latter in the EDCs was integral to employment distribution across sectors. Moreover, the wage rate in the modern sector became higher than in the traditional sector. In India, the sectoral composition of employment in 1981 was comparable to that in the US in 1820. However, between 1981 and 2001, i.e. in just two decades, her sectoral composition had changed in a manner that took 43 years to mature in another Asian but EDC, i.e. Japan, between 1870 and 1913 (Maddison 1995). In India, agriculture, forestry and fisheries together lost 11 percentage points between 1981 and 2004, in terms of employment. Mining, manufacturing, construction and utilities provided 5 per cent more employment during the period, while the services sector gained a mere 5 percentage points despite a significant concurrent increase in its GDP share (Table 4.3). Since about 836 million or 77 per cent of the Indian population are still living with a daily expenditure of less than half a US dollar (to be precise, less than Rs 20), the pattern of consumer demand was unlikely to differ much from the observed one.

Moreover, unbecoming for the archetypal tertiarization, the employment elasticity of agriculture has increased over time and was a robust 1.52 at a time when the aggregate employment elasticity in the economy was less than 0.5 between 1999 and 2005 (Table 4.4). Industry as a whole has low elasticity, except in "construction". In the services economy, "trade, hotels and restaurants" and "transport, storage and communication" have near-secular declines in employment elasticity. It is only "financing, insurance, real estate and business services" that has an employment elasticity value of 0.94, after a long spell of inelasticity in the second half of the 1990s. Further, the employment elasticity of either the organized industry or the organized services sector has been negative, as noted earlier. In other words, new jobs are created almost exclusively in the unorganized economic sectors and so the Indian labour market has become more volatile: in the unorganized services sector, 60 per cent are self-employed and the rest work in such establishments as employ at least one hired labourer. In terms of the rural–urban division of the services sector workforce, rural India – where labour market volatility is greater – employs 14.1 million as against 12.5 million in the urban services economy (NSSO 2006d, Report no. 515).

Table 4.3 India: employment share of different sectors, 1981 to 2004

Year	*Agriculture, forestry and fisheries*	*Mining, manufacturing, construction and utilities*	*Services*
1981	69	13	18
1991	67	12	21
2001	60	18	22
2004–05	58	18	23

Sources: Based on GoI, Office of the Registrar General and Census Commissioner, *Census of India*, 1981, 1991 and 2001; and NSSO (2006d) Report no. 515.

Table 4.4 Employment elasticity in India

Sector	*1977–78 to 1983*	*1983 to 1993–94*	*1993–94 to 1999–00*	*1999–00 to 2004–05*
Agriculture, forestry and fishing	0.45	0.50	0.00	1.52
Mining and quarrying	0.80	0.69	0.00	0.82
Manufacturing	0.67	0.33	0.26	0.34
Electricity, gas and water supply	0.73	0.52	0.00	0.33
Construction	1.00	1.00	1.00	0.88
Trade, hotels and restaurants	0.78	0.63	0.55	0.59
Transport, storage and communication	1.00	0.49	0.69	0.27
Financing, insurance, real estate and business services	1.00	0.92	0.73	0.94
Community, social and personal services	0.83	0.50	0.07	0.28
Total employment	0.53	0.41	0.15	0.48

Sources: Rangarajan *et al.* (2007).

Further, retail and wholesale trade is the single largest subsector in the services economy in terms of income contribution, contributing more than 14 per cent to GDP while employing 6 per cent of the country's total workforce. The unorganized retailing is by far the most prevalent form of trade, while the organized trade (undertaken by licensed retailers, who are registered for sales tax, income tax etc.) accounts for a negligible part.[3] One of the principal reasons behind the ever-expanding business of retail outlets and its fragments is that it is probably the primary form of disguised unemployment and/or underemployment. Given the already overpopulated agriculture sector[4] and the employment inelastic manufacturing sector, several million of the Indian labour force have gone out of their way to migrate to the services sector. The "pull" factor does not appear strong for the services sector as the average daily wage paid to the lowest paid full-time unskilled hired worker in a service establishment is the same as, if not lower than, the agricultural wage. Since productivity growth in the services sector is faster than in agriculture, this appears as a paradox.

It is apparent that the wage variation across sectors does not follow a corresponding variation in productivity, because of disproportionality in the GDP share and employment share of different sectors (Table 4.5). The latter is directly proportional to the relative weight of the unorganized segments in each of the primary, secondary and tertiary sectors, typically characterized by vintage capital as well as low capital base. The net value added per worker in the unorganized sector is about one-third that of the organized industrial sector (based on Sundaram 2008: Table 5), and generally capital–labour relations in the former are not well defined. In the unorganized services sector, labour productivity is further lower, i.e. only 19 per cent of that in the organized counterpart.

In general, migration from one sector to another is not strictly determined by relative wages. Also, the tertiarization of the economy is hardly associated directly with the improving standards of living as Kuznets, Fuchs and many others have

Table 4.5 India: trends in sectoral labour productivity in relation to the national average (= 100)

Sector	*1981*	*1991*	*2001*	*2004–05*
Agriculture and allied activities	55	47	40	34
Industry	134	165	143	144
Services	248	232	229	230

Sources and notes: Computed from CSO, NAS, various years; Office of the Registrar General, *Census of India*, various years; and NSSO (2006d) Report no. 515. Sectoral (i-th) labour productivity is calculated as the ratio of x_i/X to l_i/L, where X and L are national GDP and employment, respectively; x_i = GDP share of the i-th sector; and l_i = employment share of the i-th sector.

predicted (Kuznets 1965; Fuchs 1968). There is, to begin with, a spillover of agricultural workforce into the rural services economy: the "residuals" get engaged in such jobs as sex workers, cooks, waiters, maids and other housekeeping service workers, sweepers, cleaners, private watchmen and gatekeepers (almost every other house in the cities and even in towns now employs a watchman/gatekeeper), hairdressers, beauticians, auto-rickshaw drivers, cycle-rickshaw pullers, in road-side makeshift food stalls, and in innumerable tea and tobacco stalls, no matter whether the earnings are comparatively lower than in agriculture. Then, understandably, one would ask: how come the services sector exhibits higher labour productivity in spite of a significant presence of the unorganized segment?

Social division of labour and weightlessness

With an ever-rising proportion of finance capital moving to the "friction free world", the capital–labour conflict does not exist there. Until a few decades ago, it was difficult to foresee that in the face of the imminent threat to its existence it would be possible for capital to launch itself into an orbit beyond the *relations of production*. Information technology has revolutionized capitalist development. Capital is increasingly becoming de-territorialized and de-materialized. A large part of finance capital can live on its own internal metabolism and circulate without any reference to an older type of content. Large amounts of stocks and shares – and derivatives of them – are traded automatically by computers rather than by a human workforce. These so-called "algo trades" (i.e. the algorithms-driven trade) accounted for as much as 40 per cent of all trades on the London Stock Exchange in 2006; on some American equity markets the figure can be as high as 80 per cent (Dodson 2008). As Dooling writes in the context of the recent US financial crisis and the bailout programme:

> Somehow the genius quants [the quantitative analysts – D.B.] – the best and brightest geeks Wall Street firms could buy – fed $1 trillion in subprime mortgage debt into their supercomputers, added some derivatives, massaged the arrangements with computer algorithms and – poof! – created $62 trillion in imaginary wealth. It's not much of a stretch to imagine that all of that imaginary wealth is locked up somewhere inside the computers, and that we

> humans, led by the silverback males of the financial world, Ben Bernanke and Henry Paulson, are frantically beseeching the monolith for answers. Or maybe we are lost in space, with Dave the astronaut pleading, 'Open the bank vault doors, Hal'.
>
> (Dooling 2008)

It is thus important to recognize that capital has significantly moved from the sphere of production to the sphere of distribution. However, it is not just the distribution of commodities but the distribution of income and wealth.

Initially, disembodied technology[5] contributed heavily to the growth in productivity in IT itself and in IT using sectors. Rapid technological progress in the hardware segment of the IT-producing industry itself raised the standard of the general-purpose technology, and now any firm could garner the benefits and make differences in competitiveness. Countries where the business sector has been quick in shifting resources toward the ICT industry and in adopting highly productive ICT equipment have been able to reap higher output and productivity growth rates than the others (Cohen *et al.* 2004). In the latter half of the 1990s, things began to take new shapes. Productivity growth that embodies knowledge, knowhow and software assumed importance. Productivity improvement no longer remained a property of just new capital investment (*cf.* Solow 1960). Market leadership came rather to depend largely on developing distinguishing software and distinguishing computer programs, and mobilizing distinguishing knowledge of human power. For an IT-using enterprise one would witness, instead of a smooth upwardly moving productivity curve, a polynomial non-linear curve of degree-3 type, or a step curve, reflecting a disproportional relation between investments and outputs in successive periods.

In India, nearly 2.8 per cent of the workforce (CSO 2005, *Economic Census*, 5th)[6] employed in financial intermediation, real estate, renting and business activities – i.e. in the distribution of income and wealth, which is what the brokerage business is all about – generate a disproportional 13.8 per cent of GDP (at constant 1999–2000 prices) (CSO 2007, *National Accounts Statistics 2005–06*). Added to this is the IT/ITes sector. About 2 million employees in IT/ITes,[7] constituting roughly 0.4 per cent of the workforce[8] and producing mainly "knowledge products", fetch 5.5 per cent of India's GDP (NASSCOM 2008b). This high ratio of value added to worker is incomparable to either agriculture or industry, and is not explained by the rate of capital accumulation alone.

Finally, it is important to recognize that the observed structural transformation in India owed more to planned development than to market forces up to the 1980s. Since the First Five-Year Plan, public sector investments in roads and telecommunications, health and education and railway transportation had been very significant. Ironically, private industrial investments had never matched the external economies thus created by the high volume of public sector investments in services. The reasons have already been explained in previous chapters. Nevertheless, the spillover effect of the accumulated public investments eventually stepped up "dematerialization", which in the EDCs, by contrast, was the result of free-market capitalist development. Demography and technology moved forward together under the wage pressure. Further, the state relentlessly intermediated to improve the conditions of living by protecting agriculture and also monitoring the conditions of the factory workers.

Shift of "place"

Quite often the *shift* of a value-added activity from the sphere of production to the sphere of services is merely one of place and not of product. In industry, for instance, activities that used to be carried out in-house such as customer support, sales and marketing, transport, supply chain management, accounting, sweeping and cleaning are now increasingly being outsourced to the ITes-BPOs as part of the flexibilization programme, whose net value added are thus accounted for in the services sector GDP.

There are also newly emerging services, such as water distribution, which were earlier treated as free public goods. These are now progressively being privatized and priced, allowing the share of the services sector in GDP to rise – indeed, an over-valuation of the sector. Massive changes in the municipal water supply systems, for example, in some countries and in a limited way in India, have taken place along with the outsourcing of the entire water sector to private companies, takeovers by foreign companies, fusion of small public companies, and the establishment of public–private partnerships. Water is not a new product, rather a heritage good, which must be protected, defended and treated as such. However, there are many players involved in promoting water liberalization in the name of injecting efficiency into the economy. They include the World Bank and its Global Water Partnership platform, the French and German multi-utility companies, and the respective trade and economics ministers and EU commissioners who push the liberalization agenda at the WTO, the EU and at national levels.

Convinced that water should be suitably priced, the World Bank has relentlessly spearheaded a campaign to push the Dublin principle (Dublin Conference on the Environment, 1992) that water is an economic, rather than social, good. The World Bank's view is that water and wastewater services are associated with several types of market failure, which require different regulatory approaches. First of all, raw water resource is a common good. Unless access is regulated, there is a risk that these resources will be overused or abused. A water resources management scheme, which integrates both quantity and quality considerations, is needed to ensure that the allocation of water among competing users, i.e. agricultural, urban and industrial, reflects its economic value.

Earlier, the local government, in some cases the central and state governments, used to supply this public good at cost-recovery prices or gratis. Now, the government and its allied lobbies have a penchant for large, capital-intensive, foreign-debt-funded water infrastructure projects. Pakistan, in South Asia, shares the same experiences even though she, like India, is not a water-stressed country (see e.g. Bengali 2003). Since water is being increasingly priced under various project schemes, the revenue that accrues to the private corporations or the government is a huge sum, inflating the figures of net value added in the services sector to that extent. "Unbundling" – using the World Bank jargon, i.e. separation of distribution from source, steeply increasing tariffs, and allocation to highest value use through the market mechanism – have artificially hiked the share of the services sector in GDP. There has been a simultaneous reduction in value added in the agricultural sector as the price of the input, i.e. water, goes up, reducing the share of agriculture in GDP.

Lending about $20 billion to water supply projects over the last 12 years, the World Bank has not only been a principal financier of privatization, it has also increasingly made its loans conditional on local governments privatizing their waterworks. The International Consortium of Investigative Journalists' (ICIJ) study of 276 World Bank water supply loans from 1990 to 2002 showed that 30 per cent required privatization, the majority in the last five years (Marsden 2003). So far, privatization has been concentrated in poorer countries where the World Bank has used its financial leverage to force governments to privatize their water utilities in exchange for loans. On another front, water companies are working closely with the EU to enforce trade barriers against any country that refuses to open its water utilities to privatization. Working with the EU trade officials, the water companies are also trying to persuade the WTO to force countries to open their utilities to free market forces. Documents obtained by ICIJ show that the EC trade office works closely with Thames, Suez, Vivendi and other private water companies to push for a reduction in trade barriers with the WTO.

A yearlong investigation by the ICIJ, a project of the Centre for Public Integrity, showed that the world's three largest water companies – France's Suez and Vivendi Environment, and British-based Thames Water, owned by Germany's RWE AG – have since 1990 expanded into every region of the world. Their revenue growth was more than proportional to their expansion across the globe. Vivendi Universal, the parent of Vivendi Environment, reported earnings of over $5 billion in water-related revenue in 1990; by 2002 that had increased to over $12 billion. The RWE, which moved into the world water market with its acquisition of Britain's Thames Water, increased its water revenue from $25 million in 1990 to a whopping $2.5 billion in fiscal 2002 (Marsden 2003). The water companies are chasing a business with potential annual revenue estimated at anywhere from $400 billion to $3 trillion. Water stocks actually do better than other utilities because of the long-term contracts that stretch for 10 to 30 years, offering a reliable and predictable return on investment. That is why a lot of pension funds as well as private individuals are willing to put money into the water business, as noted by Thames' executive Peter Spillett.

AquaFed is the international federation of private water operators, set up in 2005 as another pressure group for private water and a front group for Suez and Veolia, It brings together over 200 water service providers in 38 countries worldwide. According to Gérard Payen, the President of AquaFed, the private water sector is larger than many people think, with thousands of businesses working every day, for the most part, to implement government policies (Payen 2006).

To summarize, from global to local, it is indeed necessary to distinguish the *illusory* part of tertiarization from its *real* part in order to understand the post-industrial in the poor developing countries as well.

Transformation, a bloated "residual"

Arthur Lewis's "modern" sector is in fact relatively small in size in India, and it is likely to continue to be so in the foreseeable future, as (a) the sector is becoming more and more labour-displacing, capital-intensive and computer-aided, and thus unable to absorb the vast potential migrants from the "traditional" sector; and (b) owing to growing trade liberalization the Indian modern sector is no longer an exclusive sovereign domestic domain. In this context, the abysmally low labour productivity in Indian agriculture in comparison with many other countries has brought forward two issues. First, economic rationality prompts India to discourage agriculture and import agricultural commodities from the high-productive countries such as Argentina, Australia, Canada, France, Germany, Russia and the US who together constitute about 64 per cent of world exports of cereals (FAO, *Statistical Yearbook*, 2004). The productivity difference between India and, say, the US being 1:134, and Canada 1:107, arguably the well-being of the common people in India would improve with imported cheaper foodgrains. Although the productivity differences do not immediately get reflected in price differences because of the high rate of subsidies being given to agriculture in the North, the trade argument is sound provided the 800 million-odd people are accommodated in the industrial and services sectors so that those displaced from agriculture have the minimum income security in order to have access to imported foodgrains.

Besides, the common understanding is that economic restructuring accompanies growth. Kuznets (1965) saw income elasticity of demand as the primary reason for changes in economic structure and away from agriculture. Kaldor (1966; 1967), on the other hand, considered manufacturing as the engine of growth: agriculture, he assumed, is characterized by diminishing returns to scale – as opposed to the Kautsky-Lenin thesis[9] – and is thus not capable of sustaining increasing levels of production and income; therefore manufacturing, without such limitations on the expansion of production, is the key to sustained economic expansion.

That neither the demand-side nor the supply-side argument on its own could explain the trajectory of structural change, or the shift away from agriculture, is amply evident. In the agriculturally high-productive 23 countries, while the average per capita GDP (at constant 1995 dollar prices) increased nearly 48 per cent between 1980 and 2002, the agricultural GDP per EAP (in agriculture) grew at a much higher rate of 116 per cent. This was made possible by a synergy of industries (producing labour-saving technologies) and agriculture (providing the ground of application of those technologies), while the displaced agricultural labour force found alternative economic means to survive. As opposed to Kuznets's closed economy model, these high-productive countries could find the much needed vent-for-surplus agricultural outputs in the world market.

There were, in India, 101.3 million holdings operated during the *kharif* season[10] and 95.7 million holdings operated during the *rabi* season (October–March) in 2002–03 (NSSO 2006b, Report no. 492). The average area operated per holding reduced to 1.06 hectares in 2002–03 from 1.34 hectares during 1991–92 and from 1.67 hectares in 1981–82. In other words, there has been more and more fragmentation in operational holdings as certain sections of the EAP became progressively dependent on agriculture.[11] The size distribution of operational landholdings exhibited more or less the same concentration ratio (Gini coefficient) in 2002–03 as it was in 1991–92. Between 1980 and 2002, although the agricultural GDP per EAP in agriculture increased from $269 to $385 (at constant 1995 dollar prices) (FAO, *Statistical Yearbook*, 2004) it is still much lower than the average GDP per capita. Here is the puzzle, following Lewis: the capitalist industrial sector in India has grown relatively fast, yet the agricultural sector is still to emerge from its subsistence level. Instead of declining, economic dependence on agriculture has in fact grown. In the average low-income country, dependence among the EAP on agriculture increased by 42 per cent, whereas in India it increased 33 per cent between 1980 and 2004, from 208.3 million to 276.7 million.

The rise in the EAP in agriculture turns out to be a net global phenomenon and not just Indian, despite decline in the same measure in many countries. The world is divided grossly between the OECD (20 countries) where the share of EAP in agriculture to the total EAP is less than 4 per cent, and the LDCs where it is more than 50 per cent (see Table 1.8). Under this unevenness, if the developing countries open up to agricultural imports following the WTO negotiations the outcome will be nothing but multi-fold increase in global unemployment. Even if labour mobility across countries were made free, this would be a long way from an adequate solution to the problem of gainful employment for more than 666 million agricultural EAP in the LDCs.

Those countries that are lagging far behind the agriculturally advanced countries must make efforts to increase their productivity. There is no doubt about it, but what is ambiguous is the economic viability of capitalism in agriculture. If the European model of capitalism in agriculture were to be followed – with intensive use of labour-saving mechanized implements coupled with land concentration – there would be massive displacements from the agricultural sector in countries like India and China. Among many other repercussions, the wage rates in the primary as well as the secondary industrial labour markets, which are already below the international poverty line, would be even lower and thereby exacerbate the global race-to-the-bottom. The workers in countries with relatively high labour standards would in turn feel the pinch in this era of globalization. This is the crisis of world capitalism to-day: globalization is supposed to widen capitalism whereas it induces resistance from more than two billion agriculture-dependent people in India, China, Indonesia and other similar countries in the South (see FAO, *Statistical Yearbook*, 2004) whose livelihoods would be threatened under free trade of foodgrains, in particular, and agricultural products, in general.

Lewis's traditional sector does include, beyond agriculture, that part of the manufacturing which is not organized and also not functioning on the basis of capitalist wage–capital relations. About 93 per cent of the Indian manufacturing workforce includes self-employed and jobs in pre-capitalist unorganized manufacturing employing 10 or less hired workers per unit. The Factories Act and the labour laws protecting wage, job, work-hour contracts and social security do not include workers in the vast unorganized sector.

Table 4.6 Share of different unorganized industries (rural and urban) to total unorganized manufacturing employment in India, 2000–01

NIC-1998 Codes	*Industry*	*% of total workers*	
		Rural	*Urban*
15	Food products and beverages	21.6	12.8
16	Tobacco products (mainly indigenous cigars consumed by common people)	11.4	5.1
18	Wearing apparel	9.6	17.3
19	Leather footwear, handbags etc.	0.6	2.0
20	Wood products	18.7	5.7
36	Furniture	5.1	13.5
	Total	67.0	56.4

Source: Based on NSSO (2002) Report no. 477.

A large sector of unorganized manufacturing reflects underdevelopment of a different nature. The underdeveloped transportation networks result in small and diffused pockets of demand that lead to small-scale localized production. Following Engel's Law, underdevelopment breeds small firms: demand for simple items such as bread, apparel, footwear, metal products (like utensils, simple agricultural implements) and furniture are rather efficiently produced using non-factory methods of capital and labour combinations (Table 4.6). There is little incentive therefore for consolidating production in several large plants and incurring the extra distribution costs (for the services of the organized intermediaries).

Industry to services

More significant than agriculture–industry has been the changing balance between industry and services. By sector-wise employment, the EDCs (excluding Japan) had reached the high point of industrial development by 1950 (Maddison 1995). The GDP per capita in these countries, in 1950, had crossed $5,000, and the share of industrial workforce varied between 34 per cent (in the US) and 45 per cent (in the UK). During the following decades, the services sector dominated the economy and society in the EDCs. In the EDCs, the sectoral structure of the economy, measured in terms of either employment or GDP, looks symmetric – either way, the share of agriculture is at the most 5 per cent across EDCs, that of industry is 33 per cent and the services sector comprises the rest. However, in South Asia, especially in India and Pakistan, where about 60 per cent of the country's total workforce are in agriculture, the GDP share of the sector has reduced to less than a quarter (Table 4.7). Both of these countries, although lagging industrially far behind countries in East and Southeast Asia, have somehow excelled them in services.

Urbanization in India perhaps played an important role in the growing services sector because of increased demand for health, education and recreation, banking and finance services.[12] If there were *planned* urbanization, one might thus witness

Table 4.7 Structural changes in selected Asian countries, 1960 to 2004

Country	*Value added as % of GDP*					
	Agriculture		*Industry*		*Services*	
	1960	*2004*	*1960*	*2004*	*1960*	*2004*
China	30 (1980)	15	49	51	21	35
India	55	22	16	26	29	52
Indonesia	50	17	25	46	25	38
Malaysia	36	10	18	48	46	42
Pakistan	46	23	16	24	38	54
Philippines	26	14	28	32	46	54
South Korea	37	3	20	35	43	62
Thailand	40	10	19	44	41	46

Source: World Bank, WDR, various issues.

shifting sectoral shares in GDP despite there being no significant rise in the average income level. Between 1961 and 2001, while India's population grew at the annual compound rate of 2.15 per cent, the urban population grew at a higher rate of 3.26 per cent (see Figure 4.2).

However, it is rather misleading when the rate of urbanization in India is compared with that of some other growing Asian countries (Table 4.8). Despite a higher level of urbanization in China, Indonesia or Malaysia, the relative size (measured by GDP share) of the services economy in any of these countries is still smaller than in India (*cf.* Table 4.7). Moreover, India's per capita income is

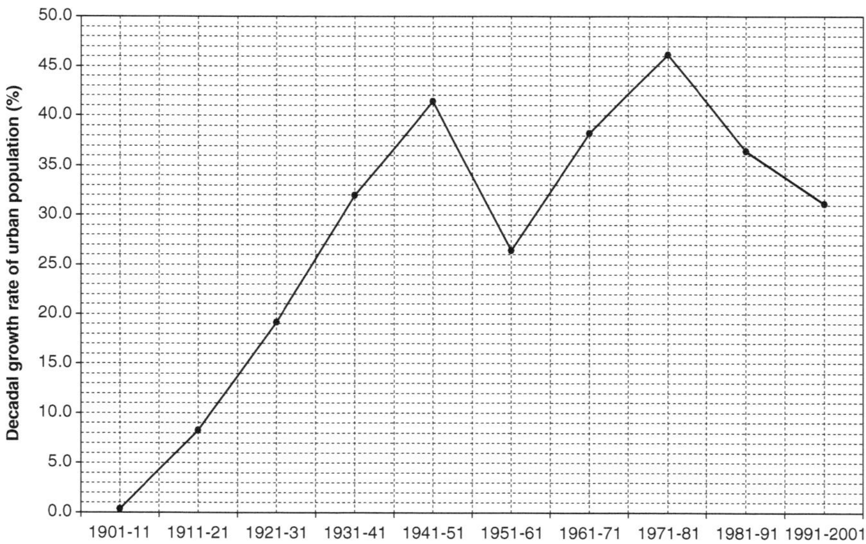

Figure 4.2 Trend of decadal growth rate (%) of urban population in India, 1901 to 2001. Source: Based on Office of the Registrar General, *Census of India*, various years.

Table 4.8 Urbanization in selected Asian countries, 1980 to 2002

Country	*Urban population as % of total population*	
	1980	*2002*
China	20	38
India	23	28
Indonesia	22	43
Malaysia	42	59
Pakistan	28	34
Philippines	37	60
South Korea	57	83
Thailand	17	20

Source: World Bank (2004).

lower than in China, Indonesia or Malaysia. To conclude, the hypothesis that growing per capita income leads to shifts in demand toward the services remains partial until and unless variables such as income distribution, interpersonal as well as rural–urban, are given due consideration.

Concluding remarks

Economic restructuring in the EDCs has been a natural fallout of the progress of capitalism – the rising income level has led to a changing pattern of consumer demand for welfare gains, and also to the changing profiles of *capital.* By contrast, the restructuring in India generally represents economic backwardness that has evolved out of the failed progress of social division of labour. Planned urbanization with an asymmetric incentive structure is one of the facilitators of the observed restructuring in India.

There has been relative stagnation in the industrial sector in India. The reach of the industrial society has largely remained confined to the upper income groups. But basic minimum services reach even to the poorest of the society in the form of health, education, transport etc., however minuscule these benefits might be. So far as the comparative advantage in international trade is concerned, India has indeed lost to countries such as Brazil, Malaysia, Mexico, South Korea and Taiwan beside North America, the EU (15 countries) and Japan in *disembodied* technology-intensive industrial goods. India is thus expected to gain in terms of well-being of the overwhelming majority by simply protecting – by tariff and fiscal measures – her labour-intensive and low-skilled unorganized manufacturing that produces mass consumption goods like garments, shoes, utensils, etc. for the domestic market, and of course for the agrarian economy (*cf.* Papola 2005).

Added to this is the emerging knowledge economy in which India has proven her competitive advantage in certain areas. From the long-term perspective, India's current development trajectory is not sustainable. The "bubble" is certainly going to burst. The level of dematerialization that is supported by the real sector economy in the EDCs could not just be replicated and grafted in a low-income

Table 4.9 India: hardware in total production of electronics and IT

Year	*Production of hardware as % of total electronics and IT production*		*Exports of hardware as % of total domestic production of hardware*
	GoI estimate (in Rupee terms)	*Nasscom estimate (in US$ terms)*	*Nasscom estimate (in US$ terms)*
2003–04	37.0	23.1	
2004–05	33.1	19.9	8.9
2005–06	29.7	19.0	8.5
2006–07	27.0	17.7	5.9
2007–08	27.8	18.8	4.2

Sources: GoI estimates are from Department of Information Technology, *Annual Report 2007–08*; Nasscom estimates are from NASSCOM (2008a).

developing country such as India. To explicate further, consider the domestic market for IT/ITes produced in India: the share of the domestic market in the aggregate value of Indian IT services is one-fourth, and it is about 13 per cent in BPO (NASSCOM 2008a). Most of the indigenous entrepreneurs in telecoms and banking, two key sectors with significant TNC participation, have significantly upgraded their levels of IT adoption to offer best-in-class services comparable to those offered by their global competitors. These two sectors together account for approximately 35–40 per cent of the domestic spending on IT services (ibid). Similar competitive pressures in other, more recently deregulated service sectors such as airlines and insurance, and the uptake in the manufacturing and industrial sectors, together with the several large e-governance initiatives launched by the government under the National E-Governance Plan (NEGP), are expected to support a secular rise in domestic demand for IT services over the next few years.

However, low tele-density,[13] low power density as well as the power supply being limited to a few hours a day in the countryside and thereby – coupled with low per capita income – the low computer density in India, low percentage of households (especially in the rural areas) having bank accounts – these are all hurdles to surmount before the domestic demand for IT-based services can take off. Still another factor going against the speedy development of IT is the lagging development of electronic hardware production in India. In its absence, the produced software needs imported hardware to be embodied. In fact, in dollar terms, the share of domestic production of hardware has been declining over the last five years and is now less than one-fifth of the total production of electronics and IT (Table 4.9). Moreover, Indian hardware products are rapidly losing the export markets.[14] This software–hardware dichotomy summarily explains the lopsidedness in the structural transformation. The failed agrarian transformation in India lies behind many such asymmetries. The social division of labour is underdeveloped because of the unsuccessful agricultural revolution.

5 Agriculture

The genesis of growing vulnerability

The world food crisis and India

In autarky, the demand for industrial goods from the very large agrarian population constitutes a critical input in industrial growth and development. Apparently, trade liberalization has rendered the effective demand problem for industrial growth as *passé*. Dismantling of the barriers to export growth as well as foreign capital inflows notwithstanding, wide fluctuations in the trajectory of industrial growth post-1991 must indicate the limitations of the "hip-hop" approach to industrialization. The relative importance of structural constraints even in a large open economy is in fact not a matter of Hobson's choice.

It is necessary to understand the dynamics of the most prolific sector in the Indian economy in order to understand the relationships between farm and non-farm in the context of the most pressing problems of unemployment and poverty eradication. About 221 million rural people were living below the poverty line in 2004–05. Most of them are in such agriculturally backward states as Bihar, Jharkhand, Madhya Pradesh, Orissa and Uttar Pradesh (GoI, Planning Commission 2007). Further, agricultural wage labourers, small and marginal cultivators and rural artisans constitute the bulk of the rural severely poor. A buoyant agriculture would raise the income level of the farm-dependent population and thereby improve their access to health and education – an insurance against government failure in public schemes aimed at improving the country's human development index (HDI).

Unless there is a required balance among the various sectors of the economy the long-term dynamics of each and every sector is likely to be affected, resulting in the crisis of *disproportionality* that we have witnessed in the previous chapter. Globally, this kind of *crisis* has in fact culminated into a more recent phenomenon: the current global food crisis and the steadily rising food prices – prices of basic foodstuffs, especially cereals, namely rice, corn and wheat, have soared as much as 130 per cent over the levels of a few years ago – have made food increasingly inaccessible to the majority of the global population. World food production must be doubled to feed a world population currently standing at 6 billion and expected to rise to 9 billion by 2050. Therefore, the urgent need – unless there is some technological revolution in food intake – is a proportionate increase in food crops production. But the central question, because of a host of interrelated issues, is: how, and in which way?

The critical problem of desirable food production has multiplied with the rise of neoliberalism. At one level, it prompts the cropping pattern in countries to follow the trend in relative market prices. Following which, one cannot call it irrational to search for carbon-free fuel for automobiles – the biofuels – in the hope of reducing greenhouse gas emissions through transport and thereby reducing global warming. But this is now put under the microscope as the programme's environmental footprint is seen as negative. Yet, production of biofuels has boomed, driven, in a sense, by rising world petroleum prices and the growing demand for energy. And this boom, by crowding out the production of grains such as maize and wheat, has contributed to the present food scarcity in many regions. Unless the remunerative prices of these grains do not increase in proportion with the prices of chemical fertilizer, pesticides, seeds and animal feed, which together have risen by more than 50 per cent in the last couple of years, crop substitution is inevitable. As state sovereignty over land-use pattern is dwarfed by free market forces, crop substitution has become smoother. Also, state minimalism in the average developing country has increasingly made the allocation of bank finance market determined. Agriculture, already at a disadvantageous position, is pushed further into competition for investible resources with other booming sectors such as real estate, no matter whether the producer countries are required to meet the needs for food of their own populations in order to avoid a global food crisis. At another level, subsidized agricultural products from the developed countries find a "green channel" to the tariff-reduced developing countries, severely affecting the latter's domestic cultivation in the absence of countervailing fiscal measures.

A structural solution to the problem of food security implies availability, access and stability of supply in countries like India having a significantly low land to person ratio. The FAO Director-General Jacques Diouf says: 'In fact, the problem of food insecurity is a political one. It is a question of priorities in the face of the most fundamental of human needs. And it is the choices made by Governments that determine the allocation of resources.'[1] The politics, at one level, is about settling within WTO the issues of agricultural subsidies, transfer of appropriate seed–fertilizer–pesticide technology from the developed countries to the developing countries, and TNC oligopoly in the farm-seeds market. At another level, the politics within some of the developing countries is about integrating the tertiary sector-based accelerated GDP growth rate with the unprotected poor and marginal cultivator-dominated agriculture.

Many in India defend the "structural solution" while others reject it in favour of the agency-based solution. The World Bank points out:

> Land markets, particularly *rental* markets, can raise productivity, help households diversify their incomes, and facilitate exit from agriculture. As farmers age, as rural economies diversify, and as migration accelerates, well-functioning land markets are needed to transfer land to the most

> productive users. But in many countries, insecure property rights, poor *contract enforcement*, and *stringent legal restrictions* limit the performance of land markets, creating large inefficiencies in both land and labour reallocation and reinforcing existing inequalities in access to land.
>
> (World Bank, WDR, 2008: 9; emphasis added)

True, insecure property rights and poor contract enforcement are mostly all-embracing in the case of tenancy cultivation and thus require new institutional arrangements. There are various types of contracts – fixed money, fixed produce, share of produce, service, usufructuary mortgage, etc. – between the landowner and the lessee for the economic rights to the land, which are often poorly enforced and in which coercion downplays the contract. In fact, the proportion of tenanted land in the total cropped area was considerably high in India. However, according to the official statistics, this characteristic of Indian agrarian structure is fast losing its intensity (Table 5.1). Tenant holdings – i.e. holdings with partly or wholly leased-in land – accounted for about 10 per cent of operational holdings[2] in 2002–03. Also, the share of leased-in land in the total operated area declined significantly to 6.5 per cent, regional variation notwithstanding (NSSO 2006b, Report no. 492).[3] In all-India, nearly 10 per cent of the holdings in the size classes larger than 1 hectare (ha) are tenant holdings, and about 70 per cent of the total tenanted land is operated by only 7 per cent of the aggregate number of operational holdings.

Moreover, the percentage of tenant holdings gives no clear direction to the variation across different holding sizes, except for the lowest size class that shows a comparatively lower incidence of tenancy. In most of the holdings groups the percentage of tenant holdings varies between 9 and 12. In the large holdings, however, nearly 14 per cent were tenant holdings in 2002–03. This notwithstanding, the percentage of tenanted (area leased-in) land in the total operated area, in general, declined in larger holdings (Table 5.2).

On the whole, the sharecropping system in the past did appear to be a strong drag on the growth of agricultural productivity as well as income distribution in rural India, since the landowners used to coerce the sharecroppers by denying

Table 5.1 India: changes in the pattern of tenant holdings by category of rural operational holdings, from 1960–61 to 2002–03

Category (landholding size in hectares)	*% of tenant holdings*				
	1960–61	*1970–71*	*1981–82*	*1991–92*	*2002–03*
Marginal (up to 1)	24.1	27.0	14.4	9.3	9.8
Small (1–2)	25.1	27.8	17.9	14.9	10.7
Semi-medium (2–4)	23.6	24.8	15.9	12.2	10.3
Medium (4–10)	20.5	20.0	14.5	13.1	7.8
Large (more than 10)	9.5	15.9	11.5	16.7	13.8
All	23.5	25.7	15.2	11.0	9.9

Source: NSSO (2006b) Report no. 492.

Table 5.2 Tenant holdings (all-India: rural): percentage of area leased in, by broad size-class, 2002–03

Size group	*% of area leased in*	*% share in leased-in area*
Marginal	8.6	30.3
Small	6.8	22.1
Semi-medium	6.3	21.8
Medium	4.2	14.6
Large	6.1	11.2
All sizes	6.4	100.0

Source: NSSO (2006b) Report no. 492.

them their fair share of the produce and thus leaving little incentive for the sharecroppers to adopt new technology and thereby augment production. Land relations in Indian agriculture have changed, partly due to productivity growth but largely because of peasant movements across the country, quite often radical, e.g. in Andhra Pradesh, Bihar, parts of Uttar Pradesh and West Bengal, and because of *de facto* land reforms in some of the states with a very high concentration of agriculture-dependent population, namely Kerala and West Bengal. This is an affirmative signal, but with a caveat: it is yet to be ascertained how much of the reduction in the relative frequency of tenancy is genuine and how much of it results from concealment – which was possible due to state inaction – of excess land over the law-defined "land ceilings" by the large landowners.

Further, two trends are now quite apparent. First, there is a rise in the share of "fixed rent" in all forms of tenancy relations, thus minimizing arbitrariness in crop-sharing. In the two most agriculturally advanced states, namely Haryana and Punjab, the most prevalent form of contract is fixed *cash* rent – a clean bargain between the principal and the agent. On the other hand, fixed *crop* rent is the most common form of tenancy in the southern states (excluding Kerala). The sloppiest contract, i.e. crop sharing, is the most prevalent form of contract, covering 35–40 per cent of the tenanted land in the erstwhile *permanent settlement* areas of the British colonial land revenue and settlement systems, namely Assam, Bihar, Orissa, the eastern Uttar Pradesh and West Bengal.

Second, wholly owned and self-operated holdings (as well as areas of operation) have grown significantly to 96–97 per cent in all size-classes of holdings (GoI, Ministry of Agriculture and Cooperation, *Agricultural Census 2000–01*). In the countryside, about 2.8 per cent of the landowning households reported leasing-out – i.e. that much of *absenteeism* – while 11.5 per cent of households reported leasing-in of land (NSSO 2006a, Report no. 491). It would perhaps not be an overstatement to say that direct cultivation has become more economic for the large landowners than it was a couple of decades ago, because of either changing *economics* of production or changing *political* relations, or a combination of both.

Finally, as we will see later, the impact as well as the feasibility of withdrawal of the existing legal restrictions on land markets – following the *WDR 2008* prescription on improving efficiencies in both land and labour allocation in the specific Indian agrarian structure – is highly ambiguous. In general, an individual's rights to utilize, obtain income from, and alienate the asset define the property rights. Legal rights, as a rule, enhance economic rights, but the former are neither necessary nor sufficient for the existence of the latter (Brazel 1989: Ch. 1). New rights are created in response to new economic forces. As the value of agricultural land rises due to, say, the extension of irrigation, or its expected proximity to a highway, economic agents tend to establish rights over it. When legal rights are difficult to obtain – due to, say, the politically sensitive land-ceiling act, or even the government-drawn land utilization maps – obtaining economic rights becomes the goal of the prospective investor who prefers to minimize risks, but not costs, because "economic rights" fetches a premium, periodically revised, provided the market is *free*.

Currently, the major problem that India confronts at the production frontier is that of comparatively lower agricultural productivity. Although 64 per cent of the net sown area is under cereal cultivation, the yield (kilos per hectare) of cereals in India is way behind that of the major cereals-producing countries in South, South-East and East Asia (Table 5.3). The yield in rice is higher than that of wheat in India, although the latter received greater coverage under the strategy of the Green Revolution with seed and fertilizer technology. The spread of the new technology in India notwithstanding, immediate neighbouring countries such as Bangladesh, China, Myanmar and Sri Lanka produce rice at a yield-rate that is higher than in India by a margin of 20–115 per cent. Besides, in terms of annual

Table 5.3 Agriculture: yield-rate (kilograms/hectare) in selected developing countries in Asia, in 2002

Country	*Cereals*		*Rice paddy*		*Wheat*	
	Yield (kg/ha) in 2002	*Annual growth rate 1992–2002 (%)*	*Yield (kg/ha) in 2002*	*Annual growth rate 1992–2002 (%)*	*Yield (kg/ha) in 2002*	*Annual growth rate 1992–2002 (%)*
Bangladesh	3,348	3.1	3,448	3.1	2,164	2.1
China	4,963	1.1	6,266	0.9	3,885	1.4
India	2,340	1.8	2,914	1.3	2,770	1.7
Indonesia	4,077	0.5	4,433	0.1		
Myanmar	3,308	1.7	3,532	1.7	981	1.4
Philippines	2,731	2.3	3,280	1.1		
South Korea	6,089	1.0	6,315	1.0	3,060	−1.5
Sri Lanka	3,712	2.1	3,827	2.0		
Thailand	2,692	2.0	2,597	1.9	615	−0.3
Vietnam	4,385	2.9	4,551	2.9		
DEVELOPED COUNTRIES (Average)	4,506	1.3	7,541	1.1	3,730	1.3

Source: FAO Corporate Document Repository.

growth rate of production between 1992 and 2002, India trailed behind such rice economies as Bangladesh, Myanmar, Sri Lanka, Thailand and Vietnam. These facts together summarize what we may term the *dilemma* India has gone through ever since the Second Five-Year Plan (FYP) (1956–61): Look to the "East" or "West"?

"Look west" policies and Indian agriculture

At the inception of the planned development in the immediate postcolonial India, in the First FYP (1951–56), public investments in agriculture, irrigation and electrification got a boost. However, they fell well short of requirements as the priority later shifted – following the Soviet model – to development founded on basic and heavy industries, beginning in the Second FYP (Table 5.4). The policy ultimately led to the saving–investment disproportionality crisis toward the end of the Third FYP (1961–66). It was inevitable, because an overwhelming part of the economy was still agricultural, more specifically subsistence agriculture, which was not equipped to generate extra savings for the industrial sector. Besides, the policy failed to make expected profits buoyant. Therefore saving, and not finance, was the ultimate constraint on the rate of accumulation, unlike what the monetary economist would try to argue.

Land reforms: the dilemmas

The paradigmatic shift in emphasis from agriculture to planned industrial development was nonetheless coupled with a few land reform measures, but with limited targets, namely: (a) to abolish the statutory landlordism (i.e. the *zamindari*

Table 5.4 India: plan outlay in agriculture and allied sectors

Plans	*% of agriculture and allied sectors to total plan outlay*
I Plan (1951–56)[(a)]	14.9
II Plan (1956–61)[(a)]	11.3
III Plan (1961–66)	12.7
Annual Plans (1966–69)	16.7
IV Plan (1969–74)	14.7
V Plan (1974–79)	12.3
Annual Plan (1979–80)	16.4
VI Plan (1980–85)	5.8
VII Plan (1985–90)	5.9
Annual Plan (1990–91)	5.8
Annual Plan (1991–92)	6.0
VIII Plan (1992–97)	5.2
IX Plan (1997–2002)	4.9
X Plan (2002–07)	5.2

Source and notes: GoI, Planning Commission.[(a)] Includes animal husbandry, special area programme, rural development, and forestry and wildlife.

estates, a hangover of the colonial rule) and provide incentives to ex-zamindars for their becoming farm entrepreneurs; (b) to secure rights of tenants and regulation of rents; and (c) to impose ceilings on private landownership by individuals or families, coupled with vest in the government of any surplus land exceeding the ceiling and redistribution of the same among small peasants and the landless (GoI, Planning Commission 1963). However, first, the *zamindars* and big landowners largely evaded the land-ceiling act by colluding with the ruling political power and administration, and thus scuttled any radical restructuring of the rural property relations. The ceiling legislation thus could not garner much *surplus* land for redistribution. Second, only rich tenants could retain land, and the smaller peasants simply lost access to it and became either tenants-at-will or landless agricultural workers. Third, the ownership distribution of rural land remained, as usual, highly skewed.[4]

The size distribution of ownership holdings in India is characterized by the predominance of virtually landless and marginal holders.[5] The lack of political determination on the part of the central government as well as most of the state governments to implement the land reform measures explains the distribution. As counter-evidence, in 1977, when the new government assumed power in the state of West Bengal it assigned top priority to the reforms of land relations, and implemented them without delay. These reforms took shape mainly in the form of (a) redistribution of vast lands already vested by the previous governments, and (b) securing of tenancy rights, which were already there in law, through a programme of universal registration of tenants called "Operation Barga" (i.e. sharecropper), in addition to the effective imposition of a stipulated ceiling on landholdings and the reduction of subinfeudation[6] through the abolition of intermediaries between the cultivator and the landlord. Major changes in tenant relations included the active official recording of registration of sharecroppers who had cultivated the same piece of land for a consecutive number of years. This registration with the department of Land Revenue (government of West Bengal) gave them permanent and inheritable rights to cultivate the land.[7] The objective was to provide security of tenure to the sharecropper so that first, her livelihood is not threatened and second, she is encouraged to make permanent and more expensive improvements on land and adopt modern technology. In addition, bestowing economic rights to land-title facilitated the sharecropper's access to institutional credit as land is the most sought-after collateral. Between 1978 and 1981, about 1.2 million sharecroppers were recorded in the state. However, the programme of sharecropper registration soon tapered off and since the mid-1980s the rate of additional registration has been negligible.[8] About 18–22 per cent of the arable land being under sharecropping, a significant part of the state's agriculture felt the wider impact of empowerment of basically marginal peasants. The latter indirectly acted as a quasi-threat to the absentee landlords, who therefore turned to direct cultivation. Later, these threatened big landlords gradually shifted their political allegiance to the ruling parties.

Initially, there was widespread scepticism among scholars and Indian planners as to the impact of *operation barga* on productivity, since the new seed–fertilizer technology requires relatively high initial investments which an average sharecropper is presumably unable to mobilize. However, in fact the small and marginal holdings turned out to be more productive than the larger holdings – the inverse size–productivity relationship once again proved itself as the right kind of conjecture in the specific conditions of Indian agriculture. Intensive use of family labour, closer supervision and motivation raised productivity. The course of development in the 1980s also belied the apprehension that the registration of sharecroppers would have adverse impact on the investment decisions of the owner-cultivators of larger holdings.

At the end of the decade, West Bengal stood distinctly above the all-India average of labour productivity in rice production. The *new* technology spread rapidly through the districts, and rice production boomed. Between 1980 and 1984 rice production increased at the rate of 5.9 per cent per annum, while the yield increased at the rate of 5.3 per cent. The growth rate declined marginally thereafter, but still increased at the rate of 4.9 per cent, and the yield rate was 3.6 per cent, from 1984–85 to 1993–94 (Banerjee 2007b).

The tempo that lasted for one-and-a-half decades has lost steam since the mid-1990s, largely because the intensification of land use was not subsequently adequately supported by the extension of irrigation facilities. In a sense, the political mobilization that once had bolstered land reforms in the 1970s and 1980s, in one way or the other, disintegrated later: large landlords themselves became part of the local ruling political elites; and energizing diesel or kerosene pump-sets with grid electricity, together with proportionate expansion of canal irrigation, lost their priorities with the neoliberal government. This happened in spite of the fact that the *Panchayati Raj* institution (PRI) had been overwhelmingly dominated, at least until 2008, by the parties whose coalition has been ruling the state uninterruptedly for the last more than three decades, ever since 1977.

These are the lessons of planning and development in India, as summarized by one of the country's renowned development planners:

> The planners were aware that major institutional changes were required in order to realize the production potential of agriculture, but they did not realize the nature and dimension of political mobilization that would be necessary to bring about the institutional changes.
>
> (Chakravarty 1987: 21)

The agricultural producers' cooperative – an institution as well as an organization – could have been one such instrument of mobilization, since unsecured land tenure coupled with small and fragmented land units often give rise to a localized monopoly/oligopoly which in turn becomes the chief source of agricultural credit as well as the leader in the local output market.

Land reforms in the "East"

The topic of land reform was first placed on the agenda of the General Assembly of the United Nations at its fifth session (1950) and was subsequently discussed in the Economic and Social Council (13th session, September 1951) as well as in the Conference of the FAO (November 1951). The suggestion that followed was: land reforms mean more than redistribution of land either by breaking up large estates or by consolidation of holdings (Raup 1967). They must include, it was suggested, a number of measures to improve the tiller-to-land relationship, including opportunities for land ownership, improved conditions of tenancy, agricultural credit at reasonable interest rates, reform of exorbitant rents and taxes, and facilities for obtaining agricultural supplies and marketing agricultural products, with emphasis on cooperatives (Andrews 1952). This concept constituted the basis of the first two UN Reports on *Progress in Land Reform*, which were subsequently circulated to member governments in 1960 in advance of preparing the Third Progress Report. The Foreword to the Third Report states:

> Land reform is treated more broadly as equivalent to agrarian reform or agrarian institutional reform. It clearly includes changes in land tenure ... But it also includes the establishment or strengthening of essential governmental, cooperative or commercial agencies or services relating to agricultural credit, supply, marketing, extension, and research. So conceived, the ideal land reform programme is an integrated programme of measures designed to eliminate obstacles to economic and social development arising out of defects in the agrarian structure.
>
> (UN, Department of Economic and Social Affairs 1962: iv)

Applied models were, however, available from countries in the East, e.g. post-revolution socialist China, and market-driven economies such as Japan, Korea and Taiwan adopted a holistic approach to land reforms similar to that stated in the UN *Foreword*. The Japanese record of agricultural production since the land reform of 1946 is highly impressive. Before World War II the Japanese output per acre was already one of the highest in the world. With less than 0.2 of an acre of cropland per person – comparable to contemporary India – the intensity of land use in Japan had reached levels that made it questionable whether any capacity remained for further increases in output. Nonetheless, the index of agricultural production (1934–36 = 100) rose from 106 in 1940 to 157 in 1964, despite a decline in acreage. Japanese farm income doubled between 1950 and 1963 (Raup 1967).

Further, Taiwan's post-WW II economic development is a typical example of W.W. Rostow's linear theory of development: agricultural take-off is the prerequisite for general economic take-off. Initially, Chiang Kai-shek had implemented a large-scale land reform immediately after his retreat to Taiwan in 1949, which redistributed roughly 13 per cent of the national wealth and laid the foundation for the "Taiwan miracle" of rapid agricultural growth based on small and marginal farmers and with income equality (Hou and Hou 2006). At the same time the government established the Agricultural Statute, by which the pre-war Agricultural Association was converted to the Taiwan Farmers' Association (FA), whose main functions included supply and marketing, propagating new technology, and of course providing credit to farmers. The role of the FA was equally important in Taiwan's reformed economy – unlike in India, where the supply and marketing functions of the limited numbers of cooperatives that could be formed turned into the stronghold of the large landowners and became sources of further discrimination. In Taiwan, over the next twenty years, as a result of the policy of "nurturing industry with agriculture", agricultural production accelerated at an impressive rate. This was soon followed by the industrialization of Taiwan in the 1970s. Subsequently, at a later stage, the plan had shifted to "developing agriculture with industry" (Hou and Hou 2006).

In Korea, nearly 3 per cent of all farm households had owned over two-thirds of all land in the late 1930s, whereas ten years later, fewer than 7 per cent of all households were landless, following land reforms. The American occupation forces groped toward land reform in response to violent peasant demands and to the Soviet example in the North. The agrarian reform of the Japanese colonial rule was pushed one stage further, and land was redistributed to the tiller. Although land-to-the-tiller in Korea never enriched the peasantry or overflowed the state tax coffers, its long-run effects were major. Reform redirected idle money away from land speculation to manufacturing and uprooted a class that had not proved to be progressive. It relieved the bottleneck in food supply, which in turn dampened inflationary pressures. Moreover, it created a far more equitable income distribution (Amsden 1989: 37).

In traditional Chinese society, a key factor affecting agriculture was the dominant position of the landed gentry. Full-time or part-time tenancy in pre-1949 China constituted 50–65 per cent of the operational holdings (Kuo-chun 1960). Before 1949, land reform had already been carried out in the previously liberated areas. Following the emergence of the People's Republic, and starting in July 1950, a radical land reform movement was carried out in the rest of the countryside. By the fall of 1950 the implementation of the programme covered 100 million peasants, of whom landlords constituted 4 per cent (Schurmann 1966). Some 43.3 million hectares of land was distributed among landless peasants and those with insufficient land (Dixin 1982). This was later supplemented by the creation of Agricultural Producers' Cooperatives (APCs). In 1955, Mao Zedong in his famous July speech ('On the question of cooperativization in agriculture') urged a decisive speed-up in the campaign of organizing APCs, which until then had countered resistance in many places from the rural elites who were against the state encroachments. By the summer of 1957, nearly 97 per cent of the total peasant population had been enlisted in one or another form of cooperative (Schurmann 1966). In brief, in her socialist economic reconstruction, China adhered to the policy of "agriculture the foundation and industry the leading factor". In planning, emphasis was placed on agriculture, light industry and heavy industry in that order, so that all three could forge ahead, unlike the Indian planning. There was impressive growth in all the sectors subsequently, and without inflation: grain production in 1973 was more than double that of 1949; the total output value of light industry in 1973 was a dozen times that of 1949 (author unknown 1975). Agriculture and light industry did provide markets and capital for heavy industry, enabling the latter to grow faster. It is important to recognize that the post-1978 Chinese development owes much to these already grown-up institutions and organizations.

The Indian government meanwhile planned for a deeper penetration into the economic life of the country as well as capturing the "commanding height" of the economy. However, it did not venture much into the land distribution system in agriculture although there was a very high frequency of tenancy cultivation, and the absentee landlords exercised their political weight over the "power" to flout the land-ceiling legislation in various parts of the country. While the structural problems remained unresolved, a major policy to protect domestic agriculture with tariffs and quantitative restrictions on trade of the non-commercial crops – similar in the nature to the protection that the Indian state provided to domestic industry – continued, however, until the 1980s.

The food crisis of the 1960s and after: production trends

The thwarted institutional reforms, coupled with the lopsided allocation of public investments, knocked down the optimism of the planners and had landed India into a grave food crisis by the end of the Third FYP. The Plan had to be discontinued for the next three years, and nearly 19 million tonnes of foodgrains were imported to avert starvation. Yet land reform, as the redistribution of holdings on the basis of political and equity considerations, did not crop up as the critical factor. Rather, agricultural growth was attempted via an exercise of utilitarian efficiency that set aside "development with justice": how best to adopt "scientific" agriculture and "modern" methods to improve aggregate production in the short run, bypassing the institutional reforms in land and the rural labour market that would have counteracted poverty directly. This was so because the latter had political costs for the ruling Indian National Congress party. The government poverty alleviation programme – conceived as a *scheme* rather than entitlement – was later announced in the early 1970s. It served as a political tool to build up the "vote bank" at a time when other designs to stimulate *aam admi* – the ordinary people – were faltering.

The "growth first" strategy included changes in the incentive structure so as to induce the rich farmers to adopt the new agricultural technology based on high-yielding variety (HYV) seeds, inorganic fertilizers and pesticides. Punjab, Haryana and the western part of Uttar Pradesh were initially selected for the implementation of the programme, since this contiguous region was endowed with rich irrigation facilities – largely developed by the British colonial government which sought to promote wheat exports (Banerjee 1999: Ch. 1) – and also had a high concentration of rich farmers (for a survey of the costs of concentration, see Rao and Storm 1998). As part of the changing incentive structure, the Agricultural Prices Commission (APC) was set up in 1965, and the Food Corporation of India (FCI) was formed to carry out the new pricing and marketing policies.

Between 1951 and 1965, during the period preceding the Green Revolution, rice production increased at an annual rate of 3.4 per cent and wheat production increased at 3.5 per cent (Table 5.5). More than anything else, the growth in output was due primarily to increased public investment in irrigation, which led to the expansion of the area under cultivation during the period. *Area* expansion as such contributed 50 per cent, while increase in *yield* contributed another 38 per cent to the output growth (GoI, Ministry of Agriculture and Cooperation, *Agricultural Statistics*, various issues). The production of foodgrains subsequently responded positively to the Green Revolution, the overall rate of growth increasing to 3.5 per cent. In this phase, area contributed proportionately less (i.e. 23 per cent), while the contribution of yield to the growth increased to 58 per cent. During the initial years of the Green Revolution (1965–73) the growth in rice output declined to 3.2 per cent, but the main carrier of the revolution, i.e. wheat, grew at an incredible rate of 10.1 per cent per annum.

As the seed–fertilizer technology adopted by the rich farmers in the developed irrigated regions made a breakthrough in wheat output, many sensed that agrarian capitalism would bring about the much-vaunted transformation through an *autonomous* propagation of the technology in newer areas, rendering agrarian class composition irrelevant. Subsequently, the agenda of land reforms – except for the consolidation of holdings,[9] which benefited the larger landholders more than others – was regarded by the government and planners (or rather, the decision was thrust upon them by the rich farmers) as making a predictably insignificant contribution to productivity growth in the country as a whole. Many regions with subsistence farming and overwhelming dominance of small and marginal cultivators thus became victims of growing unevenness. Mainly because of the "yield effect", five states, namely Gujarat, Haryana, Punjab, Rajasthan and Uttar Pradesh, raised their share in the country's total food production by the late 1970s, while the traditional paddy areas of Bihar, Karnataka, Kerala, Tamil Nadu and West Bengal together lost their previous weights in the country's rice production (see e.g. Bhalla and Alagh 1979).

The role of the rising relative prices of agriculture against industry during the initial period of the Green Revolution also could not be played down. One cannot rule out the possibility of collusive price setting by the rich farmers – at the time more than 60 per cent of the total arable land in the country was either owned or operated by barely 10 per cent of the farming community. However, even 10 per cent of the total farming population represented close to 40 million individuals, or roughly 8 million households; that so many households can come to a mutual understanding as to how farm prices are to be determined in the market would be considered as most far-fetched (Mitra 1977: 111). In a way, the domination of the public sector enterprises in the industrial sector until the 1970s in fact enabled the government to set the relative prices right with relative ease.

The new technology covering paddy, wheat, bajra, jowar and maize subsequently spread to other regions, albeit slowly. However, very soon – the Fifth FYP (1974–79) onwards – the initial momentum of the new seed–fertilizer–irrigation technology flattened. Between 1973 and 1989 the area under foodgrains as such fluctuated widely, and output growth dropped to 2.8 per cent. The rate of growth of wheat output declined drastically from the earlier rate of 10 per cent to

Table 5.5 India: trend (exponential) rate (%) of growth of area, production and yield of foodgrains, rice and wheat

Period	*Foodgrains*			*Rice*			*Wheat*		
	Area	*Production*	*Yield*	*Area*	*Production*	*Yield*	*Area*	*Production*	*Yield*
1951–2005	0.23	2.47	2.24	0.66	2.56	1.90	1.87	4.82	2.95
1951–1965	1.08	2.60	1.52	1.41	3.41	2.00	2.12	3.49	1.37
1965–1973	0.68	3.52	2.86	0.73	3.18	2.47	5.26	10.07	4.89
1973–1989	NSSG	2.83	2.76	0.48	3.09	2.61	1.39	4.88	3.50
1989–2005	(–)0.26	1.16	1.41	NSSG	1.15	0.10	0.73	1.87	1.14

Source and notes: Calculated from GoI, Ministry of Agriculture and Cooperation, *Agricultural Statistics at a Glance* (2006). Three-year moving average values of each variable, for the period from 1950–51 to 2006–07, are considered for growth rate calculation, which is based on OLS estimation of $y = ab^t$. NSSG = no statistically significant growth.

less than 5 per cent. The rate of growth of rice production declined too (Table 5.5). The earlier terms of trade favouring agriculture also turned to its disadvantage.

One thus gets the impression that Indian agriculture did have inherent structural limitations to its smooth adjustment to the changed circumstances of economic liberalization in the early 1990s, which ruptured many of the protections to the sector. Between 1989 and 2005, production of foodgrains – both rice and wheat – experienced the lowest ever growth since the early 1950s, despite successive good monsoons since the drought in 1987. The yield-rate too became lower than that which prevailed even before the Green Revolution (i.e. 1951–65) (Table 5.5).

Low growth disorder: inputs and land use pattern

Area under cultivation

Ironically, the rate of expansion of area under foodgrains was highest between 1951 and 1965 in post-Independent India. Despite the Green Revolution, the rate of area expansion slowed down. Between 1973 and 1989 there was no statistically significant growth in area. Most strikingly, between 1989 and 2005 the area under foodgrains manifestly decreased (Table 5.5). The reduction of area was not so much for rice and wheat as it was for the poor people's consumables, i.e. coarse cereals such as bajra, maize, jowar and, of course, pulses grown mostly by the SC/ST cultivators for their own consumption. The reduction in area under coarse cereals cultivation is only partially explained by the shift to oilseeds cultivation in large tracts of the rain-fed regions of Madhya Pradesh and Rajasthan.

In fact, the area under foodgrains began to decline steadily after 1983–84 (see Figure 5.1).[10] The arable land reduced by 2.4 million hectares between 1980 and

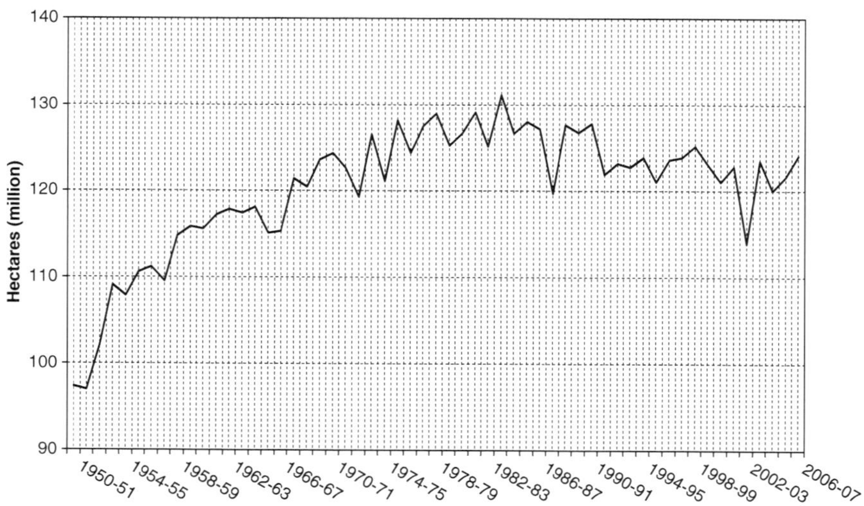

Figure 5.1 India: trend in area under foodgrains, 1950 to 2007.

2000, according to FAO. Moreover, the labour force engaged in the land was plainly displaced. Assuming 10 economically active persons engaged in a hectare of land cultivation, nearly 24 million people have lost employment in farming. Over and above this, the animal-dependent agricultural economy has also had to cope with the loss of more than 1 million hectares of pasture during the last two decades (FAO 2007: Table A2). Additionally, more than 42 per cent of the geographical area of the country comprises degraded land, a substantial part of which is human-made: the extent of degraded land is higher in the states with a larger share of rain-fed agriculture (Vyas 2004).

There are many explanations for the decline in the yield-rate: e.g. the over-dose of inorganic fertilizers which eroded the soil fertility; the quality of the irrigation water, particularly of the groundwater, which increased the salinity of the soil in many parts of the country; the reduced seed-productivity, often due to the spurious seeds supplied to the market; and so on. In many instances the agricultural extension services are to be blamed. The extension system seems to have nearly collapsed in almost all of the states because of, as part of the neoliberal policies, stringent fiscal regulation and budget management by the respective governments which deter fresh employment of extension service personnel. As a result, farmers have increasingly become dependent on the "information services" being provided by the dealers in private agricultural inputs (mostly of the TNCs), who have their own "maximizing objectives".

Not less important is the fact that the pressure on land for foodgrains has increased due to urbanization as well as market-induced shifts towards commercial crops. The land-rent has steadily increased, pushing food crop cultivation into inferior lands of lower productivity. There was a decrease of about 2.12 million hectares of net sown area in India between 1990–91 and 2003–04 (GoI, Ministry of Agriculture and Cooperation, *Agricultural Statistics* 2006). So, the average area operated per holding has reduced as the population has increased and additional employment opportunity in non-farm jobs has become irregular.[11]

Nevertheless, the part of the agricultural process, namely cultivation, which depends more on animal power than on human power is being slowly mechanized, largely in response to the depleting stock of farm animals owing to the rising fodder prices and diminishing pasture. On the other hand, mechanization has remained negligible in harvesting and thrashing – i.e. where outputs depend more on human power.[12] In the use of tractors, India is ahead of China (using 7 per 1,000 hectares in 2003, remaining almost the same since 1980), while China is way ahead of India in the use of labour-displacing harvesters and thrashers (using 2.5 per 1,000 hectares, which increased from 0.3 in 1980). China, by maintaining a certain level of livestock, could release agricultural human power for other sectors at a scale that is much greater than in India. This is one of the sources of truncated capitalism in Indian agriculture.

Irrigation, the variable

Generally, expansion of irrigation facilities leads to a rising ratio of gross cropped area (GCA) to net cropped area, and declining dependence on rainfall.

Table 5.6 India: growth of net area under irrigation, by source (per cent)

Year	*Canals*		*Tanks*	*Tubewells and other wells*	*Other sources*	*Total*
	Government	*Private*				
1950–51	39.7		17.2	28.7	14.4	100
1990–91	35.3	1.00	6.1	51.4	6.1	100
2000–01	28.6	0.37	4.4	61.4	5.2	100
2005–06	25.4	0.34	3.4	58.8	12.1	100

Source: CSO, *Statistical Abstract of India*, various issues.

Massive public thrust and planned investments to expand irrigation – 22 per cent of the public sector outlays was on irrigation and flood control – in the First FYP in India led to the expansion of the area under cultivation at a rate that could never be matched later, as noted above. Note that the major component of growth was area expansion between 1951 and 1965. Subsequently, as the implementation of the seed–fertilizer technology proceeded and success was achieved in selected regions, public investments in canal irrigation progressively declined since the mid-1980s. Moreover, owing to the lack of complementary investments in operation and maintenance, and bureaucratic mishandling of the use of this resource, the efficiency of canal water has been jeopardized (see e.g. CAG 2006). The trend is counterbalanced by private investments in small irrigation from tubewells, tanks, etc. (Table 5.6). However, the major hurdle faced by this type of irrigation is the highly fragmented plots of land; it is economic only for a farmer with consolidated holdings in the command area of the well. Moreover, exploitation of the groundwater has caused negative externalities in regions where these forms of irrigation are over-concentrated, especially in the arid and semi-arid areas where progressively larger areas are coming into the "dark zone" (Vyas 2004).

The gross irrigated area as a ratio of GCA was 17.1 per cent in 1950 and had doubled by the end of the 1980s. However, as the area under cultivation had been reducing and both the production and growth in yield rate declining, in the post-1990 period the ratio increased only marginally to 40.3 per cent in 2003–04. In other words, about 60 per cent of the GCA still depends on the rainfall. The cropping intensity (as measured by the ratio of GCA to the net sown area), which progressively increased until 1998–99 (with some exceptional years), ultimately experienced a secular decline (GoI, Ministry of Agriculture and Cooperation, *Agricultural Statistics* 2006: Table 14.2).

Regrettably, months before the start of monsoon, speculation in the central government and various ministries becomes rife as to whether it will be *normal* or not. In the so-called postmodern India, a good or bad monsoon still has such a high linkage effect throughout the economy that the speculations in the share market rely too heavily on the level of rainfall during the monsoon. "Uncertainties" in the economy as a whole would have minimized had there been a policy of allocating public investments and inducing private investments based on the linkage coefficients of different assets (in this case, irrigation). However, for predictably political reasons, the policy of various states has been to increase production through subsidies on inputs such as power, water and fertilizers, rather than by building new capital assets in irrigation. This problem is particularly severe in the backward states.

There is also the problem of equitable distribution of the available irrigation facilities over various crops. Nearly 66 per cent of the total GCA is under foodgrains. Of this, rice constitutes 22 per cent, wheat 14, coarse cereals 16, total cereals 53 and pulses 13 per cent. While the GCA under coarse cereals is greater than that under wheat, only 11 per cent of the former was under the cover of irrigation as against 88 per cent of the wheat area in 2002–03. Also, of the total area under rice cultivation – mostly concentrated in the poorer states – only 50 per cent was covered by irrigation in the same year (GoI, Ministry of Agriculture and Cooperation, *Agricultural Statistics* 2006).

One might come across a weak correlation between the rate of irrigation expansion and the growth of productivity at the district or block level. But that does not disprove the positive association between the two at the macro level. First, often the farmers' share of the irrigation water, mostly from dams, is a residual percentage after the demand from the power plant(s) or other such water-requiring industrial plants – be they private or public – has been met.[13] Second, the *variation* is explained by the relative concentration of tenancy cultivation in the district or block. The prevailing tenancy contracts have a bearing upon irrigation use and crop intensity. On the whole, for spatial variation, one has to probe into the land tenure system. Third, the official statistics on canal irrigation often do not tally with the actual availability of water at the fields; most often the irrigation potential created is much less than the irrigation-command area of a project. This is as true for one of the oldest irrigation (plus hydro-power) projects in India – namely the Damodar Valley Corporation (DVC)[14] which was constituted in 1948 as a replica of the Tennessee Valley Authority of the USA – as it is for the Sardar Sarovar Narmada Nigam (SSP), the latest but most controversial and expensive irrigation-cum-power project. On the whole, there is a huge gap of 14 million hectares between irrigation potential created and potential utilized, which needs to be plugged, according to the Planning Commission. The potential gap is due to reasons such as siltation of reservoirs and lack of field channels (GoI, Planning Commission 2005, Part II: Ch. 6).

To elaborate, Gujarat has been able to irrigate 57,002 hectares from the SSP, which is just 10 per cent of the irrigation possible in phase I of the project, because the state failed to develop the distribution network and the command area for irrigating extended areas. Among all the components of the SSP, development of the canal network right up to the field is the most expensive one. The SSP has become the costliest irrigation project in India today because of the delay in the development of the command area; the state, with an annual growth rate much above the all-India average, was hardly constrained by the fiscal resources crunch. It is perhaps due to its weighing agriculture against other sectors with the utilitarian yardstick, for the allocation of available fiscal resources, which mattered the most.

There is, of course, a limit to expanding the irrigation potential. Thus the growth of that fraction of agricultural productivity which depends on irrigation is limited. According to the Planning Commission, some states – namely Tamil Nadu for major and medium irrigation and Uttar Pradesh for minor irrigation – have already reached their critical potential (GoI, Planning Commission 2005, Part II: Ch. 6). Given the situation, it is necessary to revive and restore the traditional water bodies, particularly those that are linked to agriculture. Increasing efficiency in water use has therefore become urgent. By *efficiency*, we mean there is a frontier of production possibilities in the two-resources domain of capital and labour, and any point (a combination of capital and labour) in the space beneath the frontier has to be treated as *inefficient*. Therefore, to reach the efficiency frontier, given an adequate supply of labour, the inadequacy of capital should first be addressed.

Proliferation of subsistence farming

For nearly 82 per cent of the total number of holdings, the size of holdings is "up to 2 ha". They cover 39 per cent of the total area of operational holdings in India. Further, more than 42 per cent of the holdings are of the size "below 0.5 ha". Moreover, the share of marginal holdings (area less than 1 ha) in terms of number is 63 per cent, while in terms of area it is 19 per cent (Table 5.7).

As the tenancy holding tended to decline since the 1970s, currently with the Green Revolution, it was thought that the eternal processes of capitalist alienation and proletarianization were ultimately unleashed. However, that has not happened so far: the small and marginal peasants hung on to their holdings. Moreover, it is not yet certain that they could survive the anticipated onslaught of the capitalist processes of differentiation by increased integration with the market as grain suppliers. The regional variation in this respect is particularly noteworthy.

One of the distinct characteristics of subsistence farming is the low ratio of marketed surplus to production. It is not just the coarse cereals, which supposedly have a restricted market, but also the marketed surpluses of rice and wheat that constitute less than 50 per cent in some of the major food-producing states in India. In Uttar Pradesh, which contributes more than one-fifth to the country's total foodgrains production, less than 50 per cent of her production of rice, wheat and barley, respectively, is marketed as surplus. Similarly, the marketed surplus ratio is low in the backward states such as Assam, Himachal Pradesh, Madhya Pradesh and Rajasthan. Incidentally, the latter two states have discernibly high agricultural land inequality. The proportion of small and marginal holdings to the total in either of these two states is much smaller than in other major states, and also smaller than the national average (Table 5.8).

The distinctly low ratio of marketed surplus is directly proportional to the intensity of small and marginal cultivation in Uttar Pradesh – about 77 per cent of the total number of holdings is "less than 1 ha" in size. The marginal and small farmers together dominate Uttar Pradesh farming by cultivating nearly 37 per cent of the aggregate operational area under agriculture in the state (Table 5.8).

Table 5.7 Distribution of operational holdings: all-India

Category of holdings	*No. of operational holdings ('000)*		*Area operated ('000 hectares)*		*Average size of operational holdings (hectare)*	
	1995–96	*2000–01*[a]	*1995–96*	*2000–01*[a]	*1995–96*	*2000–01*[a]
Marginal (less than 1 ha)	71,179 (61.6)	76,122 (63.0)	28,121 (17.2)	30,088 (18.8)	0.40	0.40
Small (1.0 to 2.0 ha)	21,643 (18.7)	22,814 (18.9)	30,722 (18.8)	32,260 (20.2)	1.42	1.41
Semi-medium (2.0 to 4.0 ha)	14,261 (12.3)	14,087 (11.7)	38,953 (23.8)	38,305 (24.0)	2.73	2.72
Medium (4.0 to 10.0 ha)	7,092 (6.1)	6,568 (5.4)	41,398 (25.3)	38,125 (23.8)	5.84	5.80
Large (10.0 ha and above)	1,404 (1.2)	1,230 (1.02)	24,163 (14.8)	21,124 (13.2)	17.21	17.18
All holdings	115,580 (100.0)	120,822 (100.0)	163,357 (100.0)	159,903 (100.0)	1.41	1.32

Source and notes: GoI, Ministry of Agriculture and Cooperation, *Agricultural Census, 2000–01*. Figures in parentheses indicate the percentage of the respective column total. [a] Excluding Jharkhand.

Table 5.8 Foodgrains: marketed surplus ratio (%) in 2004 (in states where the ratio is 50 per cent or less), and distribution of agricultural landholdings

	Assam	*Uttar Pradesh*	*Himachal Pradesh*	*Rajasthan*	*Madhya Pradesh*	*All-India average*
Rice	41.3	46.5				
Wheat		50.2	29.5	27.2		
Maize			44.3			
Jowar					43.4	
Barley		45.6				21.5
Ragi						37.3
% share in country's total foodgrains production	1.8	20.7	[Wheat: 1.0 Maize: 3.7]	5.5 [Wheat: 8.5]	6.7 [coarse cereals: 13.3]	
	Size of land holding: *Less than* 1.0 ha					
% of total no. of holdings	62.6	76.9	67.3	31.8	38.6	62.9
% of total area of operational holdings	21.3	37.0	25.7	4.2	8.5	18.7

Sources and note: GoI, *Agricultural Statistics at a Glance* (2006); for the land distribution data, see GoI, Ministry of Agriculture and Cooperation, *Agricultural Census, 2000–01*. Figure in parentheses is percentage of country's total in respective crop.

They produce mainly for their own consumption, besides saving a part as "seed capital". Moreover, the propensity to take the surplus to the market depends on the nature of the crop: whether it has a common market, or a specialized market where "risks" are inbuilt. The cultivators who grow coarse cereals – i.e. the Giffen goods with a very high substitution effect – mostly do it for their own consumption. In brief, the *market* has perhaps failed to penetrate. However, the fact that ought not to be downplayed is that the large number of economically active people in agriculture themselves manage their own food security and, in that way, reduce the avowed burden of the government.

Finally, for this large population of cultivators, household savings are either "nil" or not worth mentioning. To add insult to injury, floods that recur in almost every year take away whatever little they can accumulate as durable goods. Thus, while the public expenditure on flood control assumes importance in the river basin areas, the actual allocation of funds for the purpose gets lesser priority. The net outcome is poor capital accumulation in agriculture (Table 5.9).[15] The GCF in agriculture as a ratio of GDP constitutes barely 2 per cent, while the sector is burdened with the responsibility to feeding more than a billion people in the country.

Rural credit as an instrument

The proliferation of subsistence farming is facilitated by the rural credit network. Most of the cultivators, small and marginal, are dependent on borrowed funds, as

Table 5.9 Gross capital formation (GCF) in Indian agriculture (excluding allied sectors), 2000 to 2006

Year	*GCF in agriculture as % of aggregate GCF in India*	*GCF in agriculture as % of GDP*
2000–01	8.12	1.90
2001–02	9.69	2.28
2002–03	8.61	2.12
2003–04	7.23	1.87
2004–05	6.41	2.85
2005–06	6.02	2.01
2006–07	5.78	2.01

Source and note: Computed from CSO, NAS (2008). Both GCF and GDP are at current prices.

working capital requirements for HYV seeds, fertilizer, pesticides and also irrigation are high by their standard. On the other hand, the number of rural bank offices has reduced since 1994. Moreover, the volume of deposits mobilized by the rural bank offices is generally greater than the amount of credit disbursed by those offices in the rural areas. Although there was a converging trend between the two until 1990, it ruptured in the aftermath of liberalization.

The volume of credit disbursement in fact has increased alongside the decline in the number of rural bank offices. However, if the rate of growth of rural credit between 1978 and 2002 is adjusted for the inflation rate in the economy, credit disbursement by the banks shows almost a "zero" growth in the midst of significant growth in farm activities as well as rural non-farm activities. In general, the agricultural credit (direct), in particular, has somehow stabilized around a lowered level of 11 per cent of the aggregate annual net bank credit (of public sector banks) in any particular year since the late 1990s (see RBI, *Report on Trend and Progress of Banking in India*, various issues). Nevertheless, there is significant variation across states in the disbursement ratio of the volume of short-term and term loans made by the scheduled commercial banks per hectare of GCA. Naturally, credit-constrained rural households in the laggard states, in particular, use fewer inputs than are demanded by the production possibilities frontier, and consequently have lower incomes.

Not more than 15 per cent of the working capital required in the Indian agriculture comes from the organized banking sector. Rural India, in general, and agriculture in particular, thus increasingly became dependent on various forms of informal credit relations. In the regions where land reforms have vested rights to assets which are acceptable collaterals, the availability of institutional finance is relatively easy. But even then the mortgaging of a tiny plot of land is the last resort that a poor landowner would try to take on. Eventually, the landowner gets interlocked with the private moneylenders who accept various movable assets including such non-marketable assets as labour-power and incomplete property rights as "future outputs" of the borrower. So, as agricultural growth generates more income, it simultaneously has generated a huge informal credit market where the borrowing *monthly* rate of interest is very high – the bottom line is 4 per cent and could be as high as 10 per cent or more – perpetuating perennial debt-bondage of the cultivators. A crop failure thus leads to a devastating effect on lives and livelihood (GoI, Planning Commission 2006).

The union minister of Agriculture confirmed in May 2006 that at least 100,000 farmers had committed suicide between 1993 and 2003 because of their inability to repay loans. The minister has gone on record stating that as many as 16,000 farmers continue to commit suicide each year in 32 vulnerable districts in western and southern India in the states of Maharashtra, Andhra Pradesh, Karnataka and Kerala (Guha Thakurta 2006). The debt-bondage becomes well entrenched due to, among other critical factors, the serious shortage of water for cultivation. Thus the drought-prone regions of Bundelkhand in Uttar Pradesh and Amlasole in West Bengal have also become vulnerable. Many of the contemporary drought-prone regions had an intricate network of bunds and canals that tapped surface water from numerous natural and artificial ponds. Even during the colonial rule many of such regions were kept well irrigated, the canals carefully maintained and more lakes and dams constructed. Moreover, the official figures of suicidal death could still be underestimates as suicides of debt-burdened farmers have continued but the local administration often put them down to unexplained deaths. It is also important to recognize that the cultivators who needed more working capital, i.e. the substantial farmers (holding 10–15 acres) are comparatively more affected than the small and marginal farmers who have the least social taboos against migration to such menial jobs as pay-loaders or stone-crushers, so to speak, in the peri-urban sphere.

Earlier, when tenancy cultivation was the predominant feature, land–labour–credit *interlinkages* used to determine output and productivity. The land relations have changed since then, but the credit market behaviour remained integral to the functioning of the rural agricultural output market, whether spot or future (Banerjee 2001). The rural professional moneylenders usually prefer cash-credit and cash-repayment to other forms of interlinked transactions, and fix an unusually high money rate of interest. However, the system of cash-credit but repayment in kind is quite widespread in paddy, raw jute, oil seeds, etc. – i.e. those commodities having scope for downstream value-additions at the local or regional level. The market relations are formed on the basis of the type of economic organization engaged in the post-harvest processing of each particular product. In paddy-rice, the medium-scale rice mills and the small-scale husking mills are the dominant competitive buyers. They have distinct methods of interlinking credit with commodity markets. Similarly, the supply chain of raw jute is consolidated by the oligopoly traders for a limited number of jute mills, through "cash-credit but repayment in kind" transactions. The bulk of the raw jute produced does not come to the open market posts. Similar are the exchange relations between oil-seed growers and the oil-mill owners, and so on. Spot prices, open auction, immediate payment are extremely rare in major crops and for the most part confined to petty trade.

In general, the borrower is compelled to transfer his harvests to the trader-cum-lender at a price that is 20–25 per cent lower than the prevailing market price. The cash–kind transactions largely explain the segmentation or isolation of the rural agricultural output market. To the extent that the lender, by using output market segmentation, could depress the post-harvest price, the *implicit* rate of interest – calculated on the basis of *margin* between the pre-harvest and post-harvest prices – goes up.

In brief, land relations, the variation in labour productivity across states, yield rate and land–person ratio have given rise to disparate credit relations, often in tandem with the marketing system of agricultural commodities in different regions.[16] There is a distinction between the logical properties of exchange and the institutional factors in the transformation of exchange as a social activity. So long as exchange is not a ubiquitous social activity, it distorts the credit relations. One would in turn witness significant divergence of prices in closely located rural market posts, instead of price convergence typical of a developed market economy.[17] Indian agriculture is inflicted with that many distortionary effects on price formation.

Low growth issue of terms of trade

The thesis that during the early stages of industrialization it is necessary for the agricultural sector to contribute to the development of a modern industrial sector by providing cheap labour and cheap wage goods – to help in maintaining a low product-wage and thereby a higher level of accumulation in the industrial sector – has somehow formed the basics of price and distribution policies in India; whereas the normative alternative was to accomplish agricultural revolution. The Soviet pricing policy for "socialist primitive accumulation" might have some relevance because agriculture there already had much higher land and labour productivity than was the case in India in the 1960s and 1970s. However, we should not overlook the fact that the former Russian agriculture, based on discriminatory pricing, was heading toward stagnation – a cumulative effect – in the closing decades of the twentieth century.

The terms of trade were unfavourable to Indian agriculture in the 1980s. Thereafter, they briefly improved *vis-à-vis* non-farm business until the mid-1990s, only to experience another round of secular decline (Table 5.10). The growth rate as well as the per capita availability of foodgrains declined, yet the terms of trade have not been favouring agriculture; perhaps because per capita (monthly) consumption of cereals had progressive declines: In the countryside, the monthly per capita consumption was 14.4 kilos, while in the urban areas it was 11.2 kilos in the late 1980s. Decade later, the same was found to be 12.2 kilos in the rural and 9.8 kilos in the urban areas, in 2004.

Certainly, as income moves upward beyond the subsistence level the cereals consumption declines – i.e. agricultural product has low income elasticity. Here is the paradox: The vast majority of the population while struggling with low per capita income have presumably reduced consumption of cereals. In fact, the

Table 5.10 India: index of terms of trade between agriculture and non-agriculture, 1981–82 to 2004–05 (base: triennium ending 1990–91 = 100)

Year	*Index of prices received by agriculture (IPR)*	*Index of prices paid by agriculture*			*Combined index (w = 100.0)*	*Index of terms of trade (ITT)*
		Final consumption (73.54w)	*Intermediate consumption (21.63w)*	*Capital formation (4.83w)*		
1982–83	60.3	58.8	91.1	62.6	66.0	91.4
1983–84	64.2	64.2	91.0	67.4	70.1	91.6
1984–85	68.0	66.6	92.3	72.5	72.4	93.9
1985–86	70.4	69.5	94.3	76.4	75.2	93.6
1986–87	76.7	74.8	98.7	78.8	80.2	95.7
1987–88	86.0	84.6	102.3	82.5	88.3	97.4
1988–89	90.3	90.4	96.9	90.9	91.8	98.3
1989–90	97.5	97.6	99.2	100.6	98.1	99.4
1990–91	112.3	112.1	104.0	108.5	110.2	101.9
1991–92	130.8	124.9	119.4	127.2	123.8	105.6
1992–93	138.7	131.5	139.5	137.5	133.5	103.9
1993–94	151.4	143.9	152.9	147.3	146.1	103.6
1994–95	171.1	159.0	166.1	158.4	160.5	106.6
1995–96	182.9	173.4	174.2	176.1	173.7	105.3
1996–97	190.6	185.6	181.5	188.8	184.8	103.1
1997–98	205.9	195.7	192.0	196.7	194.9	105.6
1998–99	220.8	213.8	197.1	206.8	209.9	105.2
1999–00	219.8	217.1	203.9	212.6	214.0	102.7
2000–01	225.0	220.5	230.4	227.0	222.9	100.9
2001–02	235.3	226.4	236.4	240.4	229.2	102.6
2002–03	247.9	234.9	253.2	245.2	239.4	103.6
2003–04	251.2	245.2	259.1	255.7	248.7	101.0
2004–05[a]	260.1	251.3	272.1	305.6	258.4	100.7

Source and notes: GoI, *Agricultural Statistics at a Glance* (2006). ITT is obtained by dividing IPR by the combined index and multiplying by 100. *w* = weight. [a] Provisional.

unfavourable terms of trade while kept the relative prices of agriculture fairly stable, at the same time this has restricted income growth in agriculture, directly affecting consumption of the farmer households as well as agricultural workers, and indirectly the *net* cereal buying households engaged in rural retail trade, unorganized manufacturing, etc., that is those whose fortunes are pegged to agricultural prosperity. And, these together largely explain the very high incidence of malnutrition. India is failing its rural poor with 230 million people being undernourished – the highest for any country in the world (United Nations World Food Programme 2007). Child malnourishment in India is higher than in Ethiopia and above the African average of 28 per cent. No country among the 177 countries for which HDI been compiled had higher percentage (under age 5) of underweight (for age) children than in India (47 per cent), except in Bangladesh (48 per cent) and Nepal (48 per cent), during the period 1996 to 2005 (UNDP 2007). So, no wonder why the Indian statistics on cereals consumption shows a downward trend.

The unequal terms of trade result in a differential rate of accumulation across sectors, which explains the variation in the supply response of different sectors to market signals. The terms of trade between agriculture and industry are also a problem of exchange between town and countryside. The modernist approach to economic development usually suggests that since agriculture remains the predominant economic activity, accumulation for growth has to depend primarily on the transfer of resources from the farm sector, either by taxing directly or by following the quasi-taxing method of differential prices when there is a governed price regime.[18]

On the one hand, in order to ensure a rise in farm productivity there is the need to improve technology. This entails a need for increased capital accumulation in the countryside, as has been the case ever since the rural–urban dichotomy arose. On the other hand, in a closed economy, industrialization needs a transfer of surplus from agriculture. However, when the level of technology is low, the surplus available to a small peasant, or from the petty commodity production, cannot but be meagre. Notwithstanding this, a class of rich farmers emerges out of the processes of *differentiation* in agrarian development, who could be taxed via prices, or whose savings could be mobilized via the banking system and then transferred to the urban sector. But then there should be a "dual pricing" system: one for the petty producers and the other for the surplus-generating rich farmers, for a state-supported industrialization – which is indeed a difficult political choice; a problem of governance, too.

Nevertheless, to determine the *appropriate* degree of plunder is rather complex: if the relative price keeps on shifting in favour of industry production rigidities might develop within agriculture because of price uncertainties. Consequently, farm demand for industrial products might shrink abruptly (Mitra 1977). In determining the fair prices for either agriculture or industry it is necessary first to fix the objective parameters of development, and then to find which sector has (a) greater employment elasticity; (b) greater capacity to alleviate poverty; and (c) greater propensity to export. If the relative price of agriculture remains depressed, wage rates of the agricultural workers remain depressed too. When this workforce seeks employment in the town the low wage rate is carried forward, depressing the industrial wage rate in turn.

Many economists – who are methodical about price but not value – argue for the inflationary role of a rising agricultural price and the consequent deprivation of the *net* foodgrains buyers, including those among the agricultural workforce. On the contrary, the focus ought to be on income and entitlements and the ability to command food. The high incidence of poverty and malnutrition in India without favourable terms of trade for agriculture points to the hollowness of the argument of the distributive effect of inflation on the poor; this in fact belongs to a different *genre* of the politics of economics.[19] No one would demur that raging inflation will wreck an economy, but how about 20 per cent inflation year after year, which characterized Korea's early growth phase?

The transfer payments to agriculture in the form of subsidies on industrial inputs, namely fertilizers, pesticide and power for irrigation purposes, are supportive to the farmers – usually upper-middle and large – who use these inputs more intensively. Besides, the inadequacy of the volume of subsidies in India is unquestionable, not to mention its distributive fairness. India is in no way comparable to any of the agriculturally developed countries in terms of agricultural subsidies per farmer; the subsidies per hectare in India are less than one-fourth of the amount paid in the OECD, and just about 6 per cent of that in the average EC country (*cf.* Table 2.7). It becomes difficult then to reconcile the vulnerability of Indian agriculture with the trade fetishist who finds food self-sufficiency a peculiarly obtuse way of thinking about food security and therefore has been strongly arguing against subsidies to Indian agriculture.

In order to formulate the price policy for major agricultural commodities – with a view to evolving a balance and integrated price structure in the perspective of the overall needs of the economy and with due regard to the interests of both the producer and the consumer – the government set up the Agricultural Prices Commission (APC) in January 1965.[20] The recommendations by the APC for the level of minimum support prices (MSP) and other non-price measures take into account the following factors for a particular commodity or group of commodities: (i) cost of production; (ii) changes in input prices; (iii) input–output price parity; (iv) trends in market prices; (v) demand and supply; (vi) inter-crop price parity; (vii) effect on industrial cost structure; (viii) effect on cost of living; (ix) effect on general price level; (x) international price situation; (xi) parity between prices paid and prices received by the farmers; and, (xii) effect on issue prices and implications for subsidy.

To point out the inconsistencies, the "effect on industrial cost structure" or the "effect on general price level", *ceteris paribus*, would generally be negative if the support price were to neutralize the rise in the costs of agricultural production. This perhaps explains why the government often declined to neutralize the adverse effect of the unfavourable terms of trade by giving a "fair price" to agriculture; this was because the prime considerations had been the effects on industrial cost structure and the general price level. The neoliberal view of agricultural price support can best be summarized in the following words: an increase in the MSP of wheat and rice leads to decline in overall GDP, increase in aggregate price index and reduction in investments. Even the increase in agricultural GDP resulting from higher MSP dwindles rapidly and only a minuscule positive impact on agricultural GDP remains by the third year. More importantly, in terms of welfare, the bottom 80 per cent of the rural and all of the urban population are worse off (Parikh *et al.* 2003). What this story badly misses out, apart from other intellectual issues, is that higher MSP not only gives support to the cultivators directly but also indirectly to a very large percentage of the rural workforce engaged as wage labourers in farms and in retail trading, transport of agricultural produce, unorganized manufacturing and so on, thus helping them to combat poverty.

Between 1997 and 2006, the trend rate of increase in MSP was 3.2 per cent for wheat, 3.5 per cent for rice and 4.4 per cent for coarse cereals (i.e. jowar, bajra and ragi). During this period, the wholesale price index of manufactured products increased at the rate of 3.7 per cent. As the wheat and rice growers experienced declining relative prices the MSP remained only a partial support for the foodgrains cultivators. Besides, the net benefits largely remained confined to a few pockets of Green Revolution where the marketed surplus ratio had been high. Moreover, the MSP, though it sounds paradoxical, has a very limited role in keeping a check on the exploitative private local trade that jeopardizes agricultural price stability.

Besides MSP, another important factor that explains the slow rise in relative prices of agricultural goods, especially of foodgrains, is the phenomenon of post-harvest distress selling. The small and marginal cultivators could not afford to build inventories of the non-perishable goods, because of the high cash liabilities they already have, and also because of the need to mobilize investible funds for the next sowing season. As a result, the price tends to crash immediately after harvest – a bumper crop takes the price even below the *average* of the last couple of normal crop seasons. In the specific context of demand–supply conditions of foodgrains in India, it would be rather grossly partial to analyse the latter phenomenon in terms of low price elasticity of farm products; i.e. an increase in production would lead to a drop in price, and vice versa.

In order to ensure that the farmers get remunerative prices for their produce and do not have to resort to distress sale, the federal government extends price support to paddy, coarse grains and wheat through the Food Corporation of India (FCI) and state agencies. The price support scheme also intends to make provision for the targeted public distribution system and other welfare schemes of the government that involve supply of subsidized foodgrains to the poor, and to build up buffer stocks of foodgrains. All the foodgrains conforming to the prescribed specifications offered for sale at specified centres are bought by the public procurement agencies at the MSP. The producers are free to sell their produce to FCI or state agencies, or in the open market. Foodgrains procured by the state governments and their agencies are ultimately taken over by the FCI for distribution throughout the country. Rice is also procured by the government through a statutory levy on rice millers and rice dealers. The percentage of levy rice is fixed by the state governments with the approval of the central government, taking into account the requirements for the central pool, domestic consumption and the marketable surplus. Prices of levy rice are fixed by the central government before commencement of every *kharif* marketing season.

The foodgrains procurement was, however, decentralized by the central government in 1997–98 with a view to 'effecting savings in the form of reduction in the outgo of food subsidy, enhancing the efficiency of procurement and PDS and encouraging local procurement to the maximum extent thereby extending the benefits of MSP to local farmers' (GoI, Ministry of Consumer Affairs, *Annual Report 2007–08*: 12). Under the new scheme, the state government undertakes direct purchase of paddy and wheat and procures levy rice on behalf of the federal government. The latter pays for the expenditure incurred by the state governments on the procurement operations as per the approved costing. The state governments that are presently undertaking decentralized procurement include Chhattisgarh, Karnataka, Kerala, Gujarat, Madhya Pradesh, Orissa, Tamil Nadu,

Uttar Pradesh and West Bengal, but not the agriculturally rich states like Haryana and Punjab, where the government agricultural marketing infrastructure is relatively developed.

Haryana and Punjab are much advanced states in terms of the proportion of the state's outputs of wheat and rice getting procured by the union government, and thus could reap the benefits of MSP at a greater scale. By contrast, Uttar Pradesh produces as much as 35 per cent of the country's aggregate wheat, yet the procurement ratio is a meagre 2.3 per cent of her annual wheat output. Other states such as Andhra Pradesh, Maharashtra, Madhya Pradesh, Orissa and Tamil Nadu are also marked by the low ratio of procurement. On the whole, rice procurement as a proportion of India's aggregate output is about 30 per cent. It is still lower for wheat, i.e. 21 per cent (Table 5.11). Thus, the effectiveness of the MSP system to stabilize the price behaviour of foodgrains in the producers' market rather remained peripheral.

The procurement ratio varies across regions, depending on (a) the differential and inadequate allocation of the central funds; (b) the marketed surplus, which often is low because of the credit–output interlinkages; and/or (c) the efficiency of the open market operation as against the government's own buying network. Besides, the procurement prices were often not so remunerative as to induce a greater proportion of marketed surplus.

Therefore, if the government could arrange distribution of industrial goods at subsidized rates to the poorer people in the countryside, the adverse income effect of the terms of trade would be somewhat neutralized. The system is there in the form of the public distribution system (PDS), no matter how effective it was, but the government has been minimizing its role in PDS ever since the early 1990s.

Table 5.11 Foodgrains procurement in India as a ratio of outputs, 2005–06

State	*RICE (incl. paddy)*		*WHEAT*	
	Procurement as a ratio of state's production (%)	*Share of the state in country's rice production (%)*	*Procurement as a ratio of state's production (%)*	*Share of the state in country's wheat production (%)*
Andhra Pradesh	42.5	12.8		
Chhattisgarh	65.1	5.5		
Haryana	63.9	3.5	51.1	12.8
Madhya Pradesh	7.8	1.8	8.1	8.6
Maharashtra	7.0	2.9		
Orissa	26.1	7.5		
Punjab	86.9	11.1	62.2	20.9
Tamil Nadu	17.8	5.7		
Uttar Pradesh	28.3	12.1	2.3	34.7
TOTAL	30.1		21.3	

Sources: For data on procurement, see GoI, Department of Food and Public Distribution, *Annual Report 2006–07*; for production data, see GoI, *Agricultural Statistics at a Glance* (2006).

Public distribution system as solace

The PDS reaches people with such essential commodities as wheat, rice, sugar and kerosene oil through a network of Fair Price Shops (FPS). Some of the states or Union Territories claim to have distributed additional items of mass consumption through the PDS outlets, such as cloth, exercise books, pulses, salt and tea. The PDS evolved as a major instrument of the welfare policy to ensure availability of foodgrains to the common people at affordable prices. It is an important constituent of the strategy for poverty alleviation and is intended to serve as a safety net for the poor who are nutritionally at risk. With a network of about 478,000 FPSs, the PDS is perhaps the largest distribution network of its type in the world. It is operated under the joint responsibility of the federal and the state governments. The federal government has taken responsibility for procurement, storage, transport and bulk allocation of foodgrains. The responsibility for distributing the same to the consumers (or cardholders) through the network of FPSs rests with the state governments. The operational responsibilities, including allocation within the state, identification of BPL families, issue of ration cards, supervision and monitoring the functioning of FPSs, rest with the state governments. In the end, the PDS is not intended to make available the entire requirement of any of the commodities distributed under it to a household or a section of society.

The PDS has served two purposes: it has contained substantially the rise in producers' prices for foodgrains and simultaneously ensured food access to urban consumers beside the rural net-buyers. Until 1992, the PDS was a *general* entitlement scheme for all consumers, without any specific target. As part of the fiscal management, the Revamped Public Distribution System (RPDS) was launched in June 1992 in 1,775 blocks across the country – out of a total of 5,612 blocks in 600 districts of 638,588 villages in India. In other words, RPDS has been implemented in less than one-third of the blocks. As the number of targeted beneficiaries has reduced while the claimants are greater in number, there is a huge disappointment as regards corruptions involved in the delivery system, which has largely devalued it. The PDS has thus become a somewhat partial remedy to the adverse terms of trade of agriculture.

However, as the terms of trade have moved against agriculture and growth of output has stagnated, the stocks of foodgrains are piling up with the FCI. Progressively increasing issue prices of foodgrains (distributed through the PDS) as part of the government's effort to reduce the food subsidy resulted in reduced buying by the disadvantaged. At the same time the government has been unable to utilize the buffer stocks of food for income generation and nutritional security of the poor, although a bunch of such programmes is in hand. However, given its politically sensitive nature, it may be difficult to drastically cut down the buffer food stocks as suggested by the Expenditure Reforms Commission. The central government thus has to employ a combination of policy changes and support prices for farmers to perform the tricky job of downsizing food stocks (Raghavan 2003).

Rural-urban income (albeit consumption) gaps

To address such binding issues as unemployment, rural poverty, and far from decent living of the vast majority of the rural population, the issue of terms of trade perhaps needs to be reviewed, especially at this stage of development when the "logic" of industrialization in a single closed economy has lost its earlier significance.

The rural–urban income gap has grown alarmingly since the early 1990s.[21] The diverging trends of average consumption in rural and urban India remain explicit even after the rural–urban effect on consumption is neutralized using appropriate prices (NSSO 2005b, Report no. 505: Statement 3.9). The gap is not so much between the lowest 20 per cent in the rural and that in the urban areas as it is between the two groups of consumers in the upper class (see Figure 5.2). Region-wise, the rural–urban difference in MPCE is lowest in the agriculturally advanced states, namely Punjab (where urban as a proportion of rural MPCE is 112 per cent)and Haryana (119 per cent), while it is highest in agriculturally backward states like Jharkhand (239 per cent) and Orissa (211 per cent), or in industrial Maharashtra (221 per cent). Note, although the latter is industrially the most advanced state in India, the industrial sector appears to have a poor "trickle down" effect on per capita income in the state's rural economy.

Farmers' predicament

This must be an anxious moment for the farmers. With some variation across states, nearly 60 per cent of the rural households in India are engaged in farming activity (NSSO 2005a, Report no. 496).[22] Given the current situation, as noted earlier in Chapter 1, quite unexpectedly 60 per cent of the landowning agricultural households at the all-India level reported that they liked farming as a profession (ibid.). Those who did not like farming were asked the reasons for their disaffection. The group of 40 per cent who disliked farming include 27 per cent who did not find it profitable and 8 per cent who thought it was too risky. Only 2 per cent of all the farmers disliked farming because of its lack of social status.

Ironically, in states such as Andhra Pradesh, Kerala and Tamil Nadu where a much lower percentage of rural households are farmers as compared to the all-India average, a much larger proportion of farmer households expressed their willingness to continue with farming (Table 5.12). Perhaps, as other households left farming, the rising land–person ratio made agriculture more remunerative for the rest in these states. However, in such industrially developed states as Gujarat and Maharashtra the percentage of farmers "liking farming" is higher than the all-India average, indicating weaknesses of the pull factors. It is thus important to recognize that in such agriculturally advanced states as Punjab and Haryana a greater-than-average percentage of farmers are still willing to hang on to agriculture in spite of the fact that they face a price crash with every bumper crop – note, with the same input ratios, implying rigidity of the cost structure – followed by several incidences of farmer's suicide.

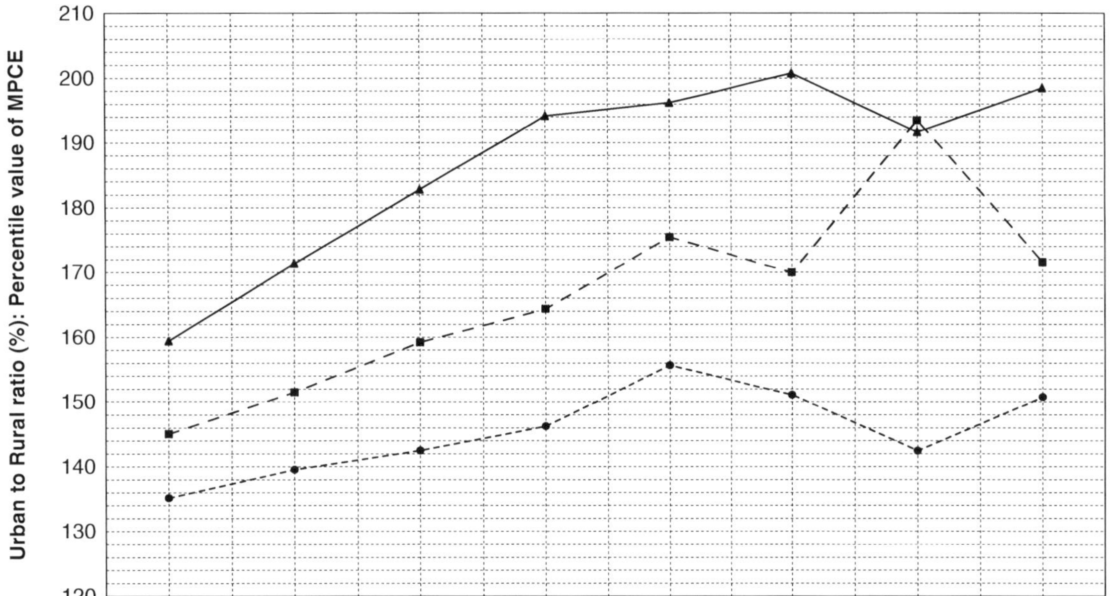

	1987-88	1993-94	1999-00	2000-01	2001-02	2002	2003	2004
20th percentile U/R ratio	135	140	142	146	156	151	142	151
50th percentile U/R ratio	145	151	159	164	175	170	193	172
80th percentile U/R ratio	159	171	183	194	196	201	192	198

Figure 5.2 Urban to rural ratio: percentile value of MPCE in India.
Source: Based on various NSSO Reports on MPCE.

Table 5.12 Farmers' decision on continuing with agriculture, in selected Indian states

State	*Percentage of farmer households*			
	Liking farming	*Not liking farming because*		
		Not profitable	*Risky*	*Other reasons*
Andhra Pradesh	76	17	5	2
Chhattisgarh	54	24	17	5
Bihar	49	36	11	4
Gujarat	67	26	5	2
Haryana	61	30	5	4
Jharkhand	53	30	9	8
Kerala	67	28	2	3
Maharashtra	61	29	7	3
Orissa	53	34	9	4
Punjab	62	28	2	8
Tamil Nadu	69	25	4	2
All-India	60	27	8	5

Source: Based on NSSO (2005a) Report no. 496.

In general, the lower the yield-rate, the higher is the propensity to quit farming, as is found in the revealed preference of the farmers in the relatively agriculturally backward states such as Bihar, Chhattisgarh, Jharkhand and Orissa. However, it is difficult to conclude straight away that farmers with lower labour productivity – because they use more animal power than diesel power to plough land – are more eager to quit agriculture.[23] Mechanization might replace human and animal power with tractors, harvesters and threshers thereby increasing the labour productivity, but its impact on land productivity is ambiguous. There must be complementary support from irrigation and credit infrastructure to efficiently utilize the available human power in cultivation in the agriculturally backward regions.

Conclusion

There is visible supply–demand imbalance in foodgrains, yet we find the paradox that growers, especially the smaller ones, are having tough times. The solution to the endless "dualism" lies in collectivization or cooperativization of small and marginal farming under the aegis of the state. One cannot overlook the "tragedy of the commons" (Hardin 1968) – i.e. in the case of commonly owned resources, each individual has the incentive to overuse the resources, regardless of what others do, thereby leading to the destruction of those resources. Only strong and appropriate intervention by the state could save the situation. There are examples of cooperative formation that have changed the face of rural India. The most striking of these is the Gujarat Cooperative Milk Marketing Federation (GCMMF, brand name "Amul"), an organization consisting of 2.7 million milk producers of 13,141 village societies, collecting 7.4 million litres of milk daily. In 2007–08, the sales turnover of Amul was US$1.32 billion. GCMMF is India's largest exporter of dairy products. It has been accorded a "trading house" status. However, this way of resolving the duality in Indian agriculture appears as utopia in the era of marked privatization that often takes the form of crony capitalism (as distinct from the "nanny state"). It is also very doubtful whether the "Wal-Mart mode" of leased farming and vertical integration, together with its highly unequal principal–agent exchange relations, has the capacity to change the backwardness of agrarian relations in the specific Indian setting.

The second-best solution is to have fair prices for agricultural produce so that the cultivators gain better entitlements to income as well as food security. Otherwise, agricultural labourers from the backward districts of Bihar would continue to migrate to, say, Punjab in crop seasons, depressing the agricultural wage rate in that state. Punjab agricultural workers subsequently would have to migrate to south Gujarat, and so on, generating circular flows of "local labour", since migrant workers are generally the easy prey. The outcome is agricultural backwardness in many respects, one of which is the convergence of agricultural wage in advanced regions to the wage in the most backward region. Perhaps improved terms of trade for agriculture would be having limited positive effects on the supply side owing to the barriers posed by the credit–output linkages of the private moneylenders, who together corner a substantial share of the harvest from the cultivators. A responsible government cannot shy away from the credit market. Still, the central question that has to be answered in the changed circumstances of deregulation is: who, within the farm sector, reaps the benefits from a rising farm price? This question is raised here because many of the Indian economists have long been arguing that a rise in farm price would actually strengthen the power of the rural rich who would then indulge in speculative trading and moneylending without any positive effect on output growth. But it is also the fact that the declining agriculture has been accompanied by unfavourable terms of trade during the last ten years. The trade-fetish might not be worried about it, but the prime development concern in the twenty-first century is human development.

As noted earlier, consumption inequality is generally much higher in the urban than in the rural areas and in the relatively industrialized states than in the laggard states. Moreover, since more than half of the labour force is dependent on agriculture in India, unless the question of inequality is addressed at the stage of development of the primary sector, the problem is most likely to spill over to the later stages of development with renewed intensity.

6 Trends in wage and earnings differentials

Global restructuring and inequality

Disparities in wages[1] and earnings are growing across countries. In a way, the phenomenon reflects upon the growing divergence between the labour value (as determined by the labour–time ratio) of a product and its price. In general, one has to appreciate the following changes in the global economy.

First, there is the relative increase in demand for skilled workers as a result of skill-biased technological changes. Automation, computerization and other technological advances change the ratio of fixed to working capital and create more demand for skilled workers in the process. This, coupled with the growing non-competitive output market, leads to divergence between value and price and thereby to wage/earnings inequality.

Second, blind adherence to trade liberalization and hence the enlarging traded sector of an economy has changed the value–price equilibrium by attracting capital as well as human resources away from the domestic non-traded sector, thereby shifting relative wages in favour of the export sector, irrespective of changes in the distribution of the skills-base of workers in different sectors. The latter actually varies according to the import intensity of an industry, especially if the imports of the intermediate and capital goods are from the North and are more technology-intensive or knowledge-intensive than those from the South.

Third, the static *comparative advantage* has in effect caused displacement of a section of workers from sectors that contract in the face of import competition, and also that are outsourced. *Outsourcing* from the North to the South has become symptomatic of globalization, loss of unionized jobs in the North, and wage losses. As the developing South has been attracting relatively low-skilled jobs from the North, the bargaining power of the low-skilled workers in the North has weakened, causing downward pressure on their wages. On the other hand, there is the self-defeating and endless pursuit among the underdeveloped countries to catch those jobs by offering a competitive wage. While many would agree that deregulated trade yields benefits to business and consumers, others endorse the theory that "freer trade costs more jobs than it creates". The outsourcing of decent jobs from the North to the countries in the South, where regular work-hours are not regulated, is destined to create proportionately fewer jobs in the world.

One worker working for 14–15 hours a day, in a offshore factory in China, India or Mexico, without overtime payments and social benefits, as against 7–8 hours of average daily regular work by a worker in the US or Europe, is tantamount to a reduction of nearly 50 per cent of the world gross "decent jobs". The labour market thus becomes volatile, while population growth rate is still positive.

The fourth source of growing earnings differentials is the shift in employment from goods-producing to service-producing industries (see, for the trend in the United States, Valletta 1997). In the services sector, the domestic help – say, the sweeper – on the one end, and the software architect on the other end of the distribution of earnings, boost up dispersion at a scale much higher than that within either industry or agriculture. The faster growth of the "dematerializing" financial service sector itself is a catalyst for increasing earnings differentials in the economy.

Finally, the trend toward monopoly pricing in varying degrees – depending on the eagerness of the purchasers to buy, and on their solvency – in different output markets leads to divergence between the *value* and the *price* (for details, see Sweezy 1946: Ch. 15). This results in distinctively different "capacities to pay" of the employers; the IT-based high-end industries are best examples. Moreover, monopoly pricing in one industry has a cascading effect in the downstream industries where circumstances are favourable to the establishment and maintenance of monopoly conditions. But there are other industries with a low ratio of fixed to working capital, and where firms are numerous, hence competitive conditions persist. These firms, on the one hand, are price-takers; on the other, they are constrained by the monopoly prices of intermediate goods. Naturally, wage depression is the only way out to survival in the market. Consequently, the inter-industry wage dispersion grows, apparently though it appears that the dispersion is caused by the capital intensity and resultant skills-level differential in different industries.

Thus it is no wonder that earnings inequality increased in almost all of the OECD countries, excepting Ireland and Spain, between 1995 and 2005. Most discernible is the dispersion between the 9th and 1st earnings deciles, although the OECD countries long ago became overwhelmingly service providers. The post-1995 phenomenon of further rise in inequality is therefore not adequately explained by the structural shifts alone.

Let us briefly examine the outliers in order to understand the factors that have raised inequality in the average OECD country. In Ireland, the ratio of 9th to 1st decile limits of earnings decreased from 4.01 in 1995 to 3.57 in 2005, while it decreased in Spain from 4.22 to 3.53 (OECD 2007: Table H). GDP grew at a rate greater than 5 per cent in Ireland between 1995 and 2005 – fastest among the OECD countries (World Bank, WDR 2006). Still significant is that it was not a "jobless" growth. Irish unemployment, which was the second highest (15.6 per cent) in the OECD as late as 1993, had fallen to 4.2 per cent in 2000, among the very lowest in OECD. The development since the mid-1990s has been led by a surge in inward investment in subsectors of the high-end services that took Ireland to the current position of the world's largest exporter of software. The tertiary sector constituted 55 per cent of Irish GDP, as against 52 per cent in India and 67 per cent in Spain, in 2004 (ibid.). Therefore, there were enough reasons for Ireland to experience growing inequality following the standard growth and development models.

The *Kuznets* inverted *U-curve* of earnings inequality lost its relevance in Ireland because, first, the employment rate for the least educated men grew noticeably. Also, the differential in employment rates declined after 1997: for women, employment at the bottom continued to grow quite strongly, and their disadvantage as compared to the most qualified stopped rising (Glyn 2005). Second, there was no minimum wage in Ireland till 2000. Once this was introduced during the boom period, the technology-induced wage differentials failed to aggravate; while employment was growing very rapidly, pay dispersion at the bottom declined. The implication is that the real wages at the bottom of the distribution grew a little faster than the average wage (ibid.). These together highlight the role of the national wage policy in mitigating earnings differentials. In fact, in Ireland, it was not only the ratio of 9th to 1st decile of earnings that declined, the ratio of 5th (median) to 1st earnings decile also went down, implying reduced differentials between the low-skilled and medium-skilled; or, maybe, between the manual and the semi-knowledge workers (like those in the BPOs).

Similarly, in Spain, employment has shown a higher rate of growth than in the rest of Europe from the start of the economic recovery of the mid-1990s (Llorente 2005). In 1995, the earnings dispersion in Spain – measured by the ratio of 9th to 1st decile limits of earnings – was highest among the OECD European countries, and was next to that in the United States. However, in the next ten years, not only the dispersion between the latter two deciles declined but the dispersion between the 5th and 1st earnings deciles also declined substantially. Studies have highlighted the role of the active labour market policies[2] in reducing the earnings differentials in Spain, where the trade union movement has a low presence in the world of work – trade union density is 19 per cent – and where, to note, the labour force is characterized by comparatively lower educational attainment (ibid.).

On the whole, the hypothesis that the formation of skills is based on formal education, and that the consequent demand for them leads to growing inequality, has only limited explanatory capacity. Despite globalization, technological change, and the structural shifts from goods-producing to services-producing in some of the countries in the developed North, the earnings differentials between the low-skilled and the semi-skilled or skilled workforce are found to have reduced primarily owing to the *active* labour market policies that are in disagreement with neoliberalism.

In fact, one has to look deeper into the *nature* of wealth creation, which consequently determines the nature of its distribution. Quite often the stability in the *Gini* inequality in India (the coefficient is around 0.34) and its lesser magnitude than in China (which is somewhere between 0.38 and 0.47) are cited as an indicator of inclusiveness and comparatively more egalitarian Indian economic growth and development. The following sections will also delve into the critical reasons for the observed *stability* of the aggregate inequality coefficient.

India: inter-personal distribution

The compound rate of growth of per capita consumer expenditure between 1993 and 2005 is found to be 6.2 per cent per annum for the high-income and 4.3 per cent for the middle-income earners, as mentioned earlier in Chapter 1. By contrast, the rate of growth of consumption of the combined group of the extremely poor,[3] poor[4] and marginal[5] had been less than one per cent (NCEUS 2007). In other words, the consumption expenditure grew at an average rate of 5 per cent for the 253 million middle and high income people, while for the 444 million people at the bottom the growth was not even 1 per cent. Obviously, the gulf between the earnings (albeit consumption) of the bottom 41 per cent and the upper 23 per cent of the population has been widening. Further, the *vulnerable*[6] expenditure class expanded from 290 million to 392 million (which is about 36 per cent of the population), and their MPCE grew at the rate of 2.8 per cent a year between 1993–94 and 2004–05. These are the disaggregated trends in earnings/consumption in a nutshell.

If we consider consumption inequality as surrogate for earnings inequality, and assume (a) wages/earnings are determined by the levels of skills,[7] and (b) there is a national average level of skills,[8] then the bottom 41 per cent of the population constitutes, so to speak, the low-skilled, the "middle" and the "vulnerable", as against 55 per cent being the semi-skilled[9] and the upper 4 per cent of the population the high-skilled workforce of the economy. We begin with this preliminary understanding of the distribution of wage/earnings, and safely conclude that, notwithstanding the growing consumption dispersion between the skilled and the low-skilled, the relatively high weightage of the middle category, i.e. semi-skilled, in the total workforce prevents the overall inequality in the economy from growing. In other words, the aggregate inequality coefficient hides more than it reveals; because of the sheer relative size of each of the skill categories. We then move on to examining the inter-personal distribution within each of the categories, and supplement the trends with inter-sectoral distribution as we find diverging trends of labour productivity in agriculture, industry and services (*cf.* Table 4.5).

Within agriculture

The rise in wage rate in the agricultural sector decelerated between 1993 and 2004, especially when compared to the rise during the 10-year period between 1983 and 1993. Wage dispersion has also been reducing. The 25th to 50th percentile ratio of wage rates declined from 1.5 to 1.4, and that of the 25th to 75th percentile declined from 2 to 1.9 between 1983 and 2004 (Abraham 2007: Table 10).[10] In other words, the sector is gradually approaching a homogenization of "skills", so to speak, missing out capitalist differentiation in spite of the growing penetration of advanced agricultural implements.

Within the organized industrial sector

A. Different earnings trajectories

The real wage in the factory sector, on the whole, increased by 20 per cent between 1974 and 1992. Thereafter, it slowed down to 12 per cent in the late 1990s.[11] There were substantial declines in the rate of growth of wage in relatively capital-intensive industries such as electrical machinery, prime movers and boilers, castings and forgings (ferrous) and petroleum refineries. In general, over the last two decades, the increase in wage rate decelerated in the high-wage industries at a rate higher than in the rest (Banerjee 2005: Ch. 4).

The real (paid) *minimum* wage,[12] industry-wise, declined in the 1980s over the previous decade – irrespective of capital intensity of the industry – in matches, tyre and tubes, cashewnuts processing, silk textiles, iron and steel, electrical accessories, and bicycle parts and assemblage, with the largest decline being in tyre and tubes. In the 1990s, wages in this group of industries marginally improved, perhaps because of rising exports, while a new set of industries emerged as the losers, most significant among these being the relatively capital-intensive industries such as electrical machinery, prime movers and boilers, castings and forgings (ferrous) and motor vehicles, i.e. the industries that faced competitive imports from abroad. So far as the *maximum* (real) wage is concerned, there was an average increase of about 18 per cent during the 1980s, followed by a decline of 4 per cent in the 1990s. Industry-wise, the maximum wage rates declined in both the 1980s and the 1990s in mass consumer goods sectors such as textile garments, footwear, bicycle, tyre and tubes, electrical accessories, and in such industries as motor vehicles. This is paradoxical to the post-1991 structural adjustment-induced economic prosperity: the mass of consumers expanded but perhaps the effective demand for mass articles declined. Alternatively, it could be a decline in the bargaining strength of workers in these industries.

B. Inter-occupational wage differentials

On the whole, occupation-wise, real wage increased for some and declined for most – neither increase nor decrease strictly followed the skill scale. The *coefficient of variation* (*cov*) of daily wage rates of different occupations in an industry gives a fair idea as to occupational distinctiveness in the labour market. A measure of occupational wage differentials in each of the 34 industries shows, for all the industries together, that the occupational wage differential at the *entry level* – measured by *cov* of minimum wage for different occupations – remained fairly stable over the last three decades of the twentieth century,[13] raising doubts about the varying demand for different skills categories in the aftermath of trade liberalization. On the other hand, the *cov* of *maximum* wage narrowed down,[14] indicating the narrowing inter-occupational wage gaps, at the upper end of the wage ladder where (a) the labour market is practically an *internal* one, and (b) the worker by this time has accumulated skills through job experience in the technology-determined specific labour process.

C. Capital intensity and inter-occupational wage differentials

The industries that were already capital intensive, requiring skilled workers and having a low wage share in the 1970s – such as motor vehicles, electrical industrial machinery, castings and forgings (ferrous), prime movers and boilers, and machine tools – and had undergone a slower automation subsequently, did not show similar trends of wage differential. The differential went up further in the 1980s and 1990s in motor vehicles and prime movers, while it declined in electrical industrial machinery and in castings and forgings (ferrous). In the machine tools industry the differential increased further in the 1980s, but declined thereafter in the 1990s. In sum, there seems to have been wage convergence in this group of industries.

D. Intra-occupational wage differentials

The narrowing vertical distance between occupations notwithstanding, the horizontal gaps – i.e. disparities in intra-occupational earnings (including wages, bonuses, overtime payments etc.) – increased in the 1990s. In the 1980s, in 29 out of the 34 groups of industries, the dispersion across individual daily earnings (all occupations) narrowed down in comparison with the 1970s. In the 1990s, the trend reversed in 19 industries, i.e. there was growing inequality, maybe because of the varying growth rate of the traded and non-traded sectors. In labour-intensive mining, wage disparities reduced during the last three decades, largely because of the significant presence of public enterprises in the sector.

Daily earnings inequality in industries having a relatively high share of exports to outputs – e.g. in castings and forgings, textile garments, woollen textiles, and glass and glass products – has declined. However, the experience is different in other export-oriented industries such as cotton textiles, cashewnuts processing etc. In the engineering industries, in general, wage dispersion increased in the 1990s as compared to the previous decade.[15]

In general, intra-occupational wage inequality between the top and bottom 10 per cent of workers increased. The all-industry average ratio of daily earnings of the 90th to 10th percentile earners (overall, for men and women together) was 2.04 during the 1970s. Thereafter, it declined to 1.98 in the 1980s, followed however by an increase to 2.12 in the 1990s. Moreover, the gender wage gap (measured as the ratio of median earnings of male workers to female workers) has increased. In those industries where the variation in daily earnings tended to increase, the overall ratio of 90th to 10th percentile for all workers (men and women together) was higher than that for male workers alone.

Intra-occupational wage disparity in textile garments, an important export industry, reduced alongside a substantial decline in wage inequality ratio in the 1980s and 1990s. However, the daily earnings inequality for male workers was lower than the overall inequality in the industry. This in fact reflects the growing gender inequality in earnings, with female workers constituting more than half of the total workforce engaged in the industry. Similar trends are found in footwear, cotton textiles and silk textiles, among others, i.e. in the relatively low technology intensive but export industries. The mining sector and petroleum refineries, being mostly in the public sector and abiding by certain norms of wage payments, exhibit less dispersion in wages of males and females.

E. Blue-collar versus white-collar

In Great Britain, the lower grades of British clerks were in the per annum earnings range of £75 to £150 between 1850 and 1880. Only some 10 to 15 per cent of the blue-collar workers of the time were in that same range of pay, and they were described as ‘highly select super aristocracy’ (Lockwood 1958: 28). In the United States, in 1900, clerical employees of steam railroads and in manufacturing establishments had average annual earnings of $1,011. In the same year, the average annual earnings of workers in these industries were less than half of that: $435 for manufacturing, and $548 for steam railroads (Fleisher 1970: 219). Since then, the relative pay scales have undergone radical changes. By the beginning of the 1970s, the usual median weekly wage for full-time clerical work in the US fell below the wage for every type of blue-collar work (Braverman 1974: 297–8; Flaim and Peters 1972). In Great Britain too the trend has been similar: by the 1950s, i.e. at the peak of industrial capitalism, the average white-collar worker became used to an income level equal to if not less than that of the average blue-collar worker (Lockwood 1958).

By contrast, in India, with regard to the occupational divisions between blue- and white-collar workers, the salary-wage dispersion in the industrial sector began to increase in the early 1990s when the “postindustrial” deepened (see Figure 6.1). The wage premium of the college graduates over the high school passed is rather a weak explanation for the economy as a whole, as the real wage is found to have been falling in non-ICT (information and communication technology) manufacturing for either college graduates or high school passed, and rising for both the groups in ICT manufacturing (Sarkar and Mehta 2007). There is of course no reason to believe that ICT manufacturing is superior to non-ICT manufacturing across the board.

On the whole, in the industrial sector, we don’t find a secular and rising trend of wage/earnings inequality despite India’s growing integration into the global market. Even where inequality has been rising, standard explanations are found to be grossly inadequate.

Services sector

Unlike agriculture and industry, wage dispersion has considerably increased in that part of the services sector which, first, has adopted ICT more intensively,

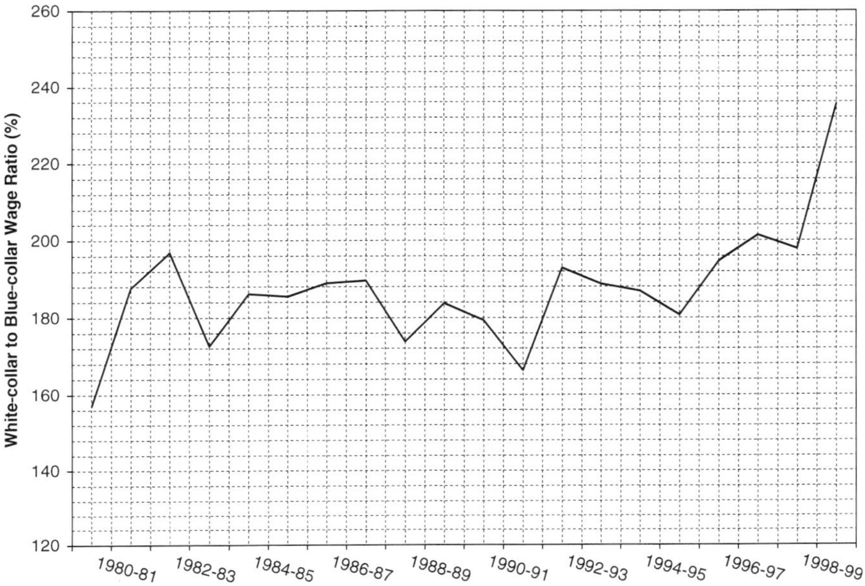

Figure 6.1 Indian organized manufacturing: ratio of white-collar to blue-collar wages, 1980–81 to 1999–2000.
Source: Computed from CSO, *Annual Survey of Industries*.

such as in financing, insurance and business services, and where, secondly, the government has a greater role to play, i.e. in community, social and personal services. In trade, hotels and restaurant – predominantly a private domain and proliferating at a greater scale – the ratio of 25th to 50th percentile of wage rates remained the same in 2004 as it was two decades earlier. Moreover, the ratio of 25th to 75th percentile declined in the latter subsector (Table 6.1). In the subsector of transport, storage and communication, which combines high (e.g. ICT) and low technologies, the ratio of 25th to 50th percentile declined between 1983 and 2004, while the dispersion between 25th and 75th percentiles increased considerably.

Table 6.1 Wage dispersion in the Indian services sector, 1983 to 2004

Subsector	*Ratio of 25th to 50th percentile*		*Ratio of 25th to 75th percentile*	
	1983	*2004*	*1983*	*2004*
Trade, hotels and restaurants	1.5	1.5	2.3	2.2
Transport, storage and communication	1.7	1.5	2.4	3.0
Financing, insurance, real estate and business services	1.5	2.4	2.1	4.9
Community, social and personal services	2.0	2.9	3.0	5.7

Source: Abraham (2007), as based on NSS unit level data.

By comparison, in finance and business services, and in social and personal services, the wage/earnings dispersion not only increased over the years but also is quite high on average. Particularly noteworthy is the ratio of 25th to 75th percentile, which was 4.9 in the finance and business services, and even greater (i.e. 5.7) in the social and personal services, in 2004. Also, the inequality between workers/ employees has grown over the last two decades. There are reasons to believe that this trend will continue to move upwardly with the shift in emphasis from the sphere of production to the sphere of distribution, in the economy.

The central government recently hiked the pay by at least 21 per cent at one go for its 5 million employees. The revised pay scales were to take effect (as and when implemented) from 1 January 2006 and the revised rates of allowances from 1 September 2008. The annual salary bill of the central government was pushed up by at least US$4.16 billion following the implementation of these changes. Added to these was an arrears payment amounting to almost US$6.86 billion. The budget deficit target for 2008–09 would be exceeded and serious fiscal risks were arising from growing off-budget liabilities, estimated at 5 per cent of GDP. At one stroke, the wage/earnings distribution in India further heightened the prevailing bias against lower percentiles.[16] As a spiraling effect, in the next round, all the state governments would implement similar pay packets for their employees and teachers in schools, colleges and universities and thus widen the earnings inequality yet again in the economy. Only a part of these sections of job-holders can claim to have investments in "embodied technology" and the status of knowledge worker.[17]

Wage differentials grow at a faster rate when technology becomes *embodied* – IT, especially, differs from the rest of the jobs in this respect – than when it is *disembodied* (Banerjee 2006),[18] as because increasing the productivity of knowledge workers seems to be far more difficult to achieve than previous productivity breakthroughs for blue-collar and agricultural workers. Thus the incentive structure is disproportional compared to others. Revolutions so far were all about sustained productivity growth in the creation of tangible products by improving the efficiency of tangible production techniques: "speed up the assembly line, the productivity of the workers would automatically increase" was the earlier method. This is, however, not applicable in economic activities based on embodied technology. The supposed breakthrough of the Information Age hinges more on an intangible knowledge-based product, which is largely the result of an equally intangible human thought process, which explains in large part the growing tangible incentives to the latter (Roach 1998). But this should not be misconstrued as a justification for the complete and unqualified rise in the earnings of the government employees, and the growing dispersion between the lower and upper deciles of the employees, especially in the background of the experience in Ireland, in particular, in recent times.

ICT services sector

Real wages/earnings have increased at a much faster rate in the IT-producing sector – i.e. at the CAGR of 5.1 per cent between 1999 and 2004 – than those in other segments of the formal or organized ICT-based services sector. Moreover, in the private ICT services sector the rate of increase in wage/earnings has been faster (i.e. 4.7 per cent) than in either the public (3.1 per cent) or the corporate sector (4 per cent), in general.

The productivity growth in the core ICT-using sectors (say, in software), where labour input tends to be cerebral and much more difficult to replace with a machine, is much slower than in ICT manufacturing (say, computer hardware). As soon as ICT is adopted in an enterprise one would find a leap forward in productivity, but it subsequently flattens and remains flat for a considerable period of time until the next cycle of rise begins. The Hicks–Marshall prototype of capital–labour substitution is thus inapplicable in the knowledge economy. The limitations on boosting the cerebral efficiency of the knowledge worker have made it extremely difficult to raise their hourly productivity on a sustained basis. Yet one finds a faster rise in wage in this sector than in the rest of the economy; perhaps *monopoly* conditions apply.

Real wage in the organized non-ICT services sector declined at the CAGR of 1.2 per cent between 1999 and 2004. But it should be noted that the rate of decline in the latter was higher than that in non-ICT manufacturing (Sarkar and Mehta 2007).[19] Further, in the *informal* non-ICT services, the decline was at the rate of 4.2 per cent. In other words, the shift of the economy toward the services sector did result in higher earnings, but only selectively, not in general.

Within the Indian ICT sector there has been a rapid employment shift from ICT goods-producing to ICT service-producing. Whatever employment growth has taken place in the ICT goods-producing sector has been mostly in the informal or unorganized sector, whereas IT and IT enabled services (ITes) employment has grown mostly in the organized sector, i.e. in relatively large establishments (Sarkar and Mehta 2007). This was followed by rapid increase at the CAGR of 5.1 per cent in wages/earnings of the ICT-based formal services employees. By contrast, in the informal sector, wages in the ICT-based services *declined* at the rate of 2.9 per cent. Unless we assume that the services in the formal and informal sectors are qualitatively different, the argument favouring wage differentiation due to embodied technology falls flat in the specific Indian conditions. Either the supply conditions of labour turn out to be the determining factor, or the costs of on-the-job training – which is negligible in the informal sector – get reflected in the differential pay packets. It may so happen also that the market share matters for a firm to determine employees' share in the total earnings irrespective of their knowledge endowments, in which respect the informal sector enterprises are at a disadvantageous position. In the end, the "island" of wage growth comprises about 2.75 million workers in the ICT sector, which is barely 0.65 per cent of the total employment in the country.

Summary

When compared with the rate of changes in wages in the manufacturing sector, two conclusions emerge: (a) the degree of dispersion is higher within the services sector than in the goods-producing sector; and (b) dispersion between these two sectors is growing, measured in terms of mean wage. But is the dispersion uniform across earnings distribution or greater in the lower half of the distribution?

On the whole, real wage (at 2004–05 prices) in the formal manufacturing sector (excluding ICT-related manufacturing) declined at the CAGR of 1.7 per cent between 1999 and 2004. The decline had been higher in the informal manufacturing (non-ICT) sector – at 7.2 per cent.[20] Therefore, the wage/earnings gap between formal and informal manufacturing has been widening.

Active labour market policy is, however, found to have a positive impact on wages. In the public-sector manufacturing enterprises, wages/earnings (at 2004–05 prices) increased disproportionately on average between 1999 and 2004. While in the other-than-ICT public-sector manufacturing enterprises wages increased at the CAGR of 2.8 per cent, those in the private sector *declined* at the rate of 5.1 per cent. The Indian private corporate sector also followed a *wage squeeze*, as reflected in the decline of real wage/earnings by 2.4 per cent.

Presumably, the technology-intensive sector has a relatively greater demand for higher educated and skilled workers/employees, and this should be reflected in the entry-level wages. However, with a different (from OWS) database, i.e. NSS unit level data, it is found that the ICT workers are not differentiated from the non-ICT workers at the entry level (Sarkar and Mehta 2007). The divergence between these two groups becomes visible only at the middle level of career. This is because, when technology is disembodied, the type of industry – ICT, petrochemicals or automobiles – makes no difference to the entry-level wage. On-the-job training does improve the skills of the workers/employees as appropriate to the specific production lines, leading to inter-industry wage differentials at the middle level. The *scale* of difference is given by the costs and duration of in-job training (or, re-skilling); the higher the costs, the greater are the wages, often in order to reduce the attrition rate.

Thus, at the more concrete level, we are confronted with more conflicting situations. The wage and productivity gap in the factory sector as a whole has been growing – i.e. workers are not compensated for productivity gains. Naturally, the distribution of manufacturing income disfavours wage, the inter-industry wage differentials are not stable, inter-occupational wage gaps are reducing and intra-occupational wage differentials growing. Thus the simple narratives based on technology and trade are inadequate to explain the discouraging trends in wages in India. Technological change, leading to skills mismatch between jobs and workers, is not an adequate explanation for the recent trends. Direct measurement of technological change is having a hard time accounting for changes in wages and employment.

Inter-sectoral distribution

Suppose l_a, l_i and l_s are employment and w_a, w_i and w_s the wage rates in agriculture, industry and services sectors, respectively, and L is the aggregate employment in the economy. Then, the wage-share of each of the sectors is: $w_a \frac{l_a}{L}, w_i \frac{l_i}{L}$ and $w_s \frac{l_s}{L}$. When $\frac{l_a}{L} = \frac{l_i}{L} = \frac{l_s}{L}$ and $w_a = w_i = w_s$, the society can be called egalitarian or democratic. Along with economic growth and development, however, the latter society generates disequilibrium. When $\frac{l_a}{L} > \frac{l_i}{L} > \frac{l_s}{L}$ and $w_a < w_i < w_s$, the economy becomes lopsided. Overall inequality in wage/earnings in the economy thus could also be measured in terms of inter-sector distribution using two variables, namely (a) sectoral employment share and (b) wage rate in different sectors. In the end, it provides a better understanding of the dynamics of the economy when put alongside the productivity curve of each of the sectors.

As the employment share of the agricultural sector declined from 69 per cent of the national total in 1981 to 58 per cent in 2004, the proportion of low-wage–low-skilled workforce in the national total also became smaller. As noted earlier, the declining combined share of, the extremely poor, poor and marginally poor in the total population – from 50 per cent in 1993 to 46 per cent in 1999, and further to 41 per cent in 2004 – is the corollary of such a change in economic structure. Hence, overall earnings inequality seems to have declined proportionately as the earnings share of the tail-end workforce in the total earnings in the country has been declining. Briefly, the structural shift away from low-wage agriculture presumably has a sinking effect on the overall earnings inequality.

The share of manufacturing in aggregate employment has been declining too since the early 1980s. The number of workers as well as the total persons employed tended to decline after 1996 in the organized factory sector. The (real) wage-bill in organized manufacturing, after reaching a peak in the mid-1990s, tended to decline, and has virtually stagnated since 1999 (see Figure 6.2). The real wage rate itself moved downward (see Figure 6.3). Moreover, relative to the national average, the labour productivity in the industrial sector – organized and unorganized sectors taken together – has been declining, like agriculture (*cf.* Table 4.5). Thus there might be technical improvements here and there but not in the industrial economy as a whole so as to tilt the balance of relative wage shares in favour of industry.

The casualization and informalization of the organized factory workers, together with proportionately greater employment growth in the labour-intensive export sector – garments, gems and jewellery, leather etc. – whether in the informal or the organized sector, determines wage redistribution. Since the mid-1990s the growth in manufacturing as well as industrial employment has been wholly in the unorganized sector, which is an open labour market for nearly 93 per cent of the Indian manufacturing workforce. Their wages are not protected by any active labour market policy while labour supply to this market is unhindered at the prevailing wage rate. In fact, the declining rate of real wage at 7 per cent plus went hand in hand with a *positive* rate of employment growth in the unorganized manufacturing sector between 1999 and 2004.

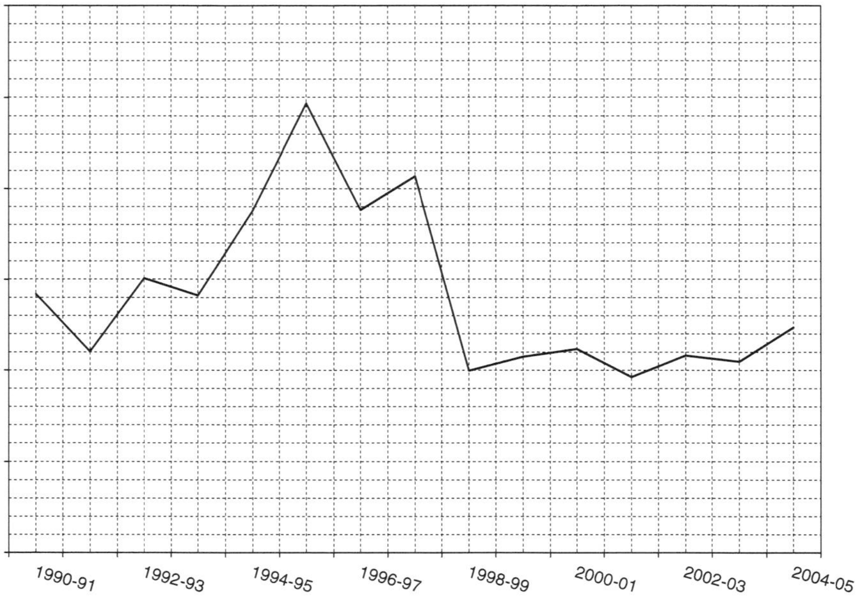

Figure 6.2 Trend in real wage-bill in the Indian organized factory sector, 1990 to 2004.
Source: Computed from CSO, *Annual Survey of Industries* (ASI).
Note: Yearly nominal wage-bills for the factory workers as available in CSO, ASI are deflated by the consumer price index (for workers) at base 1982 = 100.

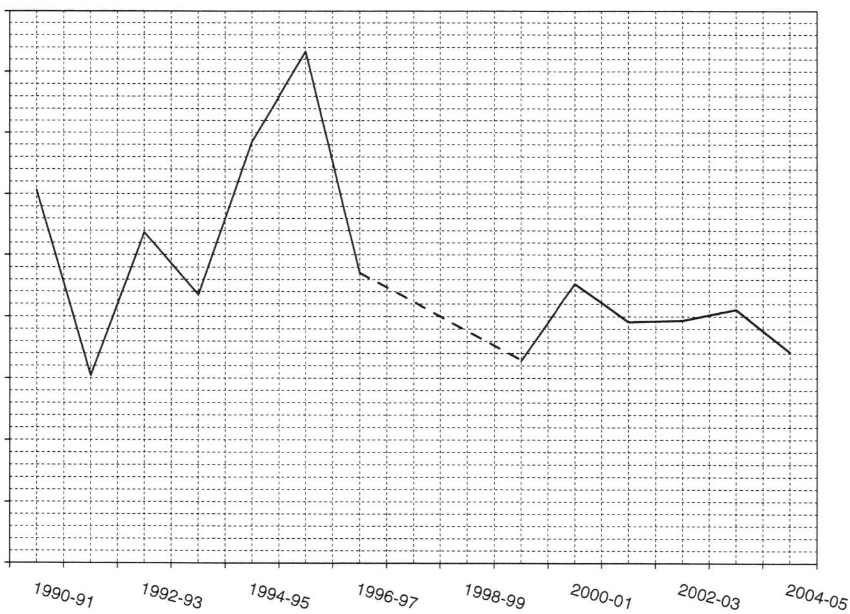

Figure 6.3 Trend in real wage rate (per person-day) in the Indian organized factory sector, 1990 to 2004.
Source: Computed from CSO, *Annual Survey of Industries*.

As a result, as the productivity gap between agriculture and industry has been closing, the wage/earnings *gap* between the sectors has reduced. To corroborate, the manufacturing wage was 2.4 times the agricultural wage in 1983. It remained almost the same during the following ten years. However, in 2004, the ratio was found to have declined to 1.9 (Abraham 2007: Table 10).[21] As a whole, the relative weight of the industrial sector in the national earnings distribution has been declining, thus restricting the overall inequality from growing.

Shifts from goods-producing to service-producing jobs

Studies based on the US data on earnings and employment demonstrate that service-producing jobs pay less than goods-producing jobs (see e.g. Blackburn 1990; Valletta 1997). The average earnings are lower – but earnings inequality higher – in service-producing jobs than in goods-producing jobs. And, for both reasons, an increasing share of service employment in the national total may increase earnings inequality. Also, based on the trend of earnings inequality in the United States, studies suggest that the shift from goods to services would lead to a declining middle class (Bluestone and Harrison 1982, 1988). In India, there is a significant and growing shift from goods-producing to service-producing economy, notwithstanding the size of the middle income group. The middle expenditure class (2PL to 4PL) increased from 15.5 per cent of the aggregate in 1993 to 16.7 per cent in 1999 and further to 19.3 per cent in 2004 (NCEUS 2007). Of course, the increasing wage differential between the white-collared and blue-collared workers in the Indian organized manufacturing gives us a hint. But that is only a partial explanation so long as the larger part of the middle class is employed in the services sector.

Most of the new jobs created in the Indian tertiary sector during the last couple of decades are in the low-skills category.[22] Presumably, the mean earnings in the jobs that are backed by the stipulated and also effective minimum wages would be higher than the rest at the lower end of the earnings distribution. As it stands, the average daily earnings of about 61 per cent of the casual workers in urban manufacturing were below the national minimum wage in 2004–05. Similarly, the average daily earnings of 68 per cent in trade and related sectors, and 73 per cent in "education, health, other services, etc.", are found to be lower than the respective national average (NCEUS 2007: Table A3.2). Therefore, the *difference* in mean earnings due to different standards of minimum wages in the industry and services is negligible and does not have much statistical significance.

Further, the government-stipulated minimum wages in the services sector might have reduced wage differentials, but at the lower end of the distribution. However, the *standard deviation* of earnings in the services sector as a whole has increased with the increasing proportion of knowledge workers in the sector. Most noteworthy is the radical increase in the standard deviation of the mean earnings in the services subsectors of "finance" and "personal services" (see Table 6.1). High mean earnings of the knowledge workers and the consequent high standard deviation in the services sector have tended to make earnings distribution more skewed in the whole of the economy, though the relative weights of the other two sectors have tended to neutralize the effect.

The future

Taking into account diverse factors, the rapid growth of the Indian middle class, unlike the trend in the United States, needs an explanation. Prima facie, more than 81 per cent of this expenditure class consists of organized-sector workers who are beneficiaries of the various labour and employment rules and regulations. But there is evidence that a large part of this expenditure (or income) group have been losing in terms of wage/earnings as those rules and regulations are becoming *de facto* ineffective. On the other hand, the retail equity investor base reached 3.5 million individuals in 2007. These individuals were directly buying equities on their own behalf. When those investing indirectly through either mutual funds or unit-linked insurance plans are included, the total estimated number of individuals participating in equity markets in 2007 turned out to be 8 million. In addition, a large part of "transfer incomes", namely public resources allocated to various social welfare projects and implemented through decentralized administration or the *Panchayati Raj* institution, are getting siphoned off by the local elites, political as well as social, thereby burgeoning the "middle class" (see various CAG Reports, in particular). While the size and prosperity of the stock-market-dependent middle class might tumble down with volatility in the market, the Keynesian remedies for stabilization would keep the avenue of prosperity of the middle class wide open.

In brief, inter-personal earnings distribution is an attribute of the social division of labour in the economy. There is, however, a loophole: a few segments in the *middle* of the distribution remain unexplained by the usual economic processes of prosperity. The huge "black income" generated as a result of execrable governance in various pockets of the economy plugs the loophole.

Besides, four major changes on the cards are likely to have deeper impact on the current trend in wage dispersions. First, significant agricultural (labour) productivity gaps between India and most of the OECD countries as well as Argentina constitute a threat to work and livelihood of the Indian cultivators. Once the trade barriers to imports of foodgrains are removed following the current negotiations in the WTO, agricultural wages in India, *ceteris paribus*, are likely to decline. A significant out-migration of the agricultural workforce to the sectors overseas having higher *mean* earnings is not within the realms of possibility.

Second, the technological backwardness of small-scale industry (SSI) – the lifeline of most of the industrial workforce – has been paying a heavy toll in the aftermath of deregulation. Domestic large and medium industries are sourcing their inputs through cheaper imports. There were an estimated 4.4 million SSI units employing nearly 23.8 million in 2007–08.[23] As a result of the deceleration that the SSI sector has been witnessing, the number of units in the sector has reduced to around 4 million and employment generation has shrunk to 22.5 million workers, leading to a decline of about 10 per cent in the contribution of SSI to manufacturing value added as well as a 7–8 per cent decline in exports. These are *net* losses of the economy to the world outside. The downward trend would continue until and unless the SSI credit policy is changed in a manner that could induce technological upgrading in the sector. Till then, the earnings disparity in the economy would grow, because the weight of the SSI is much larger than that of the large and medium industries taken together.

Third, once foreign direct investment (FDI) in the retail sector for multi-brand products is opened up alongside already approved FDI in retail for single brand, there would be a huge loss of employment in the traditional sector, although the wage gains in the sunrise sector are ambiguous. Global retail giants such as Wal-Mart, Tesco, Kingfisher, Carrefour and Royal Ahold, along with Indian corporate houses, are gradually making inroads into the retail arena. Currently, there are 25 million or more employed in retail trade in India (CSO, *Economic Census* 2005). Also, retailing is probably the primary form of disguised employment or underemployment in the country. It is almost certain that most of these retail businesses would not be able to compete with the highly computerized world retail chains.[24] If oligopoly capital-driven retailers were to take 20 per cent of the Indian retail trade there would be a job loss of more than 5 million persons employed in the unorganized retail sector. Creation of new jobs would amount to a tiny proportion of the total jobs lost in the process. And the changed occupational categories of the new jobs would render most of the job-losers unemployable in these retail chains. This makes the retail business dissimilar to, say, the BPO services, where *net* additional jobs are created in spite of the shift of "place" of the services from one form of organization to another.

In a startling econometric exercise on poverty in the United States, it comes out that – holding constant the initial (1989) poverty rate – counties with more Wal-Mart stores in 1987 had a higher poverty rate in 1999 (or a smaller reduction in the rate) than did counties with fewer or no Wal-Mart stores in 1987 (Goetz and Swaminathan 2004). Equally noticeable is that counties in which new Wal-Mart stores were built between 1987 and 1998 also experienced higher poverty rates, *ceteris paribus*. But how does Wal-Mart affect county poverty rates? First, the retail workers displaced from existing mom-and-pop-type stores because of "low-wage Wal-Mart" have no alternatives. Second, Sam Walton Foundation's philanthropy may not be as extensive or effective as that which the displaced mom-and-pop stores would have provided. A third and perhaps more subtle effect may be that, by destroying the local class of entrepreneurs, the Wal-Mart chain also destroys local leadership capacity as well as reducing social capital levels locally (ibid.). This is a lesson which corroborates the hypothesis (as pointed out in Chapter 1) on the pitfalls of "increasing returns to scale" in the absence of corrective public policy measures.

Finally, in India, with the growing weightlessness of the economy – i.e. an ever-increasing proportion of capital transcending to the "friction free world" – capital moved largely from the sphere of production to the sphere of distribution before the former attained a critical stage. This is seen not just in the distribution of commodities but also in the distribution of income and wealth. Therefore, in the future, an ever-increasing proportion of aggregate earnings would be accumulated in the upper deciles of the distribution, resulting in increased dispersion.

To conclude, explanations pertaining to the discipline of economics of the visible trends in wage/earnings dispersion are grossly partial. For a comprehensive account, one perhaps cannot overlook the politics of relations between the state, capital and workforce, which certainly has not transcended traditional boundaries (of coercion) to liberal democracy (of productivity-wage economic and social relationships) that the EDCs had experienced in the late nineteenth century and until the mid-1970s. Notwithstanding this, all of a sudden the *relations* in India embraced neoliberalism, prompting a minimal role of governance, which gave rise to several asymmetries between distribution of wage/ earnings and the social division of labour in the economy.

7 Development as governance

More evidence from the social sector

Why governance?

Many countries in the world with a similar time-trend of investment ratio have been experiencing different GDP growth rates. A positive coefficient on the contemporaneous investment ratio in a growth regression may reflect the positive relation between growth opportunities and investment rather than the positive effect of an exogenously higher investment ratio on the growth rate. This reverse effect is especially likely to apply for open economies (Barro 1997: 32–3). It is also on record that the radical changes in property relations (e.g. in many socialist countries) have not produced economic growth as distinct from the capitalist economies, except for a very brief period. Governance, similarly to investment, is a critical input in growth. It is important to recognize that even if global capitalism is a single genus, it becomes a distinct species in each specific country, depending on the latter's specific history of development that is inseparable from the history of governance. Japanese capitalism, US capitalism or, for that matter, Scandinavian capitalism have distinguishing features of capital and labour relations. In other words, all the developed countries have distinct social structures of accumulation; the relative substantive representation of various class forces in the state and its various institutions and organizations influences the processes.[1]

Governance ultimately is about creating positive externalities. To elaborate, Adam Smith's system of "natural liberty" refers to political and economic freedom, but within a set of rules supported by public intervention and public institutions. The classical economists, while highlighting the virtues of the market as an allocating instrument, also indicated the demerits of the free play of self-interested economic agents. People are at times unable to see their own best interests or to take adequate care of them, thereby justifying certain paternalistic actions by government. Hence there is the need for workplace safety regulations, health regulations and so on, and, of course, various restrictions on freedom of contract (Sidgwick 1887).[2] There are many instances in which private enterprises will not provide goods and services owing to their inability to appropriate sufficient returns to justify the investment (ibid.). Sidgwick stood with John Stuart Mill – a staunch advocate for *laissez faire* and freedom of individuals who, at the same time, was aware of drawbacks and disadvantages of the government – in contending that governmental corrective actions could counter many of the negative effects of self-interested behaviour when self-interested agents fail to take into account the full social impact of their activities (Medema 2003).

The analysis of the potential for market failure by Sidgwick gained strength as Pigou examined: 'how far the free play of self-interest, acting under the existing legal system, tends to distribute the country's resources in the way most favourable to the production of a large national dividend, and how far it is feasible for State action to improve upon "natural" tendencies' (Pigou 1932: xii). In the end, the Pigovian welfare analysis demonstrated that perfect markets work perfectly, imperfect markets work imperfectly, and perfect government can cause imperfect markets to also function perfectly. The inefficiencies of both market and government in a given set of circumstances have become the focus in later days, following Ronald Coase's argument that the divergence between private and social costs occurred owing to the failure of government to assign rights over the resources in question and that, once such rights were assigned, externalities would be efficiently resolved through negotiation (Coase 1960).

In India, most of the reports on human development have taken the "administrative state" as the unit of comparison, plotted the scatter, and come up with conflicting conclusions on the relationship between per capita income (or economic prosperity) and selected indices of human development. Since most of the Indian states broadly share the same structure of economy, what distinguishes one from another with respect to human development is the mode of *governance*. This is particularly true at a lower level of per capita income, since the latter is inadequate for buying one's own health or education. Both aspects of governance – quantity as well as quality management – are equally important. But, so long as the relationship between *quantity* and *quality* is not directly proportional, the latter relies more on the public delivery system.

At the microeconomic level failure of the market as well as the government often gets rectified by peoples' referendum, as happened in, say, Singur or Raigad (see Chapter 1). At the macroeconomic level, on the other hand, stability failure is recurrently rectified by the government through its stabilization policy. In September 2008, for instance, the US government worked out a Wall Street bailout aimed at keeping credit flowing and saving the nation's shaky economy from collapsing into a crippling recession. The nationalization of Fannie Mae and Freddie Mac, the two largest financial institutions the world has ever known, signalled the complete failure of the biggest, most dynamic, most innovative and competitive markets that have existed in the history of capitalism – the Wall Street stock market and the market for US bonds. Even more than the mind-boggling \$5,500 billion size of the two US mortgage companies, it was the political significance of their nationalization that marked it out as an historic turning point. This was, after all, the biggest expropriation of private property undertaken by a government outside the former socialist world, yet there was absolutely no protest, nor even discussion, about the terms imposed by the US Treasury. Overnight some \$20 billion of shareholder wealth was wiped out by the US government without any objection from business to this anti-capitalist coup

(Kaletsky 2008). In addition, the US Senate has passed trillions of dollars of financial rescue packages. In a similar manner, the Indian capital market too is frequently bailed out by the government – this rarely, if ever, applies to the labour market – in the so-called deregulated regime to restore public confidence, but without putting checks on future reckless behaviour. In the midst of the recent financial crisis, the government of India urged banks to prop up failing businessmen.

But, at the meso-level, i.e. in between the micro and macro, or at the broad community level, the Indian government is uncertain on the distribution failure – in health, education, social security and political power. The uncertainty is not so much about the government's capabilities[3] as it is about its aptitude for supplying collective goods. However, this is often conditioned by the public *demand for better* delivery of public services, or their awareness about their rights to better public services. The characteristics of "supply" and "demand" jointly make governance different across countries. As the GDP growth rate failed to appear as proxy for prosperity in India, "development as governance" is worth pursuing. While the preceding chapters have directed us toward this end, in the following sections some selected cases of the social sector are taken up for further corroboration.

Health and workers

The well developed health system for Indian workers – part of the social security system – is fast disintegrating because of lackadaisical governance. As a background, there has been renewed concern for health inequalities as globalization and economic reforms are found to have negative impact on income inequality, breeding inequality of access to health (and also education) (see e.g. World Bank, WDR 2005). Studies have discovered that more lethal than cigarettes, obesity, alcohol, pollution, AIDS, vehicle accidents, suicides and homicides, is the gradient of inequality in our societies (see e.g. Kawachi *et al.* 1999; Wilkinson 2005). In the *World Health Report 2000*, the World Health Organization (WHO) proposed principles by which the performance of national health systems should be assessed. For this, WHO prefers to measure health inequality across individuals rather than across groups, similar to the way *Gini* income inequality is measured. However, since the individual approach cannot provide results that distinguish health inequalities having natural causes from those that have social causes, the WHO formula is questionable on various counts (Asada and Hedemann 2002).

If we assume the access to health is directly proportional to access to income, then the occupational health hazards of the colliery workers, the workers in traditional industries, the stone-crushers or the condemned-ship-breakers, which are found to be different from people in the same income group yet performing safer jobs (say, office assistants), remain unexplained. The plantation workers are exposed to different kinds of diseases which the agricultural workers are not generally prone to. In other words, health expectancy of different occupational groups, yet in the same income group, is different even in an equality-oriented health service. Certainly, there is a need to reduce greatly the burden of excess mortality and morbidity suffered by the poor. But the poor are not an undifferentiated "lot"; there are, in underdeveloped countries, "industrial" poor as distinct from "agricultural" poor as well as the poor in the services sector, like transport workers. Thus, it is important to find the most efficient way of combating diseases through identification of the sources within the social reproduction of labour. In this respect advancing health status seems to be more important than finding out the statistically foolproof measure of health inequality, which perhaps has little analytical significance, as is the case for income. The variables frequently used to categorize social groups can be useful in targeting policy and indicating identifiable population groups that require specific medical attention because their underlying social characteristics are likely to make it more difficult for them to be healthy (Braverman *et al.* 2000).

The WHO approach to health equality is perhaps best represented in the National Polio Surveillance Project (NPSP) – a government of India–WHO collaboration for universal immunization – launched in India in 1997 as a vertically driven scheme, affecting the routine immunization programme that was initiated in 1986. There are a host of partner agencies too from Canada, USA, Italy, Denmark, UK and Japan, the World Bank and the United Nations Children's Fund (UNICEF). Nearly one billion US dollars were spent on the programme up to 2005, excluding the extra budgetary expenditures incurred by the WHO and UNICEF on the appointment of 1,000 consultants in the country to monitor the programme and the amounts being incurred by the UNICEF on information, education and communication (Rao *et al.* 2005: 249). Currently, nearly 9 per cent of the health budget of the government of India is allocated for the polio eradication programme alone. It is estimated that one drop of polio vaccine given during the project is almost 30 times more expensive than the drop given in the routine programme (ibid.). In the end, what is worrying is that the total number of new cases of acute flaccid paralysis (AFP) in children has gone up since 2006.[4] More alarming is the fact that increased numbers of new polio cases are getting concentrated in a smaller number of districts, mostly in the most backward regions such as Bihar and Uttar Pradesh (GoI, NPSP).

As to health inequality, in the following section we focus on the industrial workforce in India. In order to address the question of how equally or unequally different aspects of health are distributed in a population, it is perhaps necessary first to locate differential *entitlements* of the different subgroups of population to health. Indian factory workers, in particular, have certain entitlements to health status – the social security system known as the Employees' State Insurance (ESI) Scheme by an Act of 1948 – which in many ways are radically different from those of other earners in the same income group in the country. Being contributory in nature, the ESI scheme is unique. All the employees in the factories or establishments to which the Act of 1948 applies are insured in a manner provided by the Act. The contribution payable to the ESI Corporation – the apex body of this scheme – in respect of an employee comprises the employer's as well as the employee's contribution at a specified rate. However, despite the Citizens' Charter – i.e. a social contract – of the social security scheme for the workers many fissures have developed in the system, increasing the health *risks* of the insured workers and also creating more numbers of *invisible* patients, but none because of any lack of resources. In the two years between 2003 and 2007 reserve funds and investments of ESIC funds in India have grown by 73 per cent to become US$3,254 million (or Rs 141.9 billion, as on 31 March 2007).

The "risks" approach[5]

Health inequality is generally defined as the variation in health status of individuals in a population. Health equality can be the equality of healthy lifespan: we would like all members of a cohort to live the same number of years, and for them to have had on an average the same health status during their lives. However, three factors cut short the expected lifespan of an economically active person. First, there is the personal health endowment at the point of entry to the labour market that represents the socioeconomic background of the individual, and no amount of compensation could rectify the shortcomings, if any. Second, there is the occupational health hazard in the labour process the individual gets engaged into. For instance, the incidence of permanent disablement per year is significantly high in Indian textiles – more than 3 per 1,000 employees as compared to, say, 0.7 in electronics units. Third, the remaining part of the healthy life span is conditioned by the *access* to proper health services. Take the distinctive case of a worker who entered the job at the age of 15 with a certain health endowment, could improve her health status (by dint of the ESI) – i.e. her expected healthy lifespan somewhat increased – while continuing in the job. However, she was suddenly caught up in an industrial accident that abruptly lowered her full health. Thereafter, she recovered with the support of the ESI scheme until she caught tuberculosis (TB) at the age of 40 and developed diabetes at the age of 50 years. Soon after that she somehow lost the coverage of the ESI scheme and died prematurely at the age of 60 (see Figure 7.1).

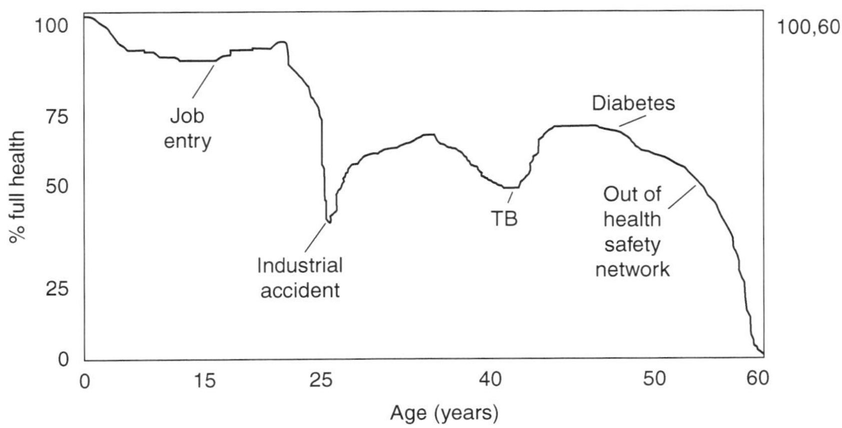

Figure 7.1 Healthy lifespan of a typical industrial worker in volatile labour market conditions.

Notes: Based on Gakidou *et al.* (1999). The area under the curve represents the individual's healthy lifespan.

It is important to distinguish between an individual's expected healthy lifespan and a set of health risks that he or she is exposed to at each stage of life. The expected number of years lived in full health is determined by a set of "expected" health risks arising from (a) varying accident rates across industrial units; (b) entrepreneurs' propensity to take remedial measures for reducing industrial accidents or pollution; (c) volatility in the labour market, or job security, which in turn determines the probability of losing access to health. Health equality for the industrial workforce would be achieved if (a) risk of industrial accidents *is equal to* 0 or 1; (b) remission of non-fatal outcomes is 0 or 1; and (c) risk of mortality is 0 or 1 – i.e. the solution is at either of the opposite corners of a *rectangular curve* (*cf.* Figure 7.1). Given the variability of each of these factors – which depends on the nature of the labour process, the labour standards and the varying social security network for different categories of workforce – equality of healthy lifespan cannot be an achievable goal in the short-term or even medium-term future. We thus focus our attention on that part of the distribution of health risks of the industrial workforce which is conditioned by the changing labour market conditions, and also by the governance of the safety network, i.e. the ESI scheme.

ESI scheme

The promulgation of the Employees' State Insurance (ESI) Act (1948) by the Parliament was the first major legislation on social security for workers in Independent India. Hotels, restaurants, cinemas, theatres, newspaper establishments, road transport establishments, shops and other establishments employing 20 or more persons have subsequently been brought under the purview of this scheme in addition to the large and small industries that were originally covered. The "appropriate government", state or central, is empowered to extend the provisions of the ESI Act to various categories of establishment. The objective of the ESI health service – i.e. a public health programme for a population subgroup or the social group of workers/employees below a certain income level – was initially to prevent diseases like tuberculosis (widely prevalent among workers in the early decades of the postcolonial industrialization), occupational diseases and industrial injuries. It also provides clinical services in response to demand from individual insured persons.

The ESI scheme being contributory in nature, all the employees in the factories or establishments to which the Act applies are insured in a manner provided by the Act. The aggregate contribution payable to the corporation per employee is the sum of employer's as well as employee's contributions at their respective stipulated rates, which are revised from time to time. Currently, the employee's contribution rate (with effect from 01 January 1997) is 1.75 per cent of the wage and the employer's is 4.75 per cent of the wages paid or payable to the employee in every wage period. Employees earning up to Rs 50 a day (i.e. less than a dollar a day) are exempted from payment of their part of contribution. The employer however has to contribute his or her own share for these employees. An employer is liable to pay the contribution in respect of every employee and deduct the employee's contribution from the wage bill, and shall pay these contributions at the above-specified rates to the Corporation within 21 days of the last day of the calendar month in which the contributions fall due. The wage limit – excluding overtime wages – for coverage under the Act is roughly US$221 (or, Rs 10,000) per month, with effect from 01 October 2006.

Full medical facilities for self and dependants are admissible from the very first day of entering into insurable employment. Whereas the primary, out-patient, in-patient and specialist services are provided through a network of panel clinics, ESI dispensaries and hospitals, super-speciality services are provided through a large number of advanced empanelled medical institutions on a referral basis. The state government bears one-eighth share of expenditure on Medical Benefit (MB) within the stipulated per capita ceiling per annum, and also any additional expenditure beyond the ceiling.

The contributions paid by employees and employers are deposited in a common pool known as the ESI Fund, which is utilized for payment of cash benefits to the insured persons and their dependants as well as for providing hospital medical facilities to the beneficiaries. The administrative and other expenses of the Corporation are also met from this fund. The huge accrued ESIC surplus is invested in Government of India (GoI) funds.[6] In fact, it is a soft loan given to GoI at the cost of health services to the contributing employees. In all these years, the soft loans to GoI have steadily increased. This is a continuous drain on the funds that are otherwise available for health services. Nevertheless, the GoI makes the law, the rules and regulations and reserves the power to change them at will, without having an obligation of contributing to the scheme. According to the ESI Act, a duly constituted corporate body called the Employees' State Insurance Corporation (ESIC) administers the scheme. It comprises members representing central and state governments, employers, employees, parliament, and the medical profession. The union minister of Labour acts as chairman of the Corporation whereas the Director General, as chief executive, discharges the duty of running the day-to-day administration.

Employer's benefits

The employer who comes under the purview of the ESI Act (1948) derives the following benefits from the scheme: First, she is absolved of all of her liabilities of providing medical facilities to employees and their dependants in kind or in the form of fixed cash allowance, reimbursement of actual expenses, lump sum grant, or opting for any other medical insurance policy of limited scope unless it is a contractual obligation of the employer. Second, the employer is exempted from the applicability of (a) the Maternity Benefit Act (1961) and (b) the Workmen's Compensation Act (1936) in respect of employees covered under the ESI scheme. Third, the employer finds at her disposal a healthy and productive workforce for attaining higher productivity of the firm. Fourth, the employer is absolved of any responsibility in times of physical distress of workers such as sickness, employment injury or physical disablement resulting in loss of wages, since the responsibility of paying cash benefits shifts to the Corporation in respect of insured employees. Finally, any sum paid by way of contribution under the ESI Act is deducted in computing the "income" of the firm under the Income Tax Act.

Exclusion and health risks

In 2006, the ESIC covered 9.1 million insured person (IP) family units, 8.4 million employees. The total numbers of beneficiaries was 35.5 million, insured women 1.5 million, and the number of employers was 300,718.[7] The number of IPs under ESIC is in fact greater than the total population of Denmark, Finland, Norway or Sweden. The comparison is pertinent in the sense that the Scandinavian welfare model for organizing and financing social security systems, health services and education stands out among the well-known European social security models, namely the British Beveridge model (1948) and the German model of social state, as distinguishable by its varying proportions of employees' contributions, differentiated benefits, free choice of doctors and sick pay.

On the whole, the number of IPs has been increasing since 2004, after a long period of secular decline. However, the increase is largely due to the extension of the ESIC facilities to some of the new growth locations, new occupations, and also to new categories of employees/workers who previously remained outside the purview of the scheme. Still, the annual targeted coverage of *numbers* of "new" employees under the ESI remained grossly unfulfilled in the advanced industrial states such as Gujarat, Karnataka, Maharashtra and West Bengal.[8] In fact, new establishments are coming up but older ones are closing down in large numbers, thus throwing considerable numbers of workers out of the health safety network.

Growing "free riders"

One of the by-products of the volatile labour market is that a growing number of employers evade submission of the ESI contributions collected from the employees, and also their own shares.[9] In just three years, the number of private companies against whom legal actions have been taken by the ESIC to recover outstanding ESI amounts increased from 93,067 in 2002–03 to 116,367 in 2004–05 – i.e. more than 41 per cent of the employers diverted the health support funds to their own "investible funds", or elsewhere. Most of the offending employers are located in such major ESI/industrial regions as Andhra Pradesh, Chennai, Haryana, Kerala, Mumbai, Pune, Punjab and West Bengal. As a result, the employees of these establishments are being deprived of the health safety network, even after duly paying their own part of the contribution.

Deteriorating industrial relations

In the 1980s, the annual frequency of lockouts was on average about 20 per cent of the total number of industrial disputes in Indian factories. Between 1991 and 2004 the figure almost doubled. The number of person-days lost due to lockouts also increased, and at a higher rate. Of the total person-days lost due to industrial unrest, the lockouts alone accounted for more than 63 per cent. On average, about 15 million person-days were lost per annum due to lockouts in the factories between 1991 and 2004. And about a million Indian workers in each year lost, on average, about two months' wages due to lockouts and closures of the factories during the period.[10] A factory closure for two months or more often deprives the affected workers of the medical benefits under the ESI scheme. The workers of the defaulting establishments are not entitled to any facilities being offered by the ESIC. There are two contribution periods, each of six months' duration, and two corresponding benefit periods, also of six months' duration.[11] Thus most of the workers who are employed in factories, which are locked out for more than 180 days are afterwards most likely to be deprived of the ESI benefits. Moreover, the loss of wages for two months in a year has its usual impact on their own and family nutritional status, particularly when real wage is hovering around the poverty line.

Finally, the state minimalism *de facto* has encouraged the setting up of some types of factories which would have been impossible to run had the Factories Act or the country's labour laws been effectively implemented by the Factory Inspectors. Particular reference can be made to the ferroalloy and sponge-iron units being set up with crude technology in recent years in states such as West Bengal, violating the norms of pollution, work conditions, remuneration and work-hours, and practically ghettoizing the captive male workers along with their spouses and children within the factory premises. The workers in the ferroalloy units are exposed to metal fume hazards and contact pulmonary fibrosis and silicosis. Those in sponge-iron units face hazards of working in intense heat and show signs of carbon poisoning. Those among them handling fly ash are exposed to silicosis (Nagarik Mancha 2009). These industrial units are yet to be brought under the ESI Implemented Areas, and until then the workers will remain deprived of affordable health care facilities. If ESI had covered these units, even then most of the workers would have remained deprived of health care facilities because generally the employers do not maintain the master-roll of their workers.

Casualization

As organized trade union activism beats a retreat from the labour market outcomes, ever-increasing numbers of workers are employed on a contractual basis, violating the Contract Labour (Regulation & Abolition) Act (1970). The employers, by the provisions of the Act, are restrained from employing contract labour in jobs that are permanent or semi-permanent in nature. Instead of confirming casual workers as permanent, it has become a common practice since the mid-1990s to route employment through a labour contractor on a purely temporary and casual basis in large enterprises. Now, in an average factory, for every three direct regular workers there is one casual worker. These contract workers perform most of the hazardous jobs inside the factory premises, but without any package of compensation, be it health or pecuniary. Over and above, there is job outsourcing (to a non-factory sector) that puts health security at stake. These workers are denied ESI health facilities. Although, by rule, the employer has to ensure that the contribution is paid in respect of all contract labour, this does not apply to *badli* and casual workers whose wages are below the stipulated ceiling. Ever since most of the state governments trimmed factory inspections, and the system of inspection was replaced by "self certification" by the employer, the latter finds it easier to flout the ESI rules and regulations.

Between 2000 and 2005, the industrial growth rate was highest in the state of Gujarat, and it owes considerably to casual employment. Consequently, the number of employees covered under ESIC in Gujarat gradually reduced from 548,880 to 484,180. Vapi, for instance, in the Surat sub-region of ESIC, is one of the largest industrial estates in India and a significant foreign exchange earner. However, the number of IPs did not increase while the economy was growing significantly. The "excluded" ultimately become the liability of the public health system. This is of course the social cost of corporate growth.

Increasing work load on reduced strength of workers

As the already weakened workers in the factories are compelled to work beyond the stipulated regular working hours, the earlier balance of the "work–rest" cycle gets disrupted, and in turn the motivation of the workers is affected. Apart from the increasing uncertainties in the labour market, the "work–rest" cycle has its toll on the worker's body in the form of *job stress*. This can be defined as the harmful physical and emotional responses that occur when the requirements of the job do not match the capabilities, resources or needs of the worker. In other words, job stress results from the mismatch of the human conditions of the worker and the workplace conditions. According to the National Institute for Occupational Safety and Health (NIOSH, part of the US Department of Health and Human Services), exposure to stressful working conditions can have a direct influence on worker safety and health. Stress sets off an alarm in the brain, which responds by preparing the body for defensive action. The nervous system is aroused and hormones are released to sharpen the senses, quicken the pulse, deepen respiration and tense the muscles. The diseases that are usually related to stress – without denying that chronic diseases take longer time to develop and can be influenced by many factors other than stress – are skin disorders, alcoholism, allergies, asthma, colitis, diarrhoea, migraine, heart disease, stroke, hypertension, ulcers, cancer, nervous breakdown, psychosis, neurosis etc. During the five-year period from 1999 to 2004, there has been an increase in stress-related diseases among the Indian industrial proletariat (Table 7.1). This disease rate is found to be higher than the incidence of the same types of disease among the common urban people.[12]

Low wages

The real wage declined below the one-dollar-a-day line in 1998–99. The health consequences of poor wages are that, among others, anaemia became endemic in

Table 7.1 Selected disease-wise incidence of morbidity/number of new cases per 1,000 IPs under the ESIC in India, 1998 to 2007

Disease	*1998–99*	*1999–00*	*2000–01*	*2001–02*	*2002–03*	*2003–04*	*2004–05*	*2006–07*
Hypertensive disease	27.8	18.1	14.52	16.30	13.36	16.30	17.03	18.65
Chronic rheumatic heart diseases	1.5	1.4	2.68	0.92	0.71	1.18	1.39	1.40
Arteriosclerosis and degenerative heart diseases	0.7	1.2	2.01	0.77	0.70	1.14	1.05	1.01
Asthma and allergic disorders	98.5	67.8	74.49	75.54	56.39	53.57	54.48	43.39
Benign neoplasm, all sites	0.6	2.4	0.55	0.40	0.50	0.95	0.92	0.22
Boil abscess cellulites and other skin infections	81.7	52.4	52.23	49.31	40.21	42.42	40.59	34.48
Diarrhoea and enteritis	78.1	48.5	43.75	43.36	33.74	38.06	32.86	25.32
Diseases of stomach and duodenum	119.7	52.5	38.82	39.24	31.88	36.07	32.62	30.23
Malignant neoplasm, all sites	0.2	0.4	0.34	0.43	0.27	0.45	0.37	0.21
Psychoneurosis and psychosis	1.5	2.0	2.16	1.08	1.09	2.40	2.31	7.78

Source and notes: ESIC, various years. From the data in ESIC, it was not possible to separate 'Asthma' from 'Allergic disorders'.

Table 7.2 Number of new cases of anaemia, per 1,000 IPs and 1,000 family (IP) units under ESIC

Year	*Anaemia*	
	Insured Persons	*Families*
1999–00	48.70	65.70
2000–01	52.66	70.24
2001–02	56.91	69.98
2002–03	42.91	53.53
2003–04	39.70	49.62
2004–05	41.79	50.61
2006–07	35.12	74.18

Source: ESIC, various issues.

Table 7.3 ESIC: incidence of tuberculosis among workers (number of new cases per 1,000 IPs/family units)

Disease	*Insured Persons*					*Family*			
	1997	*1999*	*2001*	*2003*	*2004*	*1999*	*2001*	*2003*	*2004*
TB of respiratory system	4.0	9.6	8.76	5.58	5.18	9.1	9.73	5.75	5.93
TB (other forms)	1.6	3.5	6.39	5.34	3.95	5.1	6.49	5.07	4.10

Source: ESIC.

workers' families (Table 7.2). The incidence of new cases of TB is still very high among the workers (Table 7.3). In a single state, namely West Bengal, having a large-scale presence of the traditional industries, about one-fourth of all the patients who die in the ESI hospitals are found to be victims of TB (of the respiratory system). In the industrialized West, the incidence of TB among the working class significantly declined even before the potent drugs became available. Thus, the contemporary growing incidence of the disease in India points to the limitations of the theoretical approach that ignores the social determinants of health.

To conclude, it is not the financial hitches that prompt the deteriorating health conditions of the workers. It is the changing labour market that has created more numbers of invisible patients. But ESIC has the strategic capacity to improve the health status by extending its coverage to greater numbers of formal as well as informal workers/employees. For this to happen, the state must come out of its current indifference and regulate the powerful employers in most of the industrial centres across the country who have become "free riders". Otherwise, the ESI health system will soon turn out to be cost-inefficient with high capital assets – as a system as well as unit IP treatment cost-wise – and, in the process, degenerate the public health status of the country as a whole. The occupancy of hospital beds in the ESI hospitals in the regions having a high concentration of extraction industries, e.g. in Jharkhand, is less than 20 per cent, and in Madhya Pradesh it is 45 per cent. In Surat (known for diamond processing by low-paid workers) the occupancy rate is 32 per cent, and it is 27 per cent in Vapi (known for the high concentration of hazardous chemicals industries), both being in the state of Gujarat. Likewise, in Maharashtra (the leading industrial state in India), the hospital bed occupancy is found to be a mere 43 per cent. On the other hand, the morbidity rate among workers, in general, has been increasing. To conclude, a large part of the workers who desperately need access to the health safety network of the ESI have remained excluded, largely because the governance failed to deliver.

Distribution of "power"

The National Rural Employment Guarantee Scheme (NREGS) – one of the most ambitious development programmes in the contemporary world – was finally launched on 2 February 2006 after years of debate between neoliberals and the humanitarians, in order to diffuse rural unemployment and also indirectly to improve the rural wage level. In the first phase, it planned to cover the 200 most backward districts. Subsequently all the 604 rural districts in the country were brought under the purview of the scheme on 1 April 2008. Under the NREG Act, the mandate is to ensure that all rural households are able to exercise their rights to employment. The Act provides a legal guarantee of 100 days of unskilled work in a year to every household who wants it. The projects to be undertaken must create durable community assets that would improve the rural infrastructure. The *Panchayati Raj* Institution (PRI) or the local elected self-government has the principal role in planning and implementation of the scheme.

Until March 2007, nearly 21.2 million households demanded employment under the NREGS, but only a fraction – 10.1 per cent by official statistics, and even less than that according to various social audit reports – got 100 days of employment.[13] Since the number of days of wage employment available annually to rural agricultural labourers is around 227 for males and 184 for females, was it then the dearth of schemes available in rural India? Of course not, because the permissible works under NREGA are plenty, e.g. water conservation, drought proofing (including plantation and afforestation), flood protection, land development, minor irrigation, horticulture and land development on the land of SC/ST/BPL and land reform beneficiaries, rural connectivity, and so on. It was not the lack of funds, either. The all-India average utilization of allocated funds during the financial year 2006–07 was only 73 per cent, including the huge financial irregularities found in the implementation of the scheme. The rate of utilization has been lower than the national average in the poorer states – e.g. in Bihar it was 60 per cent, in Jharkhand 72 per cent, in West Bengal 63 per cent. It is all the more surprising to find that one of the most industrially advanced states, namely Maharashtra, remained one of the worst performers among the states in implementing NREGS despite the fact that rural poverty there was more severe than in the average Indian state.[14] Maharashtra could spend not more than 36 per cent of the funds allocated to the state under the scheme in 2006–07.

According to the guidelines of the scheme, the inventory of projects has to be prepared following the priority list as articulated by the *Gram Sabha* (GS, a village council consisting of persons whose names are included in the electoral rolls for the *panchayat* at the village level). As per the rule, every GS (a) shall approve of the plans, programmes and projects for social and economic development before such plans, programmes and projects are taken up for implementation by the panchayat (the elected body representing a cluster of villages) at the village level, and (b) be responsible for the identification or selection of persons as beneficiaries under the poverty alleviation and other programmes. Every panchayat shall be required to obtain from the GS a certificate of utilization of funds for the plans, programmes and projects (GoI, Ministry of Panchayati Raj). In sum, NREGS *de jure* has at once bolstered democracy at the grassroots level. At least 50 per cent of works have to be allotted to village panchayats for execution. The wage to material ratio has to be maintained at 60:40.[15] The use of contractors and labour-displacing machinery is prohibited. All these measures may sound quite proactive but have turned into a major hurdle for the scheme in the deeply penetrated *contractor raj*.

As it stands, the scheme is most ineffective in areas where there is a strong collusion between local self-government, the local well-to-do landlords and the political parties at the local level. In these localities or regions the agricultural wage rate is much lower than the NREGS-stipulated daily wage rate for project work, thus threatening the existing largely semifeudal labour-use pattern by the "satraps" (see Box 7.1).[16] These are the facts that unfold the political economy and explain the exceedingly uneven implementation of NREGA across districts in the country.

Box 7.1 Impact of NREGS on labour supply to tea gardens: Report from Guwahati (Assam)

There are about 110 registered tea gardens in Assam's Barak or Surma Valley, requiring large number of plantation workers a day during the peak plucking and pruning season from April–December. However, since the implementation of NREGS less than half of the required workforce turned up in the tea gardens. A wage difference of Rs 30 is the main reason for this. While tea gardens offer Rs 48.65 a day to plantation workers, NREGS ensures them Rs 77 per day. 'The situation is getting out of hand', said the secretary of the Surma Valley branch of the Indian Tea Association, 'we have nothing against issuing job cards to plantation workers under the Central scheme, but the least the government can do is ensure that the gram panchayats (the bottom-level body of local government) target tea garden labourers only during the off season'. In fact, the secretary revealed that the panchayats had earlier refrained from issuing job cards to both permanent and casual plantation workers numbering around 75,000 across the Barak Valley.

Source: Karmakar (2008).

Among other social sector schemes that are either pretty old, or refurbished and implemented through PRI, are: the *Intensive Child Development Services* (ICDS) scheme to improve the nutritional and health status of children under the age of 6 years; the scheme called *Indira Awas Yojana* (IAY) that aims to provide dwelling units free of cost to poor SC, ST, freed bonded labourer households and also to the non-SC/ST but BPL rural households; the *Swarnajayanti Gram Swarozgar Yojana* (SGSY) whose objective is to bring the assisted self-employed rural poor above the poverty line by providing them income-generating assets through bank credit and government subsidy; the *Sampoorna Grameen Rozgar Yojana* (SGRY) to provide additional wage employment in the rural areas and also food security, alongside creation of durable community, social and economic infrastructure (the programme was later subsumed entirely in NREGS with effect from 1 April 2008). Yet one would come across unusually high incidences of malnutrition, shelter-less people across the board, poor sanitation, high infant mortality, lack of gainful employment, premature ageing in at least 7 out of 10 people in the countryside as well as in the urban areas.

Further, the under-five mortality rate (MR) (per 1,000 live births) – i.e. the probability of dying between birth and exactly five years of age – was 76 in India as compared to 13 in Sri Lanka or 24 in China, in 2006. Infant MR (per 1,000 live births) – i.e. the probability of dying between birth and exactly one year of age – was 57 in India as against 20 in China and 11 in Sri Lanka (UNICEF 2007). However, what remains invisible in the summary statistics is the still worse under-5 MR among the disadvantaged SC/ST population: it is 119 for SC and 127 for ST (National Advisory Council, NAC, 2005). India's rank is 49th in the world for under-5 MR, while some other poorer South Asian countries' performance looks better – namely Nepal's rank is 63 (with MR of 59), Bhutan 54 (MR: 70), Bangladesh 55 (MR: 69); the exception is Pakistan, which with a MR of 97 ranked 42 (ibid.). Note that both Pakistan and India, having bad records in human development, spend more than 3 per cent of GDP on military purposes.[17] Maybe the country's sovereignty is at the top of the priority list. Or perhaps it is the failure on the human front that leads to militarization. Anyway, the literature that puts growth in per capita income at the top in the priority list — and human development should follow — ignores the historical lessons from countries across the globe. Hard economics does not take into account the enormous potential of a healthy labour force for augmenting social productivity. And, to that extent, it lets pass the lessons of Korean or Japanese economic development, among others.

Among the under-fives, 43 per cent suffer from being underweight, 20 per cent from wasting and 48 per cent from stunting, during 2000–06. Poverty of course it is; but, the phenomenon goes beyond and engulfs the "vulnerable" households that are above the poverty line. The least developed countries outdo high-growth India on these accounts (Table 7.4). This was unexpected since the central government has two entitlement feeding programmes, two food subsidy programmes and one social food assistance programme and several other food-related schemes (see Box 7.2). Over and above, there is considerable "buffer stock" of food in possession of the government.

Table 7.4 Nutrition: India and the least developed countries compared

	Per cent of under-fives (2000–06) suffering from:			
	Underweight		*Wasting*	*Stunting*
	Moderate and severe	*Severe*	*Moderate and severe*	*Moderate and severe*
India	43	16	20	48
LDCs	35	10	10	42

Source and notes: UNICEF (2007). *Underweight*: Moderate and severe: below minus two standard deviations from median weight for age of reference population; severe: below minus three standard deviations from median weight for age of reference population; *Wasting*: Moderate and severe: below minus two standard deviations from median weight for height of reference population; and *Stunting*: Moderate and severe: below minus two standard deviations from median height for age of reference population.

Box 7.2 Food-related schemes of the government of India

In an order dated 28 November 2001, the Supreme Court converted the benefits of nine food-related schemes into "legal entitlements" and directed the state governments to fully implement these schemes as per official guidelines. These schemes can broadly be divided into the following categories:

Entitlement Feeding Programmes

- Integrated Child Development Services: covers all children under the age of six, pregnant and lactating mothers and adolescent girls.
- Mid Day Meal Scheme: Covers all primary school children.

Food Subsidy Programmes

- Targeted Public Distribution System: Provides 35 kg per month of subsidized food grains at half the cost of the economic price to all families identified as living below the poverty line (BPL families).
- *Antodaya Anna Yojana*: Provides 35 kg of rice per month at Rs 3 per kilo or 35 kg of wheat per month at Rs 2 per kg. This is to around 40 per cent of the poorest of poor families.

Employment Programmes

- *Sampoorna Gramin Rojgar Yojana*: A food-for-work programme that is being phased out and replaced by the NREGA.
- National Rural Employment Guarantee Act: Guarantees 100 days of employment at minimum wages.

Social Assistance Programmes

- National Old Age Pension Scheme: Provides a monthly pension to all BPL adults above the age of 65.

- National Family Benefit Scheme: Provides compensation of Rs 10,000 in case of death of breadwinner of BPL families.
- *Annapurna Yojana*: Provides 10 kg of free food grain for destitute poor who are not covered under the National Old Age Pension Scheme (this scheme is now being revised as the national old age pension scheme has been recently revised to cover poor old people).

These are some of the trying outcomes at the end of billions of dollars of public expenditure in the social sector, the bulk of which is spent through the decentralized governance of PRI. India is closely following most of the sub-Saharan African countries in this respect, in spite of the huge disparity between the latter group of countries and India in terms of economic growth rate. Many other welfare schemes are equally victims of "truncated democracy": flows of funds are regular, yet the beneficiaries are not the same people for whom the schemes are floated. In fact, feudalism may be gone but the emerging class of "feudal lords" corners the bulk of the "transfer incomes" from the state exchequer that are targeted to millions of poor people and designed to be spent through the PRI.

No wonder why about one-third of India – the most backward regions with a high concentration of SC/ST population – is under the influence of poor and marginalized SC/ST villagers turned rebels, who are running almost a parallel government of their own. The "red corridor" is now spanning 167 districts. However, though apparently conflicting, the NREGS, like many other social improvement schemes in these districts, turns out to be a non-starter. This is not because the militants are opposed to the project, although this has become an excuse for government officials for not implementing it.[18] There is little effort made by various state functionaries to redress the grievances of the disadvantaged in these areas in a non-violent manner, although the union ministry of Home Affairs admits in the official reports: '[N]axalism is not merely a law and order problem; it has deep socio-economic dimensions' (GoI, Ministry of Home Affairs, *Annual Report 2006–07*: 24).[19] As a result, areas of deprived and destitute people are increasingly coming under the influence of the rebels, presenting a great challenge to the formal democracy (ibid.). Yet India is spending a huge sum of public revenue – annually, $250 million or so – on anti-Naxal measures like modernization of the police force and deployment of more forces in these areas while actually cutting back on development spending. To conclude, the decentralization of power through PRI has *de facto* turned out to be "decentralized corruption" to a great extent, in the absence of complementary reforms in agrarian relations and social reforms in general.

Mass education and quality: the hope

When the experiment with decentralization of *power* fails to deliver the desired outputs, the role of education in society once more comes to the fore: through it, peoples' demand for better public services gets articulated and effective. The latter alternative is a paradigmatic shift from the idiosyncratic notion of education as facilitator for finding gainful, remunerative and productive jobs (*cf.* Becker 1975). In other words, the paradigm of "education for enrichment" narrowly relates education to mere job market and overlooks its desired social role – Rabindranath Tagore, the "conscience" of India, wrote on the problem in the early twentieth century (see Tagore 1906).

The official literacy statistics of India show improvements, as the adult literacy rate (persons aged 15 and above) is found to be 61 per cent (as in 2005; UNDP 2007: Table 1). Ironically, about 50 per cent of the rural and 20 per cent of the urban households had no *literate* among the female members of age 15 years and above (NSSO 2006e, Report no. 517). Moreover, in about 26 per cent of the households in the rural and 8 per cent of those in the urban areas, there was not a single member of age 15 years or above who could read and write a simple message with understanding in at least one language. This proportion is more than 50 per cent among the marginally poor, 60 per cent among the poor, and about 70 per cent among the extremely poor in rural India.

Further, measures such as the *mean* years of schooling of a population and school-life expectancy adequately capture educational attainment. It is evident that the average years of schooling of rural agricultural workers is 2.8, and that of agricultural labourers 1.8, as compared to rural non-farm workers who are having 4.6 years of schooling on average. Moreover, the gender disparity in mean years of schooling – two years – is striking for all workers (NCEUS 2007).[20]

Mass demand for delivery of better public social services is thus a distant possibility; the public opinion or "mind" is generally fractured or dominated by the propaganda machinery of the power blocks. Take for instance the NREGA, whose significance lies in the fact that it creates a rights-based framework for wage employment programmes and makes the government legally accountable for providing employment to those who ask for it. In this way, the legislation goes beyond providing a social safety net towards guaranteeing the right to employment. According to the NREGA, employment will be given within 15 days of application for work by an employment-seeker. If employment is not provided within 15 days, a daily unemployment allowance (at the rate of stipulated daily minimum wage) in cash has to be paid – which was supposed to work as a pressure tactic for the non-performing state. Moreover, liability for payment of unemployment allowance is that of the state governments. As it happened, an average household which demanded employment got only 43 days of employment instead of the stipulated 100 days, taking all states together, in 2006–07. There are even worse performing states such as West Bengal where only 14 days of employment were created for an average household. Also, the unemployment benefits to which the employment seekers are entitled remain elusive to them. In most cases the job-card holders are just not aware of their rights and become easy prey. There are no official statistics yet showing how many employment seekers received the benefits (see e.g. Pankaj 2008).

To give yet another instance, the *Indira Awaas Yojana* (IAY), the housing scheme for the poor that was initiated in the mid-1980s, is funded on a cost-sharing basis of 75:25 between the central government and the states. In 2007–08 about US$1 billion (i.e. Rs 40,327 million) was allocated under the scheme for construction of 2.13 million houses, but only 0.94 million houses could be constructed (GoI, Ministry of Finance, *Economic Survey 2007–08*). The funds crunch probably never was the problem because generally the fund utilization ratio hovered at around 60 per cent. On the demand side, there are still millions of people without shelter or who are living in makeshift arrangements.

Given the decrepit condition of the public good delivery system, it would perhaps do more justice if the huge public funds available for distribution at the grassroots level through the PRI or the public administration were rather transferred directly to the target groups of population, by opening accounts in the names of the beneficiaries at post offices or banks. At least the "drainage" of funds could have been minimized by this measure. However, problems are still there: identification of the poor, and the BPL people. The PRI is entrusted with the job of making a door-to-door census survey and identifying BPL households in the rural areas. The lists are still incomplete and fraught with excluded genuine claimants, while many economically and socially privileged people get their names included by dint of their proximity to the ruling political power at the local level.

India follows a two-step procedure using two distinctive methodologies, databases and processes, to identify BPL: the Planning Commission's private consumer expenditure statistics based on the NSSO are used to measure the *incidence* of poverty. In the process, the maximum number of poor per state is fixed by the Planning Commission. Each state government then autonomously carries out the physical *identification* of the poor using household indicators derived from the "BPL Census multi-dimensional indicators" as prepared by the union ministry of Rural Development. Thus, exclusion or inclusion of any family in the *poverty category* is the prerogative of the state (or the PRI where applicable). Since the *number* of poor people always exceeds the periodic estimation of the Planning Commission, the state government finds the opportunity – because of mass indifference in the absence of mass awareness – to exercise its discretionary power. As a result of arbitrariness and discretionary politics the entire exercise to identify BPL households is spoilt. Maybe, India would need direct help from the United Nations to monitor the census of BPL households.

Further, the underutilization of funds due to the lack of public accountability in the internationally well-known Tsunami Rehabilitation Programme – the four-year programme was launched in 2005–06 – is a case in point. Over the past three years, a combined amount of about US$0.9 billion (or, Rs 35.5 billion) has been spent in five affected states and Union Territories, working out to roughly 39 per cent of the total outlay. Enmeshed in inefficiency, bureaucratic red tape and procedural issues involving the centre–state relations, the programme is threatening to collapse, with over 60 per cent of the total outlay remaining unutilized (Jha 2008).

Collective reasoning

So, what is the lacuna, especially in a system of representative democracy where the people's representatives are elected to the policymaking bodies by the majority of the voters who are otherwise invisible? The answer perhaps is, as Socrates argues: democracy needs citizens who can think for themselves, and who can reason together about their choices (see e.g. Kraut 1984: Ch 7, Socrates and democracy). '[W]hen politicians bring simplistic propaganda their way', Nussbaum argues, 'young people will only have a hope of preserving independence and holding the politicians accountable if they know how to think critically about what they hear, testing its logic and its concepts and imagining alternatives to it' (Nussbaum 2008: 15).

Among the basic weaknesses in public collective reasoning is, first, that a large proportion of the Indian population is deprived of basic literacy. The enrolment figures are impressive. Yet, getting lost in the jungle of statistics is the rather unnerving *quality* of education that the children get: over 40 per cent of children in Class 5 are unable to read Class 2-level text; a large number of children progress to the next level without learning basic skills. Nearly 45 per cent of kids enrolled in upper primary classes cannot read their own mother tongue. Over 40 per cent of upper primary school children do not know how to subtract. More than 80 per cent of 6–8-year-old school kids could not solve, when asked by the survey teams, simple problems regarding money by subtracting numbers from a sum of Rs 50 that they were given, and so on (Pratham Resource Centre 2008).[21] So, how the collective mass reasoning to the poor public services delivery system be gelled?

It is high time that – as Tagore (1906), among other writers, had drawn to our attention – critical thinking as a discipline is taught as part of a school's curriculum. Nowadays, school textbooks are giving increasing space to "contemporary icon" building and "education for enrichment", deadening people's moral imaginations, intellectual self-reliance and freedom. The nation is thus heading towards a poor state of critical reasoning. This ultimately gets reflected in another foremost field of operation, i.e. the poor performance of India's R&D irrespective of there being no dearth of science and engineering graduates, national institutes of higher learning, and adequate funds for the university departments to undertake R&D. Perhaps, all these are giving the present state of governance some kind of stability in the midst of so many social anomalies.

Governance as accountability

The second most fundamental remedial measure for many of the ailments of economic and social development is to enhance the accountability of the system at large, using the office of the Comptroller and Auditor General (CAG). The Constitution of India amply delineates the role of CAG, in Part V, Chapter V, Articles 148 and 151. The CAG undertakes audits according to the Duties, Powers and Conditions (DPC) of the Services Act of 1971. However, this Act has become archaic, as the Comptroller and Auditor General notes: 'a lot of the clauses in the Act are inadequate in today's context'.[22] One of the problems is that the state executives increasingly show indifference to the CAG audit reports, although the Constitution says there must be a CAG audit. The CAG makes its observations, places them before the Parliament, which refers them to the ministries concerned. The fact is that one-third of the 9,000 audit paragraphs – to which the concerned executive has to respond – placed in the last 14 years, for instance, 'have not even received the first response from the government or different departments' (Rai 2008). So the intent of the Parliament itself was being negated. A still more important issue is the unchanging jurisdiction of the CAG, while the economy has been drifting away fast from the domination of the public sector undertakings (PSUs). Now there has emerged the public–private partnership (PPP) model – through which more and more government activities are being channeled – and the number of BoT (build-operate-transfer) projects is increasing. Further, progressively more public resources are being canalized through the PRI. None of these, however, is listed in the DPC Act (1971). Whether in a PPP or a BoT project – being implemented by a private promoter – the authority of the CAG gets diluted.

The destabilization of this institution of accountability of resources use will *de facto* raise the capital–output ratio in the economy as a whole, besides increasing the probability of missing the targets of beneficiaries in the government social projects. In the UK, for example, the CAG is an officer of Parliament, which means that if he or she is asking an executive or enterprise for a document and if that is not complied with, it is considered a breach of parliamentary privilege. By contrast, in a similar situation in India the CAG is helpless. In the US system, if the CAG does not get a document from the ministry the holder of the office can go to a federal court and register a complaint. Within 20 days the ministry has to produce the document. Otherwise, the officer is liable for, yes, criminal procedure, unlike in India. In Canada, the CAG is an officer of Parliament. In France, the CAG is a court – a quasi-judicial body. Australia and New Zealand are similar to these cases. 'These are just examples of other democracies, of how over a period of time they have empowered the CAG' (Rai 2008). Democracy after all is built on a few foundation pillars. The worrying naivety is that which fails to recognize these pillars on the way to economic as well as human development. Market and credit-rating agency conjointly provide only a very weak substitute.

8 Epilogue

[I]

Which one is a sound representation of "development": rise in per capita income, improvement in human development index, or a rise in the composite index of "happiness"? Rise in per capita income – gross income divided by population – in India is of course marred by income inequality and thereby fails to truly represent development. As income inequality breeds inequality of access to the basic components of better livelihood, human development does not follow a rise in GDP. "Happiness" would have been a better indicator but for the problem with measurement; a better composite index needs to be developed. Following the UNDP rank-table of HDI, Norway is positioned in the second place, while 66 per 100,000 Norwegians were in prison in 2007 (UNDP 2007). Similarly, Australia is placed at the third position in the HDI rank, yet her prison population is 126 (per 100,000 people). Further, the United States' HDI rank is 12, but the ratio of prisoners to total population is unusually high, i.e. 738. In general, the industrially developed countries witness considerably high prison population. By contrast, though India is poor in the record of HDI rank, yet only 30 per 100,000 people were in prison in 2007. This is no mean achievement when compared with another late developing country that is emerging as a "giant" as well as a superpower, i.e. China, where 118 people per 100,000 are in prison, while her HDI rank is 81. Admittedly, a single indicator for a complex matter of "mind and body" has its pitfalls.

There might be alternative explanations of the phenomenon of "prison population ratio". One line of argument would be that in countries where the prison to total population is high, the institutions protecting personal and property security are *de facto* effective as compared to countries exhibiting a remarkably low *ratio*. In other words, in the former group of countries crime and justice coexist as strong counterforces, while in India, say, crimes might have gone scot-free. The second line of argument is that crime is systemic in most of the industrialized economies; the system provokes the unhappy self to "unlawfully" maximize his or her personal gains – the frequency of both the problems of "moral hazard" and "free riding" tends to be high in a market economy. Current global meltdown partly began with the failure of the US financial market to keep in check the latter kinds of problems. Third, if the proportion of "excluded and marginalized" to the total population was high, the sense of relative deprivation would tend to result in high crime frequency. The law would fail to act as deterrence whatever efficiency the judicial system had. Briefly, one may use the proportion of prison population as a metaphor for the unhappiness in the society. However, the ways in which people relate to each other and the extent to which they are effectively engaged in helping each other are strongly related to their satisfaction with life, and could be countervailing forces. This might be the case in agrarian India, explaining the low crime rate despite a very high rate of destitution and deprivation.

The other problem, apart from the choice of indicator, is: how to translate economic prosperity (as measured by per capita income) into human development? Many think the debate on the *means* of achieving the target of development is a closed chapter, and the increasing returns to scale-based *industrialization* is the solitary way left for the developing countries. The Indian case poses a dilemma. In a country with high population density and a large percentage of the workforce being farm-dependent, why do we draw a closure on such possibilities as growth and development of the agrarian economy, together with tertiarization, and on market-based industrial investments which will be socially feasible, economically viable and politically acceptable?

In the course of economic development over the last sixty years, many more people have been "included". The combined purchasing power (at PPP dollars) of the thriving Indian middle class is enviable by many of the EDCs. The retail equity investor base rose to 3.5 million individuals in 2007. These individuals were directly buying equities on their own behalf. If those investing indirectly through either mutual funds or unit-linked insurance plans are included, the total estimated number of individuals participating in equity markets turned out to be 8 million in 2007. However, at the same time, even larger numbers of people – the casual employees and workers, the unorganized-sector workers and the BPL people – are included only to be excluded forthwith. As the GDP growth rate picked up Indian planners assured the nation of a better future – i.e. an "inclusive growth".

The poverty rate is many times the chronic unemployment rate in India. The main reason is that a large number of the working population are otherwise disguisedly unemployed – i.e. their individual marginal productivity is much lower than the respective sectoral average productivity, and unemployment has compelled them to renegotiate their "reservation wage" down to the level of the BPL wage. Therefore, the prime objective of "inclusive" development ought to be to reduce and ultimately eliminate disguised unemployment.

The common understanding is that Indian agriculture still remained the "breeding ground" of disguised unemployment. The low land-to-person ratio in agriculture has rendered a large number of the working population "surplus" who could be moved away from agriculture without affecting agricultural outputs. This understanding is consistent with the presumption that Indian agriculture has exhausted its potential. Since Independence in 1947, the realization had been that diversification of economic activities is the answer to India's economic backwardness.

But somehow the target has remained elusive over the last six decades. It is equally important to recognize that the diversion of the workforce from more productive to less productive occupations results in rather increased numbers of disguisedly unemployed.

The diversification of economic activities, in other words the expanded *social division of labour* requires, first, a wider distribution of the means of production – capital, labour (hired) and knowledge – among larger numbers of independent productive agents. Second, the division is directly related to the size of the market for the product produced by a particular community – the larger the size of the market, the greater is the specialized line of work. Third, the upward mobility of different producer communities reinforces the expanded division of labour. In reality, the distribution of both capital and knowledge is extremely skewed; self-employed instead of hired labour is the predominant feature; upward mobility is very much restricted, especially as we find most of the socially disadvantaged are also economically poor and vulnerable; and, while the unorganized sector dominates Indian manufacturing, the market size for each of the unorganized production establishments is extremely small. Briefly, the underdeveloped social division of labour implies that the forces of production – the means of production as well as the wage–profit relations – still remain well below the level at which competition is viable.

The options available to the progressive government for diversification of economic activities are: (a) land reforms; (b) to promote employment-augmenting micro and small enterprises (i.e. the "market entrepreneurs"); and (c) industrialization based on large-scale industries. The government failure in (a) and (b) is unambiguous in India. In case (c), it has been both a government failure and a market failure, since the roles of planning and the public sector have been replaced progressively by market and subsidized private investments (often the "political entrepreneurs").

[II]

Why is industrial growth slow in India or, for that matter, in some of the developing countries or regions? Some scholars argue differently: it is the legislative institution that has impeded labour market flexibility and thereby industrial investments. The revival and recent growth of interest in the economics of labour law is an outcome of the contemporary policy debates over regulation versus deregulation, and over privatization versus the role of the state in ensuring growth and human development. It is "revival" in the sense that private property rights of capital, workers' rights, international competitiveness and all the related issues were widely debated in nineteenth-century Europe, or during the first half of the twentieth century in the US. Ultimately, the liberal project of modernity coupled liberty with equality. Liberty without equality is nothing but the invisible hand of the market, and is barbaric. Karl Marx in *Das Kapital* summarized in a precise manner the historical role of the working-class movement and the labour regulations. The pressure from below by the workers led to a series of inventions and innovations in nineteenth- and early twentieth-century Europe, which then moved far away from the poorer countries. This is of course only one of the few most important factors of the relative backwardness of the late-developing countries.

The economics of labour law was widely practised in the early decades of industrial development in Europe in the nineteenth century before the labour movement acquired enough strength to compel the state to legislate welfarist laws. The political power of labour became central to legal and regulatory design only in the late nineteenth and early decades of the twentieth century. In Great Britain, modernization and rationalization in cotton mills – the most important industry that was driving the Industrial Revolution – and also in the coal mines owed much to the Factory Act of 1833, and to a series of acts beginning with the English Factory Act of 1802.

Many of the acts had a selective impact. For instance, those cotton magnates who had made the transition to steam, because it was considered likely to disadvantage their competitors who remained dependent on waterpower, supported early British legislation on the length of the working day. There is strong evidence of producers seeking to gain a competitive advantage by embracing labour standards that would disadvantage rivals who were using a more vulnerable technology. On the other hand, the idea that was crystallizing then is that certain social guarantees of stable employment and protection against risks arising from injury, illness, unemployment and old age are required to legitimize the inequality within the enterprise. However, it was not until the early decades of the twentieth century that the concept of "contract of employment" was definitively established as the foundation of the law governing the labour market (Deakin and Wilkinson 2005).

The recent growth of interest in the economics of labour law is the direct outcome of the coming to dominance of the Chicago school of law and economics, in the early 1980s, which upholds the free market as a means of organizing resources, and stands for scepticism about government intervention into economic affairs. Liberalism in Europe, over a period of three centuries, gradually separated two aspects of social life: accumulation of capital and political democracy. The primacy of accumulation of capital was often blurred in the course of social development over the last century and more in Europe and elsewhere (Amin 2004). Two parts of society experienced autonomous development to a great extent, if not mutually exclusive. Neoliberalism, however, once again started putting the clock back and pushing hard to put the two separated parts of society into one whole; political democracy is made subservient to the accumulation of capital.

The idea that economics could best be politically governed thus seems to have been rejected by the neoliberals. The flexible labour market has been highlighted in numerous Fund-Bank and OECD reports, and has generally meant policies designed to decentralize labour relations and cut protective and pro-collective regulations. One of the chief concerns was to tackle unemployment in Europe, which to the neoliberals was due to labour market rigidities. The US labour market is now upheld as the paradigmatic example of the flexible labour market policy approach. However, first, the vast majority of the job growth in the US during the last two decades of the twentieth century actually occurred in the private services sector, with the remainder in the local government sector, leaving the industrial sector trailing far behind. Second, the US economy, as against popular belief, is not moving to a completely fluid labour market and to completely fluid careers for all workers. A large number of employees continue to be employed in the same organization for long periods of time. The job tenure has declined but the median tenure is still about five years for workers in the age range 35–44 and 10 years for those in the age range 55–64. Third, by the turn of the century the unemployment rate in the US started picking up alongside sluggish wage growth – and ultimately a decline in real wage in 2005 – and slowed down real GDP growth. "The Great American Job Machine", as it was proudly called during the Reagan era, has long since come to a halt.

Many scholars expressed doubts that greater flexibility would in fact achieve lower unemployment, pointing instead to low levels of demand for labour as the culprit behind Europe's higher unemployment rates. On the basis of OECD data, it is found that labour market flexibility, encouraged by low minimum wages, low benefits and weak employment protection (as reflected in high wage inequality) has *not* been the route by which some OECD countries have managed to minimize the employment disadvantage of the least qualified. Its impact appears to have been marginal compared with the overall demand for labour.

The issue of labour market flexibility in the EU is rather more centred on public governance and fiscal management than on firm-level economics. The labour market reform has gradually infiltrated the EU discourse as an ever-increasing retired workforce is becoming dependent on a decreasing number of the existing workforce. So there is an urge on the part of the state to reduce non-wage labour costs as well as the reservation wage, which is high because of unemployment and other benefits. The expansion of the European welfare state in the 1970s has led to the latter kinds of benefits, which not only grant high net replacement rates but are also of long duration. The feeling is that such generosity makes the decision to work less attractive, and in fact the unemployed are trapped in unemployment. Therefore, '… in the long term, if unemployment is to be kept low, it is vital to limit entitlements to benefit and refuse benefit to people who are not available for work' (OECD 1994: 213). This is, however, not the case in India; there is neither comprehensive employment protection nor comprehensive social benefits.

Moreover, the tradition of Common Law in India never allowed much rigidity in the labour market. One of the debates is over the provisions of Chapter VB of the Industrial Disputes Act (1947), introduced by an amendment in 1976. This chapter required firms employing 300 or more workers to obtain government permission for layoffs, retrenchments and closures. A further amendment in 1982 – which took effect in 1984 – expanded its ambit by reducing the threshold to 100 workers. It is argued that since permission is difficult to obtain, employers are unable to restructure their workforce in line with changes in technology and demand conditions, making them reluctant to hire workers.

Those who argue for a free labour market often cite the workers' right to strike – which they think the Industrial Disputes Act (1947), Chapter V, has empowered the workers with – as anti-growth as well as anti-private property rights. The Act of 1947 has remained the basis for negotiation, conciliation, settlement and adjudication in India. However, the question that still remains unresolved is: is there a constitutional or legal right to strike? The matter came up time and again in the High Courts of respective states as well as in the Supreme Court over the last five decades, but the issue of *right* is still ambiguous (Mukhija and Shah 2007). The autonomous space for decision making by the judges and the scope of judicial discretion intrinsic to common law, as opposed to codes, are most revealing as one finds the court's decision varying across similar cases.

Why, after all, does government intervene in the labour market? The theories underlying most interventions are that free labour markets are imperfect (for a summary, see Botero *et al.* 2004). As a consequence there are rents to be paid in the employment relationship. Employers abuse workers to extract these rents, leading to both unfairness and inefficiency. For example, employers discriminate against disadvantaged groups, underpay workers who are immobile or invest in firm-specific capital, fire workers who then need to be supported by the state, force employees to work more than they wish under the threat of dismissal, fail to insure workers against the risk of death, illness or disability, and so on.

On the other hand, the basic hypothesis of those who relate industrial relations (IR) to industrial growth and development is that industrial growth is dependent or determined by IR. First, no economic theory would come forward in support of the hypothesis. Second, one cannot rule out the fact that IR and some undefined (residual) problems of industrial growth are correlated. However, one then has to estimate whether IR itself is functionally related to economies/diseconomies of agglomeration. Briefly, the question of whether the industrial growth rate, say, was down due to adverse IR, or the latter is adverse because the industrial growth was down, is the kind of *causality* one has to establish before making any informed judgement.

In fact, there is adequate evidence of considerable employment flexibility, lackadaisical enforcement of labour laws, and above all weakening of bargaining power of the workers over the last two decades, although these are not reflected in the growth rate of private investments in India. To understand how far labour laws could hinder industrial employment or output growth it is perhaps important to study the political economy of law. In brief, India, having the tradition of common law, preserves the freedom of contract to a great extent and has a less generous social security system than in most of the EU countries. This also perhaps explains the multiplicity of political power or authority so far as the administration of the labour regulations is concerned. The missing vertical[1] as well as horizontal integration[2] is really the weakness of the labour laws to lay down any effective hindrance to private capital accumulation in India as a whole. Unlike in the EU countries, the *reservation wage* in India is also very low. The possibility of further decrease of that through the flexible labour market, to make room for additional employment without affecting labour productivity, is yet to be probed with detailed empirical evidence.

Further, why there has been a significant increase in lockouts? The simplest of the arguments is that it is the inflexibility instituted by the ID Act, especially its Chapter VB, and by similar other restrictive clauses in the labour laws on rationalization and expansion. Empirical data provide a different contour: during the last 20 years, a substantial amount of employment was generated in new factories the size of which attracted Chapter VB of the ID Act. In other words, new factories with 100 or more workers have surfaced steadily during the last two decades despite the so-called inflexibility clause(s) in the labour laws. Second, there has been growing casualization – and decreasing strength of regular workers – in the factories despite there being the Contract Labour Act, belittling the "inflexibility" argument. Third, if the locked-out factory is re-opened, it often reopens with a substantially reduced number of workers without inviting any judicial or administrative reprimand. Fourth, wage revisions are long overdue in many industries where wages are negotiated centrally, giving rise to an enormous amount of rent for private capital to amass. Fifth, the working hour has lengthened in many of the factories, violating the stipulated norms and allowing capital to extract more abstract surplus value from the labour power. Finally, the frequency of factory inspection has significantly reduced; a large number of factories are not inspected even once in a year. Instead, the system of "self-certification" by the entrepreneur has been introduced in many of the states by using the instrument of "Government Order", which has subjected workers to the arbitrariness of the management.

The question then logically arises: why hang on to the labour laws when critics say these (a) encourage informalization; (b) deter industrial growth rate; (c) increase worker bargaining power, thereby decreasing capital formation; and (d) raise the marginal cost of production? Each of these arguments has been scrutinized and found to be unsustainable by the "logic" of economics (Banerjee 2008). To conclude, what appears to be significant is that without labour laws labour standards would have been still poorer, whereas there is no firm ground to believe that the rate of industrial growth might have been higher had there been no public laws interrupting the free play of the economic agents. In fact, it seems that had the social, economic and political rights – instead of being mutually autonomous within the broad perimeter of the Indian Constitution – rather embedded into one and the whole like that in the social democracy of, say, the Scandinavian countries, many of the explicit disruptions that the capitals are now able to make in the wage negotiations, or in negotiations relating to the basic rights of the workers at work, could have been avoided. As a result, large external economies in industrial investments would have generated. Any scholarly judgement on the labour market institution warrants understanding of the anthropology of the Indian business community, and the legal theory of institutional evolution.

In fact, the common law that the British colonial rule grafted on the Indian judicial system has left open wider space for governmental political power, while at the same time it has tended to favour markets and contracts. The ample scope of arbitrariness and discretion in decision making by the *independent* judges and juries – unlike in the civil law or "code" tradition – have allowed very little space for a regulated labour market as well as social control of business. So long as the common law is dependent on arbitration and not guided by codes, the labour market *de facto* remains flexible in India, despite the magnanimity of the labour laws. We are yet to know how labour market flexibility would generate more employment. Are the protagonists talking about full-time job equivalents? Or are they anticipating a reduction in employment hours per person per annum, thereby generating an increased *number* in employment like Wal-Mart in the US? If yes, that goes against the very notion of decent work and is socially regressive. Workers then have the right to defend their own cause within the perimeter of the Indian Constitution, despite the drawbacks of labour regulation and its administration.

[III]

It is perhaps beyond the capacity of the government in a mixed economy to attempt, from its position of dominance, to diversify economic activities to the extent whereby the problem of surplus labour in agriculture would be diffused. Generally, as income rises – and with a fair distribution of that rising income – the consumption pattern in the economy begins to change. The income elasticity of demand for agricultural commodities eventually goes down, while that of industrial products rises; and, with further rise in per capita income, the consumer demand swings discernibly towards services, resulting in a structural transformation that broadens, *ceteris paribus*, the social division of labour. The industrialization programme of the Indian government, to the extent that it did not address the issue of income distribution – never mind resolving the issue of "fair wage", effectively implementing the minimum wages in the unorganized sector, putting into perspective the terms of trade between agriculture and industry, and so on – has failed to inject momentum into an open social division of labour. However, the asymmetric income distribution was effective in generating demand for specific kinds of goods and services which, in turn, led to a higher GDP growth rate. Yet the problem of aggregate effective demand aggravated, amplifying structural deficiencies that put a brake on steady economic growth as well as on raising human capabilities.

Trade liberalization since the early 1990s has unlocked the "vent for surplus" and thus opened up possibilities of overcoming the domestic effective demand problem. However, it has simultaneously exposed various domestic sectors to higher-productive foreign goods and services. The productivity gaps between Indian agriculture and, especially, the OECD are so large that once the barriers to imports of agricultural products are withdrawn – following the WTO negotiations – there would be a catastrophic impact on Indian agricultural employment. Without appropriate income entitlements, the food security of most of the Indian people would be immediately jeopardized. The Indian industrial sector has become equally vulnerable; the foreign import elasticity of Indian industrial goods is low when compared to that from many other developing countries.

The limiting factor in the economy is not so much the shortage of money as the shortage of real capital or capital equipment. The industrial (as well as agricultural) capabilities are highly restricted by India's pitiable performance in the field of R&D. This is largely owing to low domestic demand for Indian R&D as embodied in domestic capital equipment. The availability of surplus labour at low wages discourages the "high road" to development. Similarly, the Indian services sector lacks many of the ingredients which otherwise would have increased her share in the global trade. The structural transformation via the changing composition of consumption thus remains stunted, and often distorted. The globalized financial market has of late boosted the GDP growth rate a bit, but the buoyancy was short-lived. The manufacturing sector immediately responded with a growth rate that is almost three times lower than that achieved in the previous four consecutive years.

Maybe it is high time that development thinking, especially for such overpopulated countries as India, takes a detour. There are – and this ought to be explored for the sake of finding a solution to the imminent world food crisis – ample opportunities to augment productivity in Indian agriculture by innovative ways such as diverting to organic farming – which incidentally is sustainable and "green" – by redesigning the incentive structure in favour of cooperative or collective farming, and endeavouring to establish balanced terms of trade between agriculture and non-agriculture, among others. Millions of gainful opportunities for employment would be created at once. But then, *governance* becomes the critical factor as individual decisions and attitudes are divergent.

A high GDP growth rate is of course desirable, but its feasibility as well as its sustainability depends on scores of other issues. Besides, a high growth rate neither automatically makes it "inclusive" nor ensures an improvement in human development. The Planning Commission (PC) has stated as its growth objective to achieve an average growth rate of 9 per cent per annum for the Eleventh FYP (2007–12) (GoI, Planning Commission 2008). However, the associated macro-balances such as export, import or investment rates have no real grounding. The PC expects that the average investment rate must rise from 32 per cent in the Tenth Plan to around 37 per cent in the Eleventh Plan period, reaching 39 per cent at the end of the period. Is the rate of investment really under the control of a government which is so keen to give up all the commanding heights of the economy to the private sector, and a private sector that is extensively penetrated by foreign capital? How has the PC arrived at the estimate of an average saving rate of 34.8 per cent? Very few countries in the developing world have actually been able to achieve a 9 per cent growth rate, among which (keeping aside China) South Korea was the most prominent in the 1980s. But South Korea had accomplished some of the most crucial institutional reforms, such as changing agrarian relations, and had achieved a very high level of human development; the investment rate there was higher than targeted by the PC.

There are other peculiarities of the projections that sit badly with the objective of providing gainful employment to everybody and ending the exclusion of increasing numbers of people from the growth process. There is no projection of the growth of labour-intensive sectors and the employment to be provided by them, but there is a great deal about the need for labour market flexibility. However, only 8–9 per cent of the economy is in the organized sector to which most of the labour laws of the country would apply. How much difference would abolishing the worker-protective clauses in the rule book make in facilitating the growth of employment? In any case, there is a dearth of evidence to suggest that labour laws have hindered the growth of employment in organized industry in the country (see Papola 2008).

Instead of devising policies for encouraging the growth of labour-intensive and technologically upgraded small-scale industry and small and medium farmer-operated agriculture, the PC talks grandly of accelerating the industrial growth rate to 10 per cent and to even higher growth in manufacturing, and the agricultural growth rate to 4 per cent, as if reaching that objective alone would be enough to solve problems of poverty, malnutrition and insecurity for the mass of the Indian people. The PC emphasizes competitiveness of Indian producers all the time but seems to be innocent of the need for increasing R&D for a globally competitive economy. It does talk about the need to spend more on research by universities and research laboratories but makes no mention of the institutional mechanisms needed to forge better linkages between academic science, technological research and actual producers, especially in the industrial sector.[3]

How could all these contradictions be ironed out in the direction of a people-friendly growth? The answer is: we must give up "obsessions", to begin with, in favour of innovative development plans, holistic in nature. The twenty-first century development agenda must be different from the early capitalism in the West. In the end, it is the *happiness* of the people that would be counted as *development*. Despite faster macroeconomic growth, social instability in India seems to be on the rise and this gets reflected in the changing politics of governance. "India: the emerging giant" has injected a growing sense of insecurity in most of the people. The innumerable spontaneous protest movements in recent times across the country over such issues as unemployment, land acquisition, special economic zone, discrimination against SC/STs and minority communities, inefficiencies of the public distribution system of food, price rise, gender discrimination, and so on; growing regionalism; last but not least, the growing intolerance of the privileged sections of the "brain" of the nation to liberalism, make one bemused about the very foundations of the current high GDP growth rate. What's gone wrong? The state assures inclusivity, yet the problem is to make the people believe this. Is "inclusive growth" then a misnomer? Maybe yes, until and unless we redefine – as attempted in these chapters – the development strategy, in the light of the fact that the neoliberal prescriptions over the last two decades or so have miserably failed to postpone the imminent but unanticipated crisis in the global economy that plunged millions of the workforce in the world into obscurity.

Notes

1 Emerging India

1 In 1958–59, 1964–65, 1967–68, 1975–76, 1977–78, 1980–81 and 1983–84.
2 India had 70,000 HNWI in 2004, while Singapore had 49,000, South Africa 37,000, Hong Kong 67,000, United Arab Emirates 53,000 and South Korea 71,000 (ibid.).
3 It was 793 in 2005, 946 in 2006 and 1,125 in 2007.
4 The number of Indian billionaires rose from 9 in 2004 to 40 in 2006 and further to 53 in 2007. The US had 469 billionaires (up from 415 in 2006). Russia replaced Germany as the second-placed country, with 87 billionaires.
5 Japan had only 24, France 14, and Italy 14 billionaires.
6 China had only 42 billionaires (and Hong Kong 26).
7 With a per capita consumer expenditure above four times the poverty line (PL).
8 With a per capita consumption two to four times the PL.
9 The growth rate of output *is equal to* the growth rate of hours worked *plus* the growth rate of productivity.
10 Incidentally, the aggregate population of Europe and North America (1,123 million) was higher than that of India (1,034 million) in 2002 (US Census Bureau 2004).
11 According to a recent study by the US–India Business Council (USIBC) and Federation of Indian Chambers of Commerce and Industry (FICCI). The companies include: Tata Group, Essar, Ranbaxy, Wipro Technologies, HCL Technologies, Jet Airways, Mahindra USA, Essel-Propack, ITC Kitchens of India, Satyam, Thermax, and Wockhardt.
12 The size of the population, i.e. 836 million, that used to survive on a daily expenditure of less than half a US dollar in 2004–05 was smaller (811 million) in 1999–2000, and yet smaller (732 million) in 1993–94 (NCEUS 2007).
13 The new line of $1.25 is the mean of the national poverty lines for the poorest 15 countries in terms of consumption per capita (see Chen and Ravallion 2008).
14 India's official poverty lines for urban and rural areas were Rs 17.71 and Rs 11.71 per day, respectively, for 2004–05. Using Chen and Ravallion (2008) urban and rural PPPs for 2005, these represent $1.03 per day.
15 As based on NSS unit level data for consecutive rounds of survey of the NSSO.
16 It was 17.2 per cent in rural agriculture and 24.1 per cent in urban non-agriculture, in 2004–05 (NCEUS 2007: Table A2.15).
17 In the rural it was 20.8 per cent in 1999 and subsequently declined to 18.6 per cent in 2004. In the urban it increased from 23 per cent to 23.5 per cent during the period.
18 In the rural areas it declined from 38.7 per cent to 34.3 per cent, while in the urban areas it increased from 43.6 per cent to 46.2 per cent, between 1999–2000 and 2004–05 (Sundaram 2007).
19 The best guide to the scenario is the Reports of the Comptroller and Auditor General (CAG, Government of India) as well as the Reports of the Accountant-General (AG)

in respective states. See CAG of India, State Audit Report (Civil) for various years, available online at: http://www.cag.gov.in/.

20 This sector consists of all unincorporated private enterprises owned by individuals or households engaged in the sale and production of goods and services operated on a proprietary or partnership basis and with fewer than 10 total workers. All agricultural activities undertaken on agricultural holdings, either individually or in partnership, are considered as being part of the unorganized sector. This excludes only the plantation sector and other types of organized agriculture (corporate or cooperative farming).

21 Notable among these cities are Greater Mumbai with 54.1 per cent slum population, Nagpur with 35.9, Thane with 27.8 (all in Maharashtra, the leading industrial state), Kolkata (West Bengal) with 32.5, Meerut (Uttar Pradesh) with 44.1, and Faridabad (Haryana) with 46.5 per cent (Source: Office of the Registrar General and Census Commissioner 2001).

22 Of the remaining 65 per cent, males constitute 54 per cent and females 11 per cent.

23 The growth rate for urban males (all activities) was (–)0.39 per cent, and for urban females (–)1.05 per cent per annum (Sundaram 2007).

24 The 'Agreement between Tata Motors Ltd, Government of West Bengal and WBIDC' was partially disclosed publicly on 08/09/08, but without the crucial Annexure, and posted on the website: http://www.wbidc.com:80/ (accessed 11 September 2008).

25 Among many other undemocratic and non-transparent means adopted, perhaps the most notorious was the incidence of gang-raping and then burning alive a 17-year old girl of a local poor land-loser family. Her "fault" perhaps was that she took an active part in the farmers' protest movement. The District Court on 12 November 2008 convicted two persons and sentenced them to life imprisonment, one of whom happened to be the secretary of the zonal committee of the Communist Party of India (Marxist) – the ruling party – and the other one an activist of the party. Perhaps this was not unusual in the early period of capitalism when the African slave trade and colonial plunder constituted integral parts of its rise to becoming a global force (see Bagchi 2005).

26 In September 2008, when the West Bengal government declared a compensation package for the unwilling farmers of the already acquired land, there were hardly any takers, which indicates their unwillingness to part with the fertile agricultural land in exchange for the compensation package.

27 The Boeing 747, 767, 777 and 787 aircraft are manufactured in Everett, Washington. The site's main assembly building has grown over the years to enclose 472 million cubic feet of space (13.3 million cubic metres). Its footprint covers 98.3 acres (39.9 hectares). The original factory was completed in 1968. From its original size, it was expanded by more than 45 per cent in 1980 to house the 767 assembly line, and another 50 per cent enlargement was added in 1993 for 777 assemblies. The site, too, has grown to 1,025 acres (415 hectares), including 215 acres (86 hectares) of paved yards and parking and 282 acres (113 hectares) of building area. Approximately 25,000 people on three shifts work at the Everett site. Production rates vary with market activity, but have been as high as seven per month for the 747 and 777 and five per month for the 767. Online, available at: http://www.boeing.com/commercial/facilities/ (accessed 2 September 2008).

28 The Jamshedpur steel plant of the Tatas used to employ 85,000 workers in 1991 to produce 1 million tons of steel. In 2005 the production rose to 5 million tons, while employment fell to 44,000. Similarly, Tata Motors in Pune (Maharashtra, India) reduced the number of workers from 35,000 to 21,000 but increased the production of vehicles from 129,000 to 311,500 between 1999 and 2004. Further, the Bajaj motor cycle factory in Pune employed 24,000 workers to produce one million units of two-wheelers in the mid-1990s. But corporate downsizing reduced the workforce to 10,500 in 2004, while production increased to 2.4 million units (Bhaduri 2008).

29 The (unpublished) survey was conducted by the *Paschimbanga Khetmajoor Samiti* (West Bengal Agricultural Labourers' Organization) in 2007 in the village of Dobandi (Singur).

30 See, for example, Sen's (2008) comments on the Singur imbroglio centred on land acquisition by the West Bengal government for Tata's automobile plant: '... for the moment the political attraction of street activism seems dominant, supplemented intellectually by the old physiocratic illusion of prosperity grounded only on agriculture. The latter piece of romantic thought cannot but fade over time with the influence of realism'.

31 For a critical assessment of the "curve", see Banerjee (2005).

32 Giles *et al.* (2005) have established this by using data from a survey conducted in five large Chinese cities (namely Fuzhou, Shanghai, Shenyang, Wuhan and Xian) that employed an internationally comparable definition of unemployment.

33 Source: China National Bureau of Statistics and China Ministry of Labour (2003). Note that surplus laid-off manufacturing workers used to be included in the data prior to 1997. Data since that year do not include surplus laid-off manufacturing workers in total manufacturing employment.

34 Various reports prepared by the non-governmental organizations (NGOs) ActionAid and Laya, and the Indian Social Institute, Human Rights Documentation, New Delhi.

35 In the absence of any sort of official estimate we have to rely on the estimates of the NGOs.

36 In 1997, the Kerala High Court Bench gave the landmark anti-"bandh" judgment. The judgment was upheld by the Supreme Court, setting the stage for similar rulings from other High Courts. In the 1997 judgment, the High Court had said that no political party or organization can claim that it is entitled to paralyse industry and commerce in the entire state or nation and is entitled to prevent the citizens not in sympathy with its viewpoint from exercising their fundamental right or from performing their duties for their own benefit or for the benefit of the state or the nation. On 3 February 2009, a Supreme Court Bench headed by the Chief Justice of India termed *bandhs* as legitimate means of expressing people's feelings in a democracy, reversing a trend the judiciary has followed since 1997.

37 Source: National Institute of Malaria Research, as reported in Agarwal (2008).

38 "The rest" and "The remainder" are as classified in Amsden (2001).

39 Take a two-country model. In country 1, the per capita income is defined

as $\frac{Y}{L} = a_1 \frac{y_{agr}}{l_{age}} + a_2 \frac{y_{ind}}{l_{ind}} + a_3 \frac{y_{ser}}{l_{ser}}$,

where L (total workforce) = $l_{agr} + l_{ind} + l_{ser}$, and

$$a_1 = \frac{l_{agr}}{L};\ a_2 = \frac{l_{ind}}{L};\ \text{and},\ a_3 = \frac{l_{ser}}{L}.$$

Similarly for country 2.

40 Average agricultural GDP per EAP in agriculture in the OECD (30 countries) was, however, lower (i.e. $32,034) since such countries as Czech Republic, Greece, Hungary, South Korea, Mexico, Poland, Portugal, Slovakia and Turkey, whose agricultural productivity is comparatively lower, are included.

2 Global trade and investments

1 According to the joint secretary of Gujarat Hira Bourse, as reported in Aron (2008). To note, more than 70 per cent of India's diamond processing is done in Surat (Gujarat).

2 Unless otherwise mentioned, South-East Europe and the Commonwealth of Independent States (CIS) are excluded from this exercise. *Developed countries* include: the member-countries of the OECD (other than Mexico, the Republic of Korea and Turkey) plus the new EU member countries and Israel. *Developing countries* include: all countries and territories not included above and excluding South-East Europe and CIS.
3 UNCTAD, *Trade and Development Report* (TDR), various issues; *Handbook of Statistics* (HS), various issues.
4 The average annual growth rate of world output was 3 per cent between 1990 and 2006. In the developed countries it was around 2 per cent, while in the developing countries it exceeded 5 per cent.
5 Based on UNCTAD, TDR, various issues; WTO, *International Trade Statistics* (ITS), various issues.
6 In the mid-1960s, the North used to import 67 per cent of the aggregate merchandise exports from the North itself. During the following two decades, instead of decreasing, the ratio increased to 68 per cent in 1985. Moreover, during the high tide of globalization the intra-North trade leapt forward, to 75 per cent.
7 In the United States, nearly all ethanol is blended into gasoline at up to 10 per cent by volume to produce a fuel called E10 or "gasohol". In 2000, total US ethanol production was 1.6 billion gallons. Thereafter, its production almost doubled to 3.9 billion gallons by 2005, replacing 3.1 billion gallons of gasoline (US Department of Energy 2007).
8 However, due to an increasing number (nearly 70 per cent in 2002) of cars and trucks that use diesel fuel in France, biodiesel programmes are more promising than bioethanol programmes. The French government has shown great interest in biofuels since 1993 by significantly reducing national excise tax. France produced 365,000 MT of biodiesel in 2002.
9 Systematic data on subsidies were not available before the mid-1980s.
10 Unless otherwise mentioned, "China" refers to mainland China in this text.
11 Between 2002 and 2005, US rice accounted for 2 per cent of world production and 13 per cent of world trade; US wheat was 9 per cent of world production and 25 per cent of world trade; US sorghum averaged 18 per cent of world production and 83 per cent of world trade; and, soybeans averaged 38 per cent of world production and 44 per cent of world trade.
12 The development campaign group Oxfam International has produced a large number of country-specific studies on the impact of agricultural subsidies in the early developed countries, available online at: http://www.oxfam.org.
13 The case follows Brazil's own successful WTO suit against US support for cotton growers in 2005.
14 This is an international treaty administered by the World Intellectual Property Organization (WIPO). Generally, applicants first file a national or regional patent application with their patent office and, within the 12 months from priority date, file a PCT international application. PCT offers inventors and industry an advantageous route for obtaining patent protection internationally. By filing one "international" patent application under the PCT, protection of an invention can be sought simultaneously in each of a large number of countries.
15 Country-wise distribution of PCT filings by field of technology is available from the WIPO Statistics Database.
16 Based on data in the WTO, ITS; UNCTAD, TDR; and UNCTAD, Statistical databases online.
17 High-technology products include Standard International Trade Classification (SITC), Revision 2, codes: 524, 54, 712, 716, 718, 75, 761, 764, 77 (excl. 772, 773 and 775), 792, 871, 874, 881 (see UNIDO 2005: 155).
18 Computed from UN Commodity Trade Statistics (COMTRADE) database, Yearbook 2007. Online, available at: http://comtrade.un.org/pb/CommodityPages.aspx?y=2007 (last accessed 8 January 2009).

19 India amended her Patents Act in 2005 and introduced product patents to comply with the TRIPS agreement. This agreement, while providing a 10-year transition period (1995–2005) to developing countries to introduce a product patent regime, made it obligatory for them to provide five years' exclusive marketing rights until the patent was granted or rejected. The introduction of product patents in 2005 has been seen as a threat to the generic drugs industry.
20 Biopharmaceuticals are therapeutic or preventive medicines that are derived from living cells, using recombinant DNA technology. These include insulin, Hepatitis B vaccine, Erythropoietin and human growth hormones.
21 European Commission *et al.* (2005). Its findings reflect responses from 167 companies and 163 other institutions.
22 Notification (dated 3 January 2007) for land acquisition was issued by the Haldia Development Authority (a quasi-government body).
23 Events are the real dialectics of history. On 14 March 2007, at least 14 people including women and children were killed by the police, assisted by pro-government party activists, and many more are still missing. That did not end there. Such was the extent of tension between the government of West Bengal and the local community that even the entire area was kept inaccessible to the public media for about two weeks (during October–November 2007) when the party activists, in collusion with the state administration and the police force, unleashed armed terror as a "cleansing operation" on the protesting farmers, agricultural workers and local retail traders (read more on this in Wikipedia, The Free Encyclopedia, 'Nandigram violence'. Online, available at: http://en.wikipedia.org/wiki/Nandigram_SEZ_controversy (last accessed 16 April 2009).
24 Sinha, the former Deputy Director-General of the Geological Survey of India (2009).
25 We have similar estimates of capital to labour ratio for the existing small as well as large chemical units in the Haldia petrochemical area (West Bengal), and elsewhere.
26 From 23 per cent in the 1970s to 30 in the 1980s, 39 in the 1990s, and further to 41 per cent during 2000–03.
27 A significant part of the statistical increase in the South–South trade in manufactures seems to be due to double counting associated with intra-regional production-sharing in East Asia for products eventually destined for export to developed countries. It is also due to double counting associated with the function of Hong Kong (China) and Singapore as transhipment ports or regional hub ports.
28 The share of developing Asia (excluding Central and West Asia) in intra-developing country exports was 62 per cent in 2003, whereas the share of other developing regions in America and Africa was less than 28 and 12 per cent, respectively. On the other hand, developing Asia accounted for 70 per cent of the total intra-developing country imports (UNCTAD 2006).
29 Admittedly, the results of trade dynamism analysis are sensitive to the period chosen. But reliable export data on Asia are not available for a longer period, especially if one includes China in the data-set.
30 The first-tier NIEs and China together contributed almost 50 per cent of developing-country exports to developed countries in 2003, while it was merely 8 per cent in the mid-1960s.
31 The hourly compensation figures in US dollars provide comparative measures of *employer labour costs*, although they *do not* provide inter-country comparisons of the purchasing power of worker incomes. *Hourly compensation costs* in the compilation include hourly direct pay, employer social insurance expenditures and other labour taxes (USDOL, BLS 2008).
32 The figure for China is for the year 2004; the compensation costs data presented for China are not directly comparable with the data for other countries in this publication.
33 A number of studies on this matter are compiled in Lichtenstein (ed.) (2006).
34 The WTO Council for Trade in Services began liberalization talks in January 2000 via the "request-offer" approach, with each country requesting that other WTO members

liberalize in a particular sector by, for instance, making a sector-specific commitment to open themselves to foreign-service providers. When all requests are received, countries announce the liberalizations they are willing to offer to obtain the access to other countries' service sectors that they requested.

35 The British in 1845 were the first to compel local Ching officials to mark off an area along the Whangpoo River as the "British Concession". In 1848, the US invaders seized a section of Shanghai as a residential district for Americans. In 1849, the French also staked off a district between the north side of the Shanghai County seat and the British Concession and made it the "French Concession". Also in 1849, the Portuguese colonialists expelled the Chinese officials from Macao, refused to pay land rent and forcibly occupied this coastal port [*The Opium War* (1976)].

36 The distinction is based on the assumption that relatively high R&D intensity and shorter life-cycle of a product attribute high unit value to the product.

37 There are gross limitations of the NSSO data on employment in the sector, owing to scope and coverage.

3 Industrial capabilities

1 Note, however, that patents differ greatly in their technical and economic significance. Many of them reflect minor improvements of little economic value.

2 For a detailed study on why patent statistics are interesting in spite of all the difficulties that arise in their use and interpretation, see Griliches (1990).

3 Since the patent laws are different across countries, the numbers of domestic applications (by country of origin) are not strictly comparable across countries.

4 Inflows of FDI into India from Cyprus have increased more than 10 times in the last three years.

5 Typically, a tax haven is characterized by low or zero taxation, a lack of transparency and a refusal to provide information to foreign tax authorities. There are serious limitations on the ability of other countries to obtain information from a tax haven.

6 The most general statement of *core* labour standards, presented by the ILO, includes (a) freedom of association (no. 87) and the effective recognition of the right to collective bargaining (no. 98); (b) the elimination of all forms of forced or compulsory labour (nos. 29 and 105); (c) the effective abolition of child labour (no. 138); and (d) the elimination of discrimination in respect of employment and occupation (nos. 100 and 111).

7 If K = capital, L = labour, Y = output and w = wage rate, the simple income identity *profit* + *wage* = *total income* can be shown to be

$$\left(e\cdot\frac{1}{w}\right)\cdot\frac{K}{Y}+w\cdot\frac{L}{Y}=1$$

When w tends to w^*, K remaining constant, increased effort leads to increased productivity and, in turn, profitability; the limiting case being $w = w^*$, when e becomes 1 (i.e. normal effort).

8 Source: D. Purandeswari, union minister of state for Higher Education, as reported in the *Hindustan Times*, Kolkata, Editorial, 23 April 2008.

4 Economic restructuring

1 y_i, n_i and w_i are income, employment and wage rate, respectively, in the i-th sector; w_{agr} is the wage rate in the agriculture sector.

2 The structures of capitalism are largely being digitized: dematerialized from file folders into electronic bits in global communication networks. With this development, corporate operations are being drastically reorganized in space and time (see e.g. Menzies 1998).

3 The number of establishments engaged in wholesale trade is 0.9 million (rural 0.4 million, urban 0.5 million), whereas that in retail trade is 15 million (rural 7.8 million, urban 7.2 million). Wholesale trade employs nearly 2.13 million; of these, in the organized segment there are 0.56 million people (the data is for the year 2004–05, as available in CSO 2008), while retail trade engages a staggering 25.14 million (CSO 2005, *Economic Census*, 5th).

4 Though employment elasticity was 1.52 during 1999–2000 to 2004–05, it was preceded by perfect inelasticity during 1993–94 to 1999–2000 (see Table 4.4).

5 That is, acquisition of external technology in the form of patents, non-patented inventions, licences, disclosure of know-how, trademarks, designs, patterns, and computer and other scientific and technical services related to the implementation of technological product and process innovations, plus the acquisition of packaged software.

6 Constituting all agricultural (excluding people engaged in crop production and plantation) and non-agricultural.

7 IT services exports, BPO exports and the domestic IT industry provide direct employment to 0.87 million, 0.7 million and 0.43 million professionals respectively (in the absence of any government statistics we rely on NASSCOM 2008b).

8 Rangarajan *et al.* (2007) have projected the annual growth rate of employment as 3.29 per cent in the post-2004–05 years, based on a projected GDP growth rate of 9.13 per cent per annum. Based on this assumption, total employment in the country in 2007–08 was perhaps nearly 500 million, while it was 457.82 million in 2004–05.

9 As Lenin (1902, 1954:10) puts it: 'the "law of diminishing returns" does not at all apply to cases in which technology is progressing and methods of production are changing; it has only an extremely relative and restricted application to conditions in which technology remains unchanged. That is why neither Marx nor the Marxists speak of this "law", and only representatives of bourgeois science like Brentano make so much noise about it, since they are unable to abandon the prejudices of the old political economy, with its abstract, eternal, and natural laws'.

10 The cropping season starts with the onset of the South-West monsoon and continues along with it till October. This is the main and substantial agricultural season.

11 Marginal holdings (of size 1 hectare or less) constituted 70 per cent of all operational holdings, small holdings (size 1–2 hectares) constituted 16 per cent, semi-medium holdings (2–4 hectares) 9 per cent, medium holdings (4–10 hectares) 4 per cent, and large holdings (over 10 hectares) less than 1 per cent, in 2002–03.

12 Out of the total population of 1,027 million (as on 1 March 2001) in India, the urban population constituted 27.8 per cent. In 1961, the ratio was 18 per cent. Thereafter it increased to 19.9 per cent in 1971, to 23.3 per cent in 1981, and further to 25.7 per cent in 1991.

13 Tele-density (as on 30 September 2007): rural, 7.3; urban, 56.93 (*Source*: Lok Sabha *Starred Question* no. 247, dated 3 December 2007).

14 Hardware exports, which constituted nearly 9 per cent (in dollar terms) of domestic production in 2004–05, came down to 4 per cent in 2007–08.

5 Agriculture

1 Address by Diouf at the High-Level Conference on World Food Security: The Challenges of Climate Change and Bioenergy, held in Rome during 3–5 June 2008. The text is available online at: http://www.fao.org/fileadmin/user_upload/foodclimate/statements/fao_diouf_e.pdf (accessed 16 June 2008).

2 "Operational holding" is defined as a techno-economic unit used wholly or partly for agricultural production and operated (directly or managed) by one person alone, or with the assistance of others, without regard to the title, size or location. As distinct

from a *household ownership holding*, which is restricted to the area of land owned by a household, *operational holding* encompasses all land – owned, leased in or otherwise possessed – under physical possession of the techno-economic unit. The area under operational holdings is called the operated area.

3 In Bihar, for instance, the *share* was already quite significant, i.e. 24 per cent in 1981–82, and further increased instead of decreasing during the next two decades, to 25 per cent in 1999–2000. Thus the agricultural backwardness in the state with per capita agricultural income has either stagnated or has declined (as revealed in a field-based study; see Sharma 2005).

4 The *concentration ratio* was 0.73 in 1961–62, and remained unchanged over the next four decades; the ratio was found to be 0.74 in 2003 (NSSO 2006a, Report no. 491).

5 During 2003, the marginal holdings (less than or equal to 1 ha) and the landless (below 0.002 ha) constituted about 80 per cent of the rural households but owned only 23 per cent of the total area. The medium (owning 4 to 10 ha) and large holders (owning more than 10 ha) accounted for only 3.6 per cent of the households but had a combined share of about 35 per cent in the total land owned by all households in the year.

6 Subinfeudation, in English law, is the practice by which tenants, holding land under the king or other superior lord, carved out in their turn by sub-letting or alienating a part of their lands to new and distinct tenures.

7 Though this legal provision already existed, it was not implemented properly.

8 The total number of recorded sharecroppers in 2000 was 1.68 million, which accounted for about one-fifth of the agricultural households, covering 8 per cent of arable land in the state.

9 Overall, around one-third of the total operated area in India was reported to have been consolidated by the mid-1980s, almost all of which was in Haryana, Madhya Pradesh, Maharashtra, Punjab and Uttar Pradesh (see Bhalla 2007).

10 Nearly 17.3 million hectares of land went out of foodgrains cultivation between 1983 and 2002. Thereafter, even though about 10.21 million hectares were regained for foodgrains cultivation, there was still a shortfall of 7 million odd hectares which were under foodgrains in 1983.

11 In 1981–82 the average area operated per holding was 1.67 ha. This reduced to 1.34 ha in 1991–92, and further to 1.06 ha in 2002–03 (NSSO 2006b, Report no. 492).

12 During 1979–81 there were 2.4 tractors per 1,000 ha of arable land. By 1989–91 this had almost tripled to 6.1. The upward trend continued, and in 2003 there were 15.7 tractors in use per 1,000 ha in India. At the same time, the use of harvesters and thrashers was practically "nil" per 1,000 ha (FAO, *Statistical Yearbook*, 2004).

13 For example, three dams are planned in Vidharva (Maharashtra, where not more than 11–12 per cent of the cultivable land is covered by irrigation) – in Amravati, Yavatmal and Bhandra. But about 35 private and state thermal power projects are already eyeing them for water supply. As farmers await irrigation water from a dam of the Upper Wardha Irrigation Project in Maharashtra, the government has allocated a quarter of it to a private power plant (Jore 2009).

14 The Damodar river basin spans an area of 25,000 sq. km, covering the states of Jharkhand and West Bengal.

15 Gross capital formation (GCF) in agriculture as a ratio of the total in the country was less than 10 per cent by the turn of the century. Thereafter, it declined steadily to 5.78 per cent in 2006–07.

16 For the different marketing systems for agricultural commodities, see e.g. Harriss-White (1996).

17 For a study on price divergence in rice, potatoes and mustard oilseeds, see Palaskas and Harriss-White (1993).

18 The problem was debated at length during the early years of the Soviet Union. For a critical summary of the debate, see Mitra (1977).

19 Elsewhere I have analysed the pitfall of the same line of argument that has been instrumental in keeping the industrial wage rate deliberately much below the "fair wage" (Banerjee 2005).
20 Since March 1985 the Commission has been known as the Commission for Agricultural Costs and Prices.
21 During January–June 2004, one-half of the rural population had MPCE below Rs 471, and about 20 per cent had MPCE below Rs 340, as compared to 82 per cent of the urban population who had MPCE above Rs 500.
22 While the percentage of farmer households to total rural households is higher than average in Chhattisgarh (76), Uttar Pradesh (77), Madhya Pradesh (67), Rajasthan (76) and Jharkhand (77), the ratio is lower in Kerala (44), Andhra Pradesh (42) and Tamil Nadu (35).
23 For instance, in Andhra Pradesh 61 per cent of the farmer households plough land using draught animals, yet 76 per cent of the total still hope to continue with agriculture. In India as a whole, 52 per cent of the farmer households still plough lands using animals.

6 Trends in wage and earnings differentials

1 Wages are only a part of the total compensation package; non-wage benefits such as employer contributions towards housing, conveyance, provident fund, health insurance etc. constitute a large part of total compensation, and especially so for those high up in the earnings distribution.
2 (a) Training, which contributes to human capital formation and therefore to future productivity; (b) to keep the unemployed in touch with the world of work; and (c) giving the unemployed an income in exchange for something, be it work in a subsidized work programme or attending a training course.
3 Who have a monthly per capita consumer expenditure (MPCE) of up to three-fourths of the official poverty line (PL).
4 MPCE-wise, those between the extremely poor and the official PL.
5 Those with MPCE of only 1.25 times the PL.
6 Whose MPCE is 1.5 to 2 times the PL (see NCEUS 2007).
7 It is easier but an open question on whether the skill level of workers can be measured by their schooling level. Rather, skill measured by occupation seems to be a better method.
8 It may be determined by the level of technology in the country, or by the average level of education.
9 As this is not well defined, we assume it as the median of the skills distribution.
10 Based on NSS unit level data.
11 Based on GoI, Ministry of Labour and Employment, Labour Bureau, *Occupational Wage Survey* (OWS), Third Round (1974–79), Fourth Round (1985–92) and Fifth Round (1993–99).
12 The *minimum* wage is the entry-level rate, whereas the *maximum* wage rate represents a premium for accumulated skills and work experience.
13 29.15 in the 1970s, 27.25 in the 1980s and 29.36 in the 1990s.
14 34.03, 33.16 and 31.66, respectively, in the 1970s, 1980s and 1990s.
15 Computed from the occupation-wise daily earnings tables in OWS, three rounds.
16 The minimum salary of a central government employee would be $233.5 (or Rs 10,000) per month, whereas the *annual* per capita income in India is $696 (Rs 29,786) (as in 2007–08).
17 A knowledge worker is anyone who works for a living at the task of developing or using knowledge – someone who primarily produces, distributes or manipulates information rather than engages in the manufacture of physical products or the delivery of tangible services. In other words, a knowledge worker might be someone who works

at any of the tasks of planning, acquiring, searching, analysing, organizing, storing, programming, distributing, marketing, or otherwise contributing to the transformation and commerce of information; the term includes those (often the same people) who work at using the knowledge so produced. Knowledge workers include those in the information technology fields, such as programmers, systems analysts, technical writers, academic professionals, researchers and so on. The term is also frequently used to include people outside of information technology, such as lawyers, teachers, scientists of all kinds, and also students of all kinds.

18 That is, acquisition of external technology in the form of patents, non-patented inventions, licences, disclosure of know-how, trademarks, designs, patterns and computer and other scientific and technical services related to the implementation of technological product and process innovations, plus the acquisition of packaged software.

19 Based on NSS unit level data.

20 Based on NSS unit level data, 55th Round (1999–2000) and 61st Round (2004–05), as computed in Sarkar and Mehta (2007).

21 Based on NSS unit level data in respective years.

22 In 2004–05, "trade, hotels and restaurant" employed 47.1 million, "transport, storage and communication" 17.4 million, "financing, insurance, real estate and business services" 6.9 million, and "community, social, and personal services" 35.7 million. Most of these employees/workers are low-skilled.

23 The Associated Chambers of Commerce and Industry of India (ASSOCHAM), 10 August 2008. Online, available at: http://www.assocham.org/prels/printnews.php?id=1632 (accessed 12 August 2008).

24 The impact that Wal-Mart has on the retail sector wage and employment in the United States is thoroughly studied in e.g. Lichtenstein (2006).

7 Development as governance

1 Different aspects of this process are analysed in Banerjee (2005).

2 Henry Sidgwick was a co-founder of the Cambridge school of economics with Alfred Marshall. His *Principles* was based on solid utilitarian foundations.

3 Among many other instances, the polio immunization programme, which is immensely vast in terms of spatial coverage and management, has at least proven the capabilities of the Indian government.

4 Before the project was launched the number of polio cases was 29,709. As on week 15 in 2009, the number of new cases was 9,305. It was 8,178 in the same week in 2008. *Source*: GoI, National Polio Surveillance Project (NPSP). Online, available at: http://www.npspindia.org/bulletin.pdf (last accessed 16 March 2009).

5 This section draws heavily on Gakidou *et al.* (1999).

6 As on 31 March 2001, the special deposit with GoI was Rs 37,514.2 million (or $787 million).

7 *Source*: ESIC. Online, available at: http://www.esic.nic.in/coverage.htm (last accessed 27 August 2008).

8 See Lok Sabha *Unstarred Question* no. 3685, dated 18 December 2006.

9 In 2000–01, out of the total amount in arrears of about $142 million (or Rs 6,498 million), factories and establishments whose amount of arrears exceeded Rs 100,000 or more constituted about 76 per cent of the total. In other words, comparatively smaller firms are on the wrong side of the country's law in fewer numbers.

10 Data compiled from GoI, Ministry of Labour and Employment, Labour Bureau, *Indian Labour Statistics*, various issues.

11 For example, if a person has joined insurable employment for the first time, say on 5th January, her first contribution period will be from 5th January to 31st March and her corresponding first benefit period will be from 5th October to 31st December.

12 As one finds in NSSO, although NSSO (1998, 2006c; Report nos. 441 and 507 respectively) data are not strictly comparable with ESIC since the former are based on self-reporting of ailments.
13 GoI, Ministry of Rural Development, Department of Rural Development (2008). On the other hand, the CAG audit report shows only 3.2 per cent of registered households succeeded in securing 100 days of employment in a year. Often, the numbers of days of work actually provided are exaggerated by the local PRI and later submitted to the branch authority of the government, which ultimately passes the data to the statistical wing of the GoI.
14 About 22.2 per cent of the rural population were BPL in Maharashtra as against 21.8 per cent in all-India (GoI, Planning Commission 2007).
15 The ratio however varies across states. States that generally chose schemes of harvesting and water conservation in large numbers spent more on the wages of unskilled workers. On the other hand, states that undertook a comparatively larger number of schemes other than schemes of water conservation, harvesting, drought proofing and land development – such as schemes of rural connectivity that require culverts – spent more on material components and on the wages of skilled/semi-skilled workers (Pankaj 2008).
16 The conclusions are based on the Comptroller and Auditor General's audit reports. There are also many probing reports available in the Indian daily newspapers.
17 (SIPRI) Stockholm International Peace Research Institute, Military expenditure database; military expenditure in constant (2005) US dollars was 23.9 billion for India and 4.6 billion for Pakistan, in 2006.
18 The Prime Minister of India touched upon two deeper issues rarely discussed by policymakers during a visit to the state of Jharkhand, where nearly all the administrative districts have been designated as affected by the militants: (a) how insurgency has become a convenient alibi for non-governance; and (b) how poor governance forces migration to bigger cities, becoming an excuse for parochial movements there (as reported by N. Misra in *Hindustan Times*, Kolkata edition, 23 April 2008).
19 The affected districts are characterized by, among other things, a very low literacy rate, a high percentage of villages without a middle school within 5 km, villages without a maternity and child welfare centre within 10 km, and villages without a paved road.
20 As computed from NSSO 2006d, Report no. 515.
21 This is one of the finest reports on Indian education, based on primary survey and covering the remotest villages. It comes from the education NGO Pratham and is backed by some of the best known international as well as Indian foundations and corporate houses.
22 Vinod Rai, CAG, to Asha Ramchandran in an interview at the end of a 3-day conference in October, and published in *The Statesman*, 25 October 2008 (see Rai 2008).

8 Epilogue

1 For example, several High Courts invalidated Sections 25M and 25N of the Industrial Disputes Act, 1947. The Supreme Court eventually upheld the original Sections 25M and 25N, in 1992 and 1994 respectively.
2 Different states in India can amend the labour laws independently. Many of the states even used Government Orders (GOs) to replace various clauses of the labour laws in favour of employers.
3 Many loopholes and logical inconsistencies were pointed out when the Approach Paper to the 11th FYP was presented for public discussion (see Bagchi *et al.* 2006).

References

1. Official Publications: Government of India (GoI)

(CSO) Central Statistical Organisation, *Annual Survey of Industries, Factory Sector*, various issues, Kolkata.

——, *Statistical Abstract of India*, various issues.

—— (1998) *Economic Census*, 4th, New Delhi.

—— (2005) *Economic Census*, 5th, New Delhi.

—— (2007) *National Accounts Statistics (NAS) 2005–06*, New Delhi.

—— (2008) *Monthly Abstract of Statistics*, January, New Delhi.

(CAG) Comptroller and Auditor General of India, State Audit Report (Civil) for various years, New Delhi. Online, available at: http://www.cag.gov.in/.

—— Report of the CAG on the Union Government (2006) *Performance Appraisal: Accelerated Irrigation Benefit Programme*, Report no. 15 of 2004 (Civil) New Delhi. Online, available at: http://www.cag.gov.in/html/reports/reports/civil/2004_15/index.htm (accessed 23 July 2008).

—— (2008a) *Report no. PA 6 of 2008 (Indirect Taxes): Chapter VI – Special Economic Zones*, New Delhi. Online, available at: http://www.cag.gov.in/ (accessed 25 June 2008).

—— (2008b) *Audit Report (Commercial) West Bengal for the Year 2006-2007*, Chapter IV. Online, available at: http://www.cag.gov.in/html/cag_reports/wb/rep_2007/com_chap_4.pdf (accessed 30 January 2009).

Department of Information Technology, *Annual Report 2007–08*, New Delhi.

Department of Science and Technology (2006) *Research and Development Statistics 2004–05*, New Delhi.

Lok Sabha, *Starred and Unstarred Questions*, New Delhi.

Ministry of Agriculture and Cooperation, *Agricultural Census 2000–01*, New Delhi.

——, *Agricultural Statistics at a Glance*, various issues, New Delhi.

——, Department of Agriculture and Co-operation (2005) *Statistics at a Glance*, New Delhi. Online, available at: http://agricoop.nic.in/statistics/stock2.htm (last accessed 30 May 2008).

Ministry of Civil Aviation, *Annual Report 2007–08*, New Delhi.

Ministry of Commerce and Industry, Department of Commerce (2008) *Special Economic Zones in India*, New Delhi. Online, available at: http://sezindia.nic.in/ (last accessed 19 June 2008).

——, Department of Industrial Policy and Promotion (2008) *India FDI Fact Sheet – March 2008*, New Delhi. Online, available at: http://dipp.nic.in/fdi_statistics/india_fdi.index.htm (accessed 19 June 2008).

——, Office of the Controller General of Patents, Designs, Trade Marks and Registrar of Geographical Indications, *Annual Report 2005–06*, Mumbai.
Ministry of Consumer Affairs, Food and Public Distribution, Department of Food and Public Distribution, *Annual Report 2007–2008*, New Delhi.
Ministry of Finance, *Economic Survey*, various years, New Delhi.
Ministry of Health and Family Welfare, Directorate General of Health Services, National Vector Borne Disease Control Programme, New Delhi. Online, available at: http://mohfw.nic.in/nvbdcp%20website/home.htm.
Ministry of Home Affairs, *Annual Report 2006–07*, New Delhi.
Ministry of Human Resources Development (2007) *Selected Educational Statistics 2004–05*, New Delhi.
—— (2008) *Educational Statistics at a Glance 2005–06*, New Delhi.
——, *Annual Report 2007–08*, New Delhi.
Ministry of Labour and Employment, Labour Bureau, *Indian Labour Statistics*, various issues, Shimla.
——, Labour Bureau, *Occupational Wage Survey*, Third Round (1974–79), Fourth Round (1985–92) and Fifth Round (1993–99), Shimla.
Ministry of Panchayati Raj, *Annual Report*, various years, New Delhi. Online, available at: http://panchayat.gov.in/.
Ministry of Rural Development, Department of Rural Development (2008) *National Rural Employment Guarantee Act 2005: Report of the Second Year April 2006 – March 2007*, New Delhi.
Ministry of Science and Technology, Department of Scientific and Industrial Research (DSIR) (2007) *Research and Development in Industry: An Overview*, New Delhi.
Ministry of Tribal Affairs (2006) *The National Tribal Policy*, New Delhi. Online, available at: http://tribal.nic.in/finalContent.pdf.
(NPSP) National Polio Surveillance Project, New Delhi. Online, available at: http://www.npspindia.org.
(NSSO) National Sample Survey Organisation (1998) *Morbidity and Treatment of Ailments*, Report no. 441, New Delhi.
—— (2002) *Unorganised Manufacturing Sector in India, 2000–01*, Report no. 477, New Delhi.
—— (2005a) *Situation Assessment Survey of Farmers: Some Aspects of Farming*, Report no. 496, New Delhi.
—— (2005b) *Household Consumer Expenditure in India*, Report no. 505, New Delhi.
—— (2006a) *Household Ownership Holdings in India, 2003*, Report No 491, New Delhi.
—— (2006b) *Some Aspects of Operational Land Holdings in India, 2002–03*, Report no. 492, New Delhi.
—— (2006c): *Morbidity, Health Care and the Condition of the Aged*, Report no. 507, New Delhi.
—— (2006d) *Employment and Unemployment Situation in India 2004–05*, Report no. 515-I and II, New Delhi.
—— (2006e) *Status of Education and Vocational Training in India, 2004–05*, Report no. 517, New Delhi.
—— (2007) *Employment and Unemployment Situation in Cities and Towns in India*, Report no. 520, New Delhi.
Office of the Registrar General and Census Commissioner, *Census of India*, various years, New Delhi.
—— (2001) *Slum Population: Census of India 2001*, Series 1: India, New Delhi.

Planning Commission (1963) *Progress of Land Reform*, New Delhi.
—— (2005) *Mid-Term Appraisal of the Tenth Five Year Plan (2002–2007)* New Delhi.
—— (2006) *Report of Fact Finding Team on Vidharbha: Regional Disparities and Rural Distress in Maharashtra with particular reference to Vidharbha*, New Delhi.
—— (2007) *Poverty Estimates for 2004–05*, New Delhi.
—— (2008) *Eleventh Five Year Plan 2007–12*, New Delhi: Oxford University Press.
(RBI) Reserve Bank of India, *Handbook of Statistics on the Indian Economy*, various issues, Mumbai.
——, *Report on Trend and Progress of Banking in India*, various issues, Mumbai.

2. Official Publications: Others

China National Bureau of Statistics, and China Ministry of Labour (2003) *China Labour Statistical Yearbook 2003*, Beijing: China Statistics Press.
(FAO) Food and Agriculture Organization of the United Nations, *FAO Statistical Yearbook*, various issues, Rome: FAO.
——, Corporate Document Repository. Online, available at: http://www.fao.org/docrep/004/ad452e/ad452e0s.htm (accessed 7 September 2007).
—— (2007) *The State of Food and Agriculture 2007*, Part III: Statistical Annex, Rome: FAO.
—— (2008) High-Level Conference on 'World Food Security: The Challenges of Climate Change and Bioenergy', held in Rome during 3–5 June 2008. Text available online at: http://www.fao.org/fileadmin/user_upload/foodclimate/statements/fao_diouf_e.pdf (accessed 16 June 2008).
(ILO) International Labour Organisation (1997) 'Union investigation reveals dirty ends of the diamond and precious stone business', December, Oslo. Online, available at: http://www.ilo.org/public/english/dialogue/actrav/genact/child/part2_a/diam.htm (accessed 25 July 2003).
—— (2005) In Focus Programme on Safety and Health at Work and the Environment, 'Global estimates of fatal work related diseases and occupational accidents, World Bank regions 2005', Geneva. Online, available at: http://www.ilo.org/public/english/protection/safework/accidis/globest_2005/world.pdf.
——, *The Key Indicators of the Labour Market* (KILM) 5th edition, Geneva.
UN Commodity Trade Statistics (COMTRADE) database. Online, available at: http://unstats.un.org/unsd/comtrade/.
(UNCTAD) United Nations Conference on Trade and Development (2005) *Globalisation of R&D and Developing Countries*, Proceedings of the Expert Meeting, UNCTAD/ITE/IIA/2005/6, Geneva.
—— (2006) *South–South Commodities Trade Quantitative Report*, Geneva.
—— (2008) *World Economic Situation and Prospects* 2008, Geneva.
——, *Handbook of Statistics*, various issues, Geneva.
——, Statistical databases online, Geneva. Online, available at: http://www.unctad.org/Templates/Page.asp?intItemID=1888&lang=1.
——, *Trade and Development Report*, various issues, Geneva.
——, *World Investment Report*, various issues, Geneva.
UN, Department of Economic and Social Affairs (1962) *Progress in Land Reform*, Third Report, New York.
(UNDP) United Nations Development Programme (2007) *Human Development Report 2007–08*, New York: Palgrave Macmillan.

UNDP India Homepage, 11 August 2004. Online, available at: http://www.undp.org.in/ (accessed 20 November 2004).

UNESCO Institute for Statistics (2006) *Global Education Digest 2006*, Quebec.

——, S&T database (on-line), Quebec. Online, available at: http://stats.uis.unesco.org/unesco/TableViewer/document.aspx?ReportId=143&IF_Language=eng.

——, UIS Statistics in Brief, Education in India, Quebec. Online, available at: http://stats.uis.unesco.org/unesco/TableViewer/document.aspx?ReportId=121&IF_Language=eng&BR_Country=3560&BR_Region=40535 (accessed 10 November 2008).

UNICEF (2007) *The State of the World's Children 2008*, New York.

(UNIDO) United Nations Industrial Development Organization (2005) *Industrial Development Report 2005*, Vienna.

United Nations World Food Programme (2007) *World Hunger Series 2007: Hunger and Health*, London: Earthscan.

(USDOL) US Department of Labour, Bureau of Labour Statistics (BLS) (2008) *International Comparisons of Hourly Compensation Costs in Manufacturing, 2006*, Washington, DC. Online, available at: http://www.bls.gov/fls (last accessed 30 April 2008).

US Census Bureau (2004) *Global Population Profile: 2002*, International Population Reports WP/02, Washington, DC: US Government Printing Office.

US Department of Energy, Energy Information Administration (2007) *Annual Energy Outlook 2007*, February, Washington, DC.

US International Trade Commission (USITC), Washington, DC. Online, available at: http://www.usitc.gov/.

US Office of Immigration Statistics (2009) *Annual Flow Report*, April, Washington, DC. Online, available at: http://www.dhs.gov/xlibrary/assets/statistics/publications/ois_ni_fr_2008.pdf (accessed 13 April 2009).

(WHO) World Health Organisation (2000) *The World Health Report*, Geneva.

(WIPO) World Intellectual Property Organization, *The International Patent System: Yearly Review*, various issues, Geneva.

——, WIPO Industrial Property Statistics, Geneva. Online, available at: http://www.wipo.int/ipstats/en/statistics/patents/filed/source.html (last accessed 4 March 2008).

(WTO) World Trade Organisation, *International Trade Statistics*, various issues, Geneva.

——, Statistics database (on-line). Online, available at: http://stat.wto.org/Home/WSDBHome.aspx?Language=.

3. Others

(Author unknown) (1975) *New China's First Quarter-Century*, Beijing: Foreign Languages Press.

(Author unknown) (1976) *The Opium War*, Beijing: Foreign Languages Press.

Abraham, V. (2007) 'Growth and inequality of wages in India: recent trends and patterns', *Indian Journal of Labour Economics*, 50(4): 927–41.

Agarwal, G. (2008) 'War against malaria', *Span*, 49(2): 40–3.

Aghion, P. and P. Howitt (1992) 'A model of growth through creative destruction', *Econometrica*, 60(2): 323–51.

Akerlof, G.A. and J.L. Yellen (1990) 'The fair wage-effort hypothesis and unemployment', *Quarterly Journal of Economics*, 105(2): 255–83.

Aksoy, M.A. (2005) 'Global agricultural trade policies', in M.A. Aksoy and J.C. Beghin (eds) *Global Agriculture Trade and Developing Countries*, Washington, DC: The World Bank.

Alexander, A. (2008) *The Arc of Japan's Economic Development*, London and New York: Routledge.
Amin, S. (2004) *The Liberal Virus: Permanent War and the Americanization of the World*, New York: Monthly Review Press.
Amsden, A.H. (1989) *Asia's Next Giant: South Korea and Late Industrialization*, Oxford: Oxford University Press.
—— (2001) *The Rise of 'The Rest': Challenges to the West from Late-Industrialising Economies*, New York: Oxford University Press.
Andrews, S. (1952) 'FAO mobilizes for increased food production', *Foreign Agriculture*, 16(2): 32–3.
Annam, S. (2008) 'Taking on Goliath', *The Sunday Statesman Magazine*, May 25.
Aron, S. (2008) 'Diamonds not forever?', *Hindustan Times*, June 23.
Asada, Y. and T. Hedemann (2002) 'A problem with the individual approach in the WHO health inequality measurement', *International Journal for Equity in Health*, 1(2): 1–5.
(ADB) Asian Development Bank (2005) *Key Indicators 2005*: (Special Chapter) *Labour Markets in Asia: Promoting Full, Productive, and Decent Employment*, Manila.
Bagchi, A.K. (2005) *Perilous Passage: Mankind and the Global Ascendancy of Capital*, Lanham: Rowman & Littlefield.
Bagchi, A.K., D. Banerjee and A. Chakraborty (2006) 'A critique of the Approach Paper to Eleventh Five-Year Plan in India', *Economic and Political Weekly*, 41(31): 3346–51.
Banerjee, D. (1999) *Colonialism in Action: Trade, Development and Dependence in Late Colonial India*, New Delhi: Orient Longman.
—— (2001) 'Non-institutional rural credit in West Bengal: analysis of interest rate variation', in S. Sau and P.S. Das (eds) *Fifty Years of Rural Development in India*, Kolkata: Firma KLM.
—— (2003) 'Concentration and investment behaviour of Indian corporate manufacturing: an institutional approach', in A.K. Bagchi, M. Chattopadhyay and R. Khasnobis (eds) *Economy and Quality of Life: Essays in Memory of Ashok Rudra*, Kolkata: Dasgupta.
—— (2005) *Globalisation, Industrial Restructuring and Labour Standards: Where India Meets the Global*, New Delhi: Sage.
—— (2006) 'Information technology, productivity growth, and reduced leisure: revisiting "end of history"', *Working USA: Journal of Labour and Society*, 9(2): 199–213.
—— (2007a) 'Liberalized trade, foreign investments and labour standards: can or should they converge in a new international division of labour?', in D. Banerjee and M. Goldfield (eds) *Labour, Globalization and the State: Workers, Women and Migrants Confront Neoliberalism*, London and New York: Routledge.
—— (2007b) West Bengal State Development Report 2007, unpublished report prepared for the Development and Planning Department (Government of West Bengal) and the Planning Commission (Government of India), *mimeo*, Institute of Development Studies Kolkata.
—— (2008) *Labour Regulation and Industrial Development in West Bengal*, vol. 8, in T.S. Papola (General Editor) *Labour Regulation in Indian Industry*, vols 1-10, New Delhi: Bookwell (for ISID, EU-India, and International Institute for Labour Studies, Geneva).
Barro, R.J. (1997) *Determinants of Economic Growth: A Cross-Country Empirical Study*, Cambridge, MA: The MIT Press.

Becker, G.S. (1975) *Human Capital: A Theoretical and Empirical Analysis, with Special Reference to Education*, 2nd edition, New York: National Bureau of Economic Research.

Bengali, K. (ed.) (2003) *The Politics of Managing Water*, Sustainable Development Policy Institute, Islamabad, in collaboration with Oxford University Press.

Bengtsson, T., C. Campbell, J.Z. Lee *et al.* (2004) *Life under Pressure: Mortality and Living Standards in Europe and Asia, 1700–1900*, Cambridge, MA: The MIT Press.

Bhabha, H.J. (1966) *Science and the Problems of Development*, Mumbai: Atomic Energy Establishment, Trombay.

Bhaduri, A. (2008) 'Predatory growth', *Economic and Political Weekly*, 43(16): 10–14.

Bhalla, G.S. (2007) *Indian Agriculture since Independence*, New Delhi: National Book Trust.

Bhalla, G.S. and Y.K. Alagh (1979) *Performance of Indian Agriculture: A District-wise Study*, New Delhi: Sterling.

Blackburn, M.L. (1990) 'What can explain the increase in earnings inequality among males?', *Industrial Relations*, 29(3): 441–56.

Bluestone, B. and B. Harrison (1982) *The Deindustrialisation of America*, New York: Basic Books.

—— (1988) 'The growth of low-wage employment: 1963–86', *American Economic Review*, 78(2): 124–8.

Botero, J.C., S. Djankov, R. La Porta, F. Lopez-de-Silances and A. Shleifer (2004) 'The regulation of labour', *Quarterly Journal of Economics*, 119(4): 1339–82.

Braverman, H. (1974) *Labour and Monopoly Capital: The Degradation of Work in the Twentieth Century*, New York: Monthly Review Press.

Braverman, P., N. Krieger and J. Lynch (2000) 'Health inequalities and social inequalities in health', *Bulletin of the World Health Organisation*, 78(2): 232–34.

Brazel, Y. (1989) *Economic Analysis of Property Rights*, Cambridge: Cambridge University Press.

Bronfenbrenner, K. and S. Luce (2004) *The changing nature of corporate global restructuring: The impact of production shifts on jobs in the US, China, and around the globe*, Washington, DC: US–China Economic and Security Review Commission. Online, available at: http://digitalcommons.ilr.cornell.edu/cbpubs/15 (accessed 05 June 2006).

Brooke, E. (1898) *A Tabulation of the Factory Laws of European Countries*, London: Grant Richards.

Bulk Drug Manufacturers' Association (India), Hyderabad. Available online at http://www.bdmai.org.

Cantwell, J. and O. Janne (2000) 'The role of multinational corporations and national states in the globalisation of innovatory capacity: the European perspective', *Technology Analysis and Strategic Management*, 12(2): 243–62.

Castells, M. (2001) *The Rise of the Network Society, The Information Age: Economy, Society and Culture*, 1, London: Blackwell.

Chakravarty, S. (1987) *Development Planning: The Indian Experience*, New Delhi: Oxford University Press.

Chatterjee, P. (2008) 'Democracy and economic transformation in India', *Economic and Political Weekly*, 43(16): 53–62.

Chayanov, A.V. (1966) *The Theory of Peasant Economy*, first English edition with a new Introduction by T. Shanin, Homewood, IL: Richard D. Irwin.

Chen, S. and M. Ravallion (2008) 'The developing world is poorer than we thought, but no less successful in the fight against poverty', Policy Research Working Paper 4703, Development Research Group, World Bank: Washington, DC.

Chossudovsky, M. (1997) *The Globalisation of Poverty: Impacts of IMF and World Bank Reforms*, Penang: Third World Network.

Coase, R.H. (1960) 'The problem of social cost', *Journal of Law and Economics*, 3 (October): 1–44.

Cohen, D., P. Garibaldi and S. Scarpetta (2004) *The ICT Revolution: Productivity Differences and the Digital Divide*, New York: Oxford University Press.

Davies, J., S. Sandström, A. Shorrocks and E. Wolff (2006) *World Distribution of Household Wealth*, WIDER (World Institute for Development Economics Research of the United Nations University), New York: United Nations Secretariat.

D'Costa, A.P. and E. Sridharan (eds) (2004) *India in the Global Software Industry: Innovation, Firm Strategies and Development*, New Delhi: Macmillan.

Deakin, S. and F. Wilkinson (2005) *The Law of the Labour Market: Industrialization, Employment, and Legal Evolution*, Oxford: Oxford University Press.

Devarakonda, R.K. (2007) 'World Economic Forum: G33 pushes trade powers on farm issues', *Inter Press Service*, January 27, New York: Global Policy Forum. Online, available at: http://www.globalpolicy.org/socecon/tncs/davos/2007/0127davosdoha.htm (accessed 13 February 2008).

Development campaign group, Oxfam International, *Reports*. Online, available at: http://www.oxfam.org.

Dixin, X. (1982) 'Transformation of China's economy', in X. Dixin (ed.) *China's Search for Economic Growth: The Chinese Economy since 1949*, translated by Andrew Watson, Beijing: New World Press.

Dodson, S. (2008) 'Was software responsible for the financial crisis?', *The Guardian*, London, October 16.

Dooling, R. (2008) 'The rise of machines', *The New York Times*, October 11.

Drucker, P. (2001) 'The next society', *The Economist*, November 1. Online, available at: http://www.economist.com/surveys/ (accessed 11 November 2004).

Easterlin, R.A. (1981) 'Why isn't the whole world developed?', *Journal of Economic History*, 41(1): 1–19.

(ESIC) Employees' State Insurance Corporation, *Annual Report*, various years, New Delhi. Online, available at: http://esic.nic.in.

Engerman, S.L. (2003) 'The history and political economy of international labour standards', in K. Basu, H. Horn, L. Román and J. Shapiro (eds) *International Labour Standards: History, Theory and Policy Options*, Oxford: Blackwell.

Enkvist, P.-A., T. Nauclér and J. Rosander (2007) 'A cost curve for greenhouse gas reduction', *The McKinsey Quarterly*, (1): 35–45.

European Commission (Directorate General of Environment), McKinsey & Co. and Ecofys (2005) *Review of EU Emissions Trading Scheme: Survey Highlights*, November. Online, available at: http://ec.europa.eu/environment/climat/pdf/highlights_ets_en.pdf (accessed 9 June 2008).

Flaim, P.O. and N.I. Peters (1972) 'Usual weekly earnings of American workers', *Monthly Labour Review*, 95 (March): 28–38.

Fleisher, B.M. (1970) *Labour Economics: Theory and Evidence*, Englewood Cliffs, NJ: Prentice-Hall.

Fuchs, V.R. (1968) *The Service Economy*, New York: National Bureau of Economic Research.

Gakidou, E.E., C.J.L. Murray and J. Frenk (1999) 'A framework for measuring health inequality', WHO. Online, available at: http://whqlibdoc.who.int/hq/1999/a68869.pdf (accessed 14 January 2008).

Gao, B. (2001) *Japan's Economic Dilemma: The Institutional Origins of Prosperity and Stagnation*, Cambridge: Cambridge University Press.

Giles, J., A. Park and J. Zhang (2005) 'What is China's true unemployment rate?', *China Economic Review*, 16(2): 149–70.

Glyn, A. (2005) 'Labour market success and labour market reform: lessons from Ireland and New Zealand', in D.R. Howell (ed.) *Fighting Unemployment: The Limits of Free Market Orthodoxy*, Oxford: Oxford University Press.

Goetz, S.J. and H. Swaminathan (2004) 'Wal-Mart and county-wide poverty', AERS Staff Paper no. 371, Department of Agricultural Economics and Rural Sociology, Pennsylvania State University, PA.

Griliches, Z. (1990) 'Patent statistics as economic indicators: a survey', *Journal of Economic Literature*, 28(December): 1661–707.

Guha Thakurta, P. (2006) 'Trade India: rare unity against west's farm subsidies', India Press Service News Agency, July 27, New Delhi.

Gupta, D. (2005) 'Whither the Indian village: culture and agriculture in rural India', *Economic and Political Weekly*, 40(8): 751–58.

Hardin, G. (1968) 'The tragedy of the commons', *Science*, 162 (December): 1243–8.

Hari, J. (2008) 'Don't let the games blind us to the plight of China's workers', *The Independent*, August 07. Online, available at: http://www.independent.co.uk/opinion/commentators/johann-hari/johann-hari-dont-let-the-games-blind-us-to-the-plight-of-chinas-workers-887136.html (accessed 8 August 2008).

Harriss-White, B. (1996) *A Political Economy of Agricultural Markets in South India*, New Delhi: Sage.

Hoopes, J. (2006) 'Growth through knowledge: Wal-Mart, high technology, and the ever less visible hand of the manager', in N. Lichtenstein (ed.) *Wal-Mart*, pp. 83–104.

Hou, C.-C. and J.W. Hou (2006) 'Taiwan's agricultural development: experience and lessons', in X.-Y. Dong, S. Song and X. Zhang (eds) *China's Agricultural Development: Challenges and Prospects*, Hampshire: Ashgate.

Huang, Y. (2003) 'Is China playing by the rules? Free trade, fair trade, and WTO compliance', *Congressional-Executive Commission on China*. Online, available at: http://www.cecc.gov/pages/hearings/092403/huang.php (accessed 13 April 2006).

Jha, S. (2008) 'Tsunami rehabilitation: going, going … ', *Hindustan Times*, May 21.

Johnson, J., G. Pecquet and L. Taylor (2007) 'Political gains from trade in dirty industries: revisiting Lawrence Summer's Memo', *Cato Journal*, 27(3): 397–410.

Jones, G. (1971) *The Role of Science and Technology in Developing Countries*, London: Oxford University Press.

Jore, D. (2009) 'Dammed: who took my water, Vidharbha farmer asks', *Hindustan Times*, April 1.

Kahn, A. (2001) 'Employment policies for poverty reduction', Recovery and Reconstruction Department, Geneva: ILO.

Kaldor, N. (1966) *Causes of Slow Growth in the United Kingdom*, Cambridge: Cambridge University Press.

—— (1967) *Strategic Factors in Economic Development*, Ithaca: Cornell University Press.

Kaletsky, A. (2008) 'We're all capitalists now? Not any longer', *The Times*, September 12.

Karmakar, R. (2008) 'Workers shun tea gardens for rural job scheme', *Hindustan Times*, Kolkata edition, April 30.

Kawachi, I., B.P. Kennedy and R.G. Wilkinson (eds) (1999) *The Society and Population Health Reader*, New York: The New Press.

Keeling, F. (1914) *Child Labour in the United Kingdom: A Study of the Development and Administration of the Law relating to the Employment of Children*, London: R.S. King and Son.

Kraut, R. (1984) *Socrates and the State*, Princeton, NJ: Princeton University Press.

Kuo-chun, C. (1960) *Agrarian Policy of the Chinese Communist Party, 1921–1959*, New Delhi: Asia Publishing House.

Kuznets, S. (1965) 'Towards a theory of economic growth', in *Economic Growth and Structure: Selected Essays*, New York: W.W. Norton.

Lenin, V.I. (1902, 1954). *The Agrarian Question and the "Critics of Marx"*, Moscow: Progress Publishers.

Lewis, A.W. (1954) 'Economic development with unlimited supplies of labour', *The Manchester School*, 22(2): 139–91.

—— (1978) *The Evolution of the International Economic Order*, Princeton, NJ: Princeton University Press.

—— (1979) 'The dual economy revisited', *The Manchester School*, 47(3): 211–29.

Lichtenstein, N. (ed.) (2006) *Wal-Mart: The Face of Twenty-First-Century Capitalism*, New York and London: The New Press.

Lieten, G.K. (2004a) 'Child labour in south Asia: an account of numbers', in G.K. Lieten, R. Srivastava and S. Thorat (eds) *Small Hands in South Asia: Child Labour in Perspective*, New Delhi: Manohar.

—— (2004b) 'Child labour and work: numbers, from the general to the specific', Radha Kamal Mukherjee Memorial Lecture, 46th Annual Conference of the Indian Society of Labour Economics, Jaipur.

Llorente, R.M. de Bustillo (2005) 'Employment performance and labour market institutions: the case of Spain', in D.R. Howell (ed.) *Fighting Unemployment: The Limits of Free Market Orthodoxy*, Oxford: Oxford University Press.

Lockwood, D. (1958) *The Blackcoated Workers: A Study in Class Consciousness*, London: Allen & Unwin.

Lucas, R.E., Jr (1988) 'On the mechanics of economic development', *Journal of Monetary Economics*, 22(1): 3–42.

Maddison, A. (1995) *Monitoring the World Economy 1820–1992*, Paris: OECD.

—— (2003) *The World Economy: Historical Statistics*, Paris: OECD.

Mander, H. (2008) 'In our metropolis', *Hindustan Times*, Kolkata edition, April 08.

Marpakwar, P. (2008) 'Raigad farmers vote against SEZ', *The Times of India*, Mumbai, September 22.

Marsden, B. (2003) 'Cholera and the age of the water barons', *The Centre for Public Integrity*, February 3. Online, available at: http://www.publicintegrity.org/water/report.aspx?aid=44 (accessed 15 June 2006).

Martin, P.L. (2006) 'GATS, migration, and labour standards', *Discussion Paper* no. 165, International Institute for Labour Studies, Geneva.

Medema, S.G. (2003) 'The economic role of government in the history of economic thought', in W.J. Samuels, J.E. Biddle and J.B. Davis (eds) *A Companion to the History of Economic Thought*, Oxford: Blackwell.

Menzies, H. (1998) 'Challenging capitalism in cyberspace: the information highway, the postindustrial economy, and people', in R.W. McChesney, E.M. Wood and J.B. Foster (eds) *Capitalism and the Information Age: The Political Economy of the Global Communication Revolution*, New York: Monthly Review Press.

Merrill Lynch and Capgemini (2005) *World Wealth Report 2005*, ninth annual report, Washington, DC: Merrill Lynch, Pierce, Fanner & Smith.

Mitra, A. (1977) *Terms of Trade and Class Relations: An Essay in Political Economy*, London: Frank Cass.
Moene, K.-O. and M. Wallerstein (2003) 'Legislation versus bargaining power: the evolution of Scandinavian labour standards', in K. Basu, H. Horn, L. Román and J. Shapiro (eds) *International Labour Standards: History, Theory and Policy Options*, Oxford: Blackwell.
Mukhija, K. and R. Shah (2007) 'Right to strike: is it a legitimate countervailing power in the globalized era? A case study of India', in D. Banerjee and M. Goldfield (eds) *Labour, Globalization and the State: Workers, Women and Migrants Confront Neoliberalism*, London and New York: Routledge.
Nagarik Mancha (2009) *Sponge Iron Factories: Devastation in the name of Industrialisation*, Kolkata: Nagarik Mancha.
National Advisory Council (NAC) (2005) *Draft National Policy on Tribals: Suggestions for Improvement*, Presentation before the NAC, February 05, New Delhi. Online, available at: http://nac.nic.in/concept%20papers/draft-tribal-policy.pdf.
(NASSCOM) National Association of Software and Services Companies (2004) *Indian IT Industry: Strategic Review 2004*, New Delhi.
—— (2008a) *Indian IT Industry: Strategic Review 2008*, New Delhi. Online, available at: http://www.nasscom.in/upload/5216/Strategic_Review_Feb2008.doc (accessed 3 July 2008).
—— (2008b) *Factsheets*, New Delhi. Online, available at: http://www.nasscom.in/Nasscom/templates/NormalPage.aspx?id=2374 (accessed 3 July 2008).
(NCEUS) National Commission for Enterprises in the Unorganised Sector (2007) *Report on Conditions of Work and Promotion of Livelihoods in the Unorganised Sector*, New Delhi.
Nussbaum, M.C. (2008) 'Education for profit, education for freedom', Opening Plenary Address, Association of American Colleges and Universities, Washington, DC, January 24.
O'Brien, D.P. (2003) 'Classical economics', in W.J. Samuels, J.E. Biddle and J.B. Davis (eds) *A Companion to the History of Economic Thought*, Oxford: Blackwell.
(OECD) Organisation for Economic Co-operation and Development (1994) *The OECD Jobs Study: Evidence and Explanations. Part II: The Adjustment Potential of the Labour Market*, Paris: OECD.
—— (2003) *Agricultural Policies in OECD Countries: Monitoring and Evaluation*, Paris: OECD.
—— (2006) *OECD–FAO Agricultural Outlook 2006–2015*, Paris: OECD.
—— (2007) *OECD Employment Outlook*, Paris: OECD.
Oxfam International. Online, available at: http://www.oxfam.org.
Palaskas, T.B. and B. Harriss-White (1993) 'Testing market integration: new approaches with case material from the West Bengal food economy', *Journal of Development Studies*, 30(1): 1–57.
Pankaj, A.K. (2008) 'The National Rural Employment Guarantee Act: guaranteeing the right to livelihood', in H.M. Mathur (ed.) *India: Social Development Report 2008*, Council for Social Development, New Delhi: Oxford University Press.
Papola, T.S. (2005) 'Emerging structure of Indian economy: implications of growing intersectoral imbalances', Presidential address to the 88th annual conference of the Indian Economic Association, Andhra University, Vishakhapatnam, December 27–29.
Papola, T.S. (General Editor) (2008) *Labour Regulation in Indian Industry*, vols 1–10, New Delhi: Bookwell (for ISID, EU-India, and International Institute for Labour Studies, Geneva).

Parente, S. (2001) 'The failure of endogenous growth', *Knowledge Technology & Policy*, 13(4): 49–58.

Parikh, K.S., A. Ganesh-Kumar and G. Darbha (2003) 'Growth and welfare consequences of rise in MSP', *Economic and Political Weekly*, 38(9): 891–95.

Patranobis, S. (2007) '79% land oustees are tribals, says NGO', *Hindustan Times*, Kolkata edition, December 21.

Pattnaik, S. (2007) 'No norm for industrial land allocation', *Hindustan Times*, Kolkata edition, November 30.

Payen, G. (2006) 'Water business', *OECD Observer* (254), March. Online, available at: http://www.oecdobserver.org/news/fullstory.php/aid/1827/Water_business.html (accessed 10 August 2006).

Phillips, A.W. (1958) 'The relation between unemployment and the rate of change in money wage rates in the United Kingdom 1861–1957', *Economica*, 25 (November): 283–99.

Pigou, A.C. (1932) *The Economics of Welfare*, 4th edition, London: Macmillan.

Piore, M.J. (2000) 'Rethinking international labour standards', *mimeo*, Cambridge, MA: Massachusetts Institute of Technology.

Pratham Resource Centre (2008) *Annual Status of Education Report (Rural) 2007*, Mumbai.

Raghavan, M. (2003) 'Food stocks: managing excess', *Economic and Political Weekly*, 38(9): 873–5.

Rai, V. (2008) 'CAG needs more teeth', an interview with A. Ramchandran, *The Statesman*, Kolkata edition, October 25.

Rangarajan, C., P.I. Kaul and Seema (2007) 'Revisiting employment growth', *Money & Finance*, (September): 57–68.

Rao, J.M. and S. Storm (1998) 'Distribution and growth in Indian agriculture', in T.J. Byres (ed.) *The Indian Economy: Major Debates since Independence*, New Delhi: Oxford University Press.

Rao, S.K., S. Selvaraju, S. Nagpal and S. Sakthivel (2005) 'Financing of health in India', in National Commission on Macroeconomics and Health, *Financing and Delivery of Health Care Services in India: Background Papers*, New Delhi: Government of India, Ministry of Health and Family Welfare.

Raup, P.M. (1967) 'Land reform and agricultural development', in H.M. Southworth and B.F. Johnston (eds) *Agricultural Development and Economic Growth*, Ithaca and London: Cornell University Press.

Roach, S.S. (1998) 'No productivity boom for workers', *Issues in Science and Technology*, 14(4): 49–56.

Roll, E. (1961) *A History of Economic Thought*, London: Faber & Faber.

Romer, P.M. (1990) 'Endogenous technological change', *Journal of Political Economy*, 98(5: part II): S71–S102.

Roncaglia, A. (2005) *The Wealth of Ideas: A History of Economic Thought*, Cambridge: Cambridge University Press.

Rosenberg, N. (1970) 'Economic development and the transfer of technology: some historical perspectives', *Technology and Culture*, 11(4): 550–75.

Sankaran, T.S. (2009) 'The unorganized workers' social security act, 2008 – a critique', *Lawyers Magazine*, December 2008–January 2009. Online, available at: http://www.lawyerscollective.org/magazine/dec2008-jan2009/feature-5 (accessed 20 February 2009).

Sarkar, S. and B.S. Mehta (2007) 'Labour market patterns and trends in ICT Sector of India', paper presented in the international workshop on "Global production network and decent work", Bangalore, November 18–20.

Sen, A. (2002) 'The discipline of cost–benefit analysis', Ch. 19 in *Rationality and Freedom*, New Delhi: Oxford University Press.

—— (2008) 'Huge price of street politics', *The Telegraph*, Kolkata, September 20.

Schurmann, F. (1966) *Ideology and Organization in Communist China*, Berkeley and Los Angeles: University of California Press.

Sharma, A.N. (2005) 'Agrarian relations and socio-economic change in Bihar', *Economic and Political Weekly*, 40(10): 960–72.

Sidgwick, H. (1887) *Principles of Political Economy*, 2nd edition, London: Macmillan.

Singer, H.W. (1975) *The Strategy of International Development*, London: Macmillan.

Sinha, S. (2009) 'Man, nature and environment', *The Statesman*, Kolkata edition, February 14.

Solow, R.M. (1960) 'Investment and technical progress', in K.J. Arrow, S. Karlin and P. Suppes (eds) *Mathematical Methods in Social Sciences*, Stanford: Stanford University Press.

Stathakis, G. and G. Vaggi (2006) 'Introduction: economic development and social change in classical view and the moderns', in G. Stathakis and G. Vaggi (eds) *Economic Development and Social Change: Historical Roots and Modern Perspectives*, London and New York: Routledge.

(SIPRI) Stockholm International Peace Research Institute, Military expenditure database. Online, available at: http://www.sipri.org/contents/milap/milex/mex_database1.html.

Stolper, W.F. and P.A. Samuelson (1941) 'Protection and real wages', *Review of Economic Studies*, 9(1): 58–73.

Sundaram, K. (2007) 'Employment and poverty in India, 2000–05', *Economic and Political Weekly*, 42(30): 3121–31.

—— (2008) 'Employment, wages and poverty in the non-agricultural sector: all-India, 2000–05', *Economic and Political Weekly*, 43(2): 91–9.

Swaminathan, P. (2007) 'Decent technology for decent work/environment: social upgrading through politico-legal intervention', paper presented at the international workshop on "Global production networks and decent work", Bangalore, November 18–20.

Sweezy, P.M. (1946) *The Theory of Capitalist Development: Principles of Marxian Political Economy*, London: Dennis Dobson.

Szreter, S. and G. Mooney (1998) 'Urbanisation, mortality and the standard of living debate: new estimates of the expectation of life at birth in nineteenth-century British cities', *Economic History Review*, 51(1): 84–112.

Tagore, R.N. (1906) '*Siksha* [Education]' (collection of articles written between 1893 and 1906), in *Rabindra-Rachanabali* [Collected Works of Rabindranath Tagore] (1989), vol. 6, pp. 565–601, Kolkata: Visva-Bharati.

Tullao, T.S., Jr and M.A.A. Cortez (2003) *Movement of Natural Persons and its Human Development Implications in Asia*, UNDP, Asia Pacific Regional Initiative on Trade, Economic Governance and Human Development, Manila.

Valletta, R.G. (1997) 'The effects of industry employment shifts on the US wage structure, 1979–1995', *FRBSF* (The Federal Reserve Bank of San Francisco) *Economic Review*, (1): 16–32.

Vyas, V.S. (2004) 'Agrarian distress: strategies to protect vulnerable sections', V.V. Giri Memorial Lecture, 46th annual conference of the Indian Society of Labour Economics, Jaipur.

Wilkinson, R.G. (2005) *The Impact of Inequality*, New York: The New Press.

(The) World Bank, *World Development Report* (WDR), various years, Oxford: Oxford University Press.

World Bank (2004) *World Development Indicators*, Oxford: Oxford University Press.

Yardley, J. (2004) 'In a tidal wave, China's masses pour from farm to city', *New York Times*, Week in Review, September 12, p. 6.

Index

Printed in the USA/Agawam, MA
March 6, 2012

564547.004